SOVIET
CONSTITUTIONAL
CRISIS

Contemporary Soviet/Post-Soviet Politics

SOVIET CONSTITUTIONAL CRISIS From

De-Stalinization to

Disintegration

Robert Sharlet

M.E. Sharpe, Inc. • Armonk, New York • London, England

Library of Congress Cataloging-in-Publication Data

Sharlet, Robert S.
Soviet constitutional crisis: from De-Stalinization to disintegration/
Robert Sharlet.
p.   cm.
Includes bibliographical references and index.
ISBN 1-56324-063-7 (cloth)
ISBN 1-56324-064-5 (pbk)
1. Soviet Union—Constitutional law.
2. Soviet Union—Constitutional history.
3. Soviet Union—Politics and government—1985–
4. Soviet Union—Politics and government—1953–1985.
I. Title.
KLA2070.S43   1992
342.47′029—dc2
[344.70229]
92-5285
CIP

Printed in the United States of America
The paper used in this publication meets the minimum
requirements of American National Standard for
Information Sciences—Permanence of Paper for
Printed Library Materials, ANSI Z 39.48-1984.

BM   10   9   8   7   6   5   4   3   2   1

In Memory of My Father,
Irving Sharlet

Contents

Preface

Like so many other scholars, I have been chasing developments in the former Soviet Union for the past seven years, since Gorbachev came to power in 1985. With the dramatic collapse of the USSR that chase has ended, and in the future, attention will turn to Russia and the other successor states of the Soviet empire. But until the future reveals itself, it is essential, I believe, to study the past as prologue.

In this book I use Soviet constitutional and legal development as a framework within which to trace, from the late 1970s through 1991, the entwined processes of political reform and imperial decline in the vast Eurasian empire called the Union of Soviet Socialist Republics. In brief, this study moves along the interface of politics and law in the former USSR, the policy space in which post-Stalin Soviet leaders tried in various ways to maintain control of their closed society in a fast-changing world, first timidly and later more boldly attempting to reform the communist system.

Law and constitutional development increasingly became the leadership's instrument of choice in the quest for controlled change, beginning with the adoption of a new Soviet constitution under Brezhnev in 1977. Initially, the Communist Party saw in legal development an imposing and sturdy façade from behind which it could govern its subjects in the post-Stalin era. One might speak of this as the party dictatorship donning the more agreeable mask of law to soften its image. But in the mid-1980s, with the rise of Gorbachev, the law began to assume a modest life of its own, seeding an embryonic Soviet-style constitutionalism. In the next few years, not without difficulty, the first shoots of limited government began to push their way up through the still infertile soil of Soviet political and legal culture. A lawyer by training, as well as a committed reformer, Gorbachev concluded that constitutional forms would serve his ambitious goal of reform better than intransigent party committees. Accordingly, he assiduously nurtured and cultivated the growth of constitutionalism in the USSR.

Ultimately, Gorbachev's constitutionalism proved incompatible with Soviet authoritarianism. It became apparent that Gorbachev had not understood the irrepressible logic of the freedom he had licensed as he progressively lost control of the social forces unleashed, undermining the centralized state, immiserating the population, and subverting the system of social control. Nonetheless, Gorbachev did succeed in bringing Soviet politics out from behind closed party doors into an open constitutional arena, in the process redefining the idiom of power in the former USSR.

Will Gorbachev's constitutional legacy prove durable in the future or will Russia and the successor states relapse into new forms of authoritarianism? This question must await time (and another book). For now, my task is to provide student and scholar alike with an analysis of the Soviet constitutional crisis from de-Stalinization to disintegration.

The book begins with a brief survey of the long political struggle to introduce the forms of constitutional government into Russia, from the tsars through the Soviet period. Chapter 1 centers on the period of Leonid Brezhnev and the 1977 Constitution, consummation of the legal reforms begun by Nikita Khrushchev, which codified the extensive de-Stalinization carried out since Iosif Stalin's death in 1953. In chapter 2 the focus shifts to the politics of law under Yuri Andropov and Konstantin Chernenko and their respective attempts to revitalize and restabilize the Soviet system in the early 1980s. In chapter 3 I turn to Mikhail Gorbachev, the emergence of Soviet constitutionalism, its destabilizing effects on the communist system, and the unintended result of Gorbachev's reformist legal policy—political decline, leading in the end to the disintegration and collapse of the USSR.

At the back of the book, students will find a chronology of key events in Soviet political and legal development (1917–1991) as well as an extensive bibliography of readings for further study on the myriad aspects of the Soviet system from Brezhnev through Gorbachev.

Because the USSR Constitution of 1977 underwent so many profound revisions in the last four years of its patchwork existence, and was largely superseded in the wake of the failed coup of August 1991 by the Law on the Transition Period (see ch. 3, n. 81), I have not reproduced the document in this volume. Instead, I direct the interested reader to the following sources. For the Constitution from its adoption in 1977 to 1988 (minus the only amendment adopted during that period, a minor one in 1981), see Robert Sharlet, *The New Soviet Constitution of 1977* (Brunswick, OH: King's Court, 1978); for the extensive 1988 amendments to the Constitution, see *Review of Socialist Law*, vol. 15, no. 1 (1989), pp. 75–118; for the Constitution as it appeared after additional major amendments in 1989 and early 1990, see either F.J.M. Feldbrugge, "The Constitution of the USSR," *Review of Socialist Law*, vol. 16, no. 2 (1990), pp. 163–224, or W.E. Butler, trans. and ed., *Basic Documents on the Soviet Legal System*, 2nd ed. (New York: Oceana, 1991), pp. 3–44; and, finally, for the much amended Constitution of 1977, including the revisions from the latter half of 1990 up to August 1, 1991, see Gordon B. Smith, *Soviet Politics: Struggling with Change*, 2nd ed. (New York: St. Martin's, 1992), pp. 348–79.

For readers interested in translations of individual amendments as they occurred, see FBIS, *Daily Report: Soviet Union* (since renamed *Daily Report: Central Eurasia*); for the amendments in their immediate political context, along with excerpts from the relevant parliamentary debates, see *Current Digest of the Soviet Press*. For translations of post-coup constitutional developments through the end of 1991 and the Soviet regime, see *The New York Times*.

By way of acknowledgment, I thank King's Court Communications for permission to reprint as chapter 1, in slightly revised form, my long essay from Sharlet, *The New Soviet Constitution of 1977: Analysis and Text* (1978). I also wish to thank Praeger Publishers for permission to reprint, as part of chapter 2, my essay "Soviet Legal Policy under Andropov" from Joseph L. Nogee, ed., *Soviet Politics: Russia After Brezhnev* (1985). The chapter has been revised as well as substantially enlarged by the addition of new material on Chernenko's legal policy.

Finally, thanks are due to a number of good people who assisted me in various ways, including Patricia Kolb, Executive Editor at M.E. Sharpe, for extraordinary patience and a keen editorial eye;

Angela Piliouras, Project Editor, for calm and steady managerial guidance; and Aud Thiessen, Editorial Coordinator, for bearing with me as I learned word processing. I am also most grateful to Helen Cernik and my secretary, Marianne Moore, for inputting parts of the manuscript as well as numerous revisions, and to Eric Boehm of the Computer Center at Union College for his technical assistance. Last but not least, I am indebted to Fiona Burde, proofreader, indexer, and my significant other.

Robert Sharlet
Union College,
Schenectady, NY
March 1992

SOVIET CONSTITUTIONAL CRISIS

Introduction

Crisis and Constitutional Reform
in Tsarist Russia and the Soviet Union

History is strewn with the wreckage of empires. In the 1990s the immense Soviet empire of Lenin and Stalin, the last of the great European empires, built upon the ruins of Imperial Russia after 1917, became history's latest fatality. Even before the abortive coup of August 1991, the Soviet ship of state—or perhaps we should say the galleon of empire—was listing badly. Over the previous several years the Moscow-centered communist system had become decentered under the impact of Mikhail Gorbachev's ambitious reforms: power had begun to flow toward the periphery, to the 15 union republics then making up the USSR. In fact, the August conspirators, all top leaders, made their move against Gorbachev on the eve of the scheduled signing of an internal treaty, the fruit of difficult negotiations, which had been intended to constitutionally recognize, institutionalize, and legitimize the *de facto* redistribution of authority between the union government and its constituent republics. The conservative leaders of the attempted coup had hoped to head off and preempt this treaty in the name of preserving the union state and centralized control of society.

The plotters of course failed, and the abrupt collapse of their coup, perversely for them, only accelerated the centrifugal forces already tearing apart the imperial Soviet state, as most of the republics declared their formal independence in the days and weeks following. By 1992 only vestiges of Lenin's and Stalin's empire remained as the Russian Federation and the other republics, now only tenuously bound to each other out of economic necessity, began to shape their separate destinies.

Gorbachev, in spite of the best of intentions, was unable to reconstitute the Soviet system, reform the Communist Party and its governmental bureaucracy, restabilize society, avert the looming conservative backlash, or, in the wake of the coup attempt, to hold back the chaos. Nevertheless, he achieved much for the people of the former USSR in barely half a decade. Gorbachev began the process of peacefully transferring power and authority from the authoritarian structures of the communist system to newly emergent representative institutions.

This transition will likely be a long, slow, evolutionary process reaching into the late 1990s and beyond, with retrograde steps along the way. The outcome for the Russian Federation and its neighbors, the Ukrainians, the Kazakhs, and others, can hardly be foreseen at this moment in time, but Gorbachev's role in sowing the seeds of constitutionalism has been vital to the process itself. In retrospect, Gorbachev has perhaps been more effective as a teacher than as a politician, performing his pedagogic role as brilliantly as John Houseman played Professor Kingsfield in the film *The Paper Chase.* Incessantly lecturing the party, the parliaments, and Soviet society on the need to conduct public life civilly and constitutionally, Gorbachev transformed the universe of political discourse, if not the mindset of most of his constituents, to the extent that even his adversaries apparently felt compelled to announce their coup in constitutional language and call forth their troops to carry out their "constitutional duty to the motherland."[1]

How did this nascent constitutional process come about in the Soviet Union and to what extent did it contribute to the decline of the communist system? I propose to address this question through an analysis of the recent politics and history of constitutional development in the USSR from the late 1970s to the present. Why a constitutional approach to the study of the erstwhile Soviet system? Basically, because modern Russian and Soviet history has witnessed a lengthy quest of nearly 200 years to fashion a constitutional or legal solution during periodic moments of internal crisis. This quest to strike a balance between traditional Russian arbitrary political rule and Westernized forms of constitutional order continued into the present time, as Gorbachev and his associates struggled to hold the Soviet system and the Soviet Union together in the face of powerful forces for change that in the end pulled apart the society and the country itself.

The search for a constitutional solution to the problems of governing Russia, be it tsarist or communist, and managing its large internal empire of non-Russian peoples had failed in the past. Each time, the sovereign, whether a crowned autocrat or a Communist

Party chief, resisted encroachment on his absolute prerogatives to govern unhindered by restraints. Hence, Russia and the USSR became exemplars of the idea of a government of men not laws. Gorbachev's predecessors, nobles and commoners alike, seem to have intuitively grasped that any serious attempt to constitutionalize the country would not only weaken their power but doom the empire. Surely Gorbachev himself understood the risk he was taking, but as a person of great confidence he believed that he could control the forces for change he had unleashed, that he could ride the tiger of social revolution. He gambled that he could successfully democratize society while constitutionally transforming into a consensual union the coercive ties that historically had bound Russia's internal colonies. How did Gorbachev's relentless drive for constitutional order eventually subvert his authority and bring the country low? No doubt Boris Yeltsin and the presidents of the other newly independent states are pondering this question as they try to steer their own governments through some of the same dangerous waters in which the imperial USSR was wrecked.

The answer is not yet fully clear. Certainly, constitutional development under Gorbachev from the late-1980s eclipsed all previous efforts, but not without significant problems. The first was that Gorbachev's attempts to reform the Soviet system gave impetus to a tidal wave of nationalism that first eroded and then eventually swept away the Union of Soviet Socialist Republics as the world had known it for nearly three-quarters of a century. The second problem was that, although Gorbachev accrued to himself as president extensive constitutional powers to maintain the Soviet system as he reforged it in the crucible of systemic change, his reluctance to employ these emergency powers infuriated conservatives who saw the country dissolving before their eyes. Their brief and inept attempt to push Gorbachev aside and seize his special powers, to stem the decline and restore order, succeeded only in converting a process of controlled dissolution into a free-fall collapse of system and empire.

Let us assume for the sake of argument that some but perhaps not all of the constituent republics of the former USSR succeed in establishing themselves as independent countries: what role might a constitutional order play in this process? For those republics determined to leave the former union completely, Western-style constitutionalism might serve as a form and style of legal ideas and rhetoric for mediating and muting possible conflicts vis-à-vis Russia with its newfound nationalistic concern for the many millions of Russians in the diaspora, who now find themselves minorities in other people's homelands. For those entities that choose (or are compelled by economic circumstances) to stay in a reconfigured union of sovereign equals without a metropole, constitutionalism might mitigate suppressed grievances and gradually alleviate tension by easing Russia and its partners, in the longer run, into a loose confederative relationship. Either way, a constitution would be more an instrumental vehicle for change than a hallowed repository of intrinsic values, and constitutionalism could become a form of civilized discourse or a method of political negotiation, a transitional method for transforming a former centralized system into a decentralized confederation of equals.

Understanding Constitutionalism

The intellectual roots of constitutionalism can be found in Aristotle, the ancient Greek philosopher who posed the question of whether it was better to be ruled by an enlightened individual or through impersonal law. Resolving the question in favor of the "rule of law," Aristotle laid the philosophical foundation for constitutional (versus absolute) monarchy and, later, modern limited government in the Western tradition.[2]

Over time, rule of law—or the idea that legislator, as well as constituent, should be subject to the law—manifested itself in the concept of a constitution, which derived from three ideas: the first was the idea of a higher law, greater even than the king; next there was individual right, the idea of liberties vested in the ordinary person as the atom of the social system; and finally, there was the idea of a charter embodying an agreement or social contract between governor and governed, specifying the rights and duties of each in the political relationship. Thus emerged historically the constitution as supreme law (preferably, expressed in writing), empowering but also limiting the government and safeguarding individual rights.[3]

In the course of the eighteenth century, particularly after the American Revolution, the concept of a constitution evolved from signifying an instrument of governance to representing a process of governing, or constitutional*ism*. In the United States and other

Western democracies, modern constitutionalism is defined by three fundamental characteristics. They are: (1) a government of laws not men, i.e., limited government; (2) an independent judiciary and a well-rooted due process of law, to buffer the individual from the greater power of the state in civil as well as criminal justice; and (3) a viable legal culture, or set of supportive attitudes, beliefs, and sentiments held by both governors and governed vis-à-vis the law as a means of peacefully mediating and reconciling political, economic, and social disputes and conflicts.[4]

For the constitutionalist, a constitution—a set of "parchment barriers," in the phrase of James Madison, a leading framer of the American Constitution—is not in itself enough to secure personal freedom and limited government. The document is rooted and "grows" over time within an appropriately supportive social environment. As a constitutional scholar expresses it,

> Constitutions do not govern by text alone, even as interpreted by a supreme body of judges. Constitutions draw their life from forces outside the law: from ideas, customs, society, and the constant dialogue among political institutions.[5]

In contemporary political science, such an environment is called a "political culture," which is similar to the idea of legal culture except that it is broader, providing the ideational context for a society's political institutions, which encompass the legal subsystem as well. Some of the key attitudes, beliefs, and sentiments of the political culture of a constitutionalist system would include civil and religious tolerance, a sense of restraint in the public realm, and a willingness to compromise. In a stable political democracy such as the United States or Great Britain, in which a reasonable balance is struck between individual freedom and public order, the type of political culture is described as a "civic culture."[6]

The Quest for a Constitution in the Russian and Soviet Past

The absence of a constitutional tradition in Russia was due in large part to the fact that Russia did not experience with Europe several of the antecedent developments in Western intellectual history. A decisive factor was the invasion and long occupation of Russia in the Middle Ages by the Tatars from the East. The more than two centuries of occupation left the imprint of a harsh, centralized administrative system brought from the Orient. As a result of the Tatar occupation, Russia was cut off from the European Enlightenment and the Protestant Reformation, and thus developed little awareness of the intellectual foundations of limited government or the idea of a loyal opposition—ideas that in the West grew and flowered as the rule of law and constitutionalism. While the concept of popular sovereignty evolved within the Western democratic experience, Russian absolutism survived into the early twentieth century, long after most of the principal European monarchies had yielded to constitutional government. Hence, the source of any change or, occasionally, reform came exclusively "from above" in Russia, and later in the USSR as well. Thus the Soviet Union at the end of the twentieth century remained hampered in its quest for modernity by the long Russian tradition of a strong state dominating a weak society.

As the West modernized—politically and economically in the nineteenth century and scientifically and technologically in the twentieth—Russian and Soviet backwardness took its toll in the country's periodic military conflicts with Western and other modernized states (e.g., Japan in 1904–05). These confrontations—in the Napoleonic wars, the Crimean War, the Russo-Japanese War, World Wars I and II, and the Cold War—spawned a series of internal crises. Each time, the ruling elite responded with reforms from the throne or from the office of the Communist Party leader, but the reforms were always qualified and hedged, reflecting (to quote Andrei Amalrik) the central paradox of power in imperial and communist Russia: "In order to remain in power, the regime must change and evolve, but in order to preserve itself, everything must remain unchanged."[7]

In each of these crises, the proponents of reform tended to view the introduction of a constitution or derivative legal development as a panacea for backwardness. A brief survey of five crises, four of which involved war, defeat, and social unrest, reveals a pattern of hesitant, limited legal and social reforms from above. In the nineteenth-century crises, the perceived need was to introduce more order and system into Russian government, while in the twentieth century the underlying problem was economic weakness, which the elites attempted to address through partial legal modernization.

The initial crisis arose in the early 1800s under Tsar Alexander I in reaction to early Russian setbacks in the Napoleonic wars against France. The solution proposed to the tsar in 1809 by Mikhail Speransky, a court jurist, was the first constitution written for Russia. Speransky's constitution would have introduced a semiconstitutional monarchy; Alexander, however, was willing to accept only a Council of State to serve him as a consultative body.[8]

Several decades later, another opportunity arose in the 1850s in the wake of Russia's setbacks in the Crimean War. This time nationalist unrest was stirring in the neighboring multiethnic Austrian empire as well, and Tsar Alexander II decided on an extensive reform program, including modern judicial and legal reforms. The Romanov dynasty was still, however, unwilling to permit a constitution or to concede any limitations on the power of the autocrat. Moreover, the tsar began to vacillate on reform in the 1870s, well before his assassination, which swung the pendulum back toward repression.[9]

Russia entered the twentieth century as an absolute monarchy and it was only after defeat by Japan and the outbreak of revolution that Nicholas II, the last tsar, finally granted Russia's first constitution, in 1906. The constitution provided for the first Russian parliament, the *Duma*, a consultative body which the tsar shortly thereafter prorogued. Thus on the eve of World War I and the subsequent collapse of the Imperial Russian system, constitutional reform was once more stillborn.

The Bolshevik seizure of power in late 1917, after the collapse of the Provisional Government that had replaced the monarchy earlier in the year, ushered in a new era of absolutism in Russia. Communist absolutism, in contrast to its predecessor, would over time develop an appreciation for the cooptive and manipulative potential of a constitution and parliament along with a number of the other political and legal aspects of a modern state. However, this was not the case immediately after the Bolshevik Revolution, when Marxist utopianism reigned and minimal political and legal structures were expected to be shortlived. This was reflected in the first Soviet constitution, the Constitution of the Russian Socialist Federated Soviet Republic, adopted in 1918. It was intended for a brief transition period "during which classes would be abolished and conditions created for the complete disappearance of the state."[10] Once the state and law had "withered away," the Bolsheviks, organized into the Communist Party, would rule society directly. Another crisis, however, caused Lenin and the party to set aside their utopian vision.

This was an economic and political crisis, which arose from the combination of Russia's defeat in World War I, the terrible toll of the Civil War of 1918–20, and the numerous popular outbreaks of rebellion against the Bolsheviks' harsh economic austerity program. Like the tsars before him, Lenin made short-term concessions to shore up the system and regain the initiative. His new program, called the New Economic Policy, permitted limited rural and small-scale urban capitalism along with qualified legal safeguards for individual property rights. A new Soviet constitution was put in place; it incorporated the Treaty of Union of 1922 by which the USSR was created as pseudo-federal state. The Constitution of 1924 and the new Soviet legal system were not, however, congruent with Western-style constitutionalism. A party led by a small group of men was supreme in the USSR, not the constitution or the law. This was a government of men, not laws.

The third Soviet constitution, promulgated in 1936 and for many years called the "Stalin Constitution," perpetuated the relationship between the government (a façade) and the Communist Party (the real power). Although the 1936 document mentioned the party in two articles toward the end, thus breaking the previous constitutional silence, the immense scope of the party's power over the Soviet system could not have been divined from these references alone.

The next internal crisis to be discussed involved not defeat in war but the death of Stalin in 1953, and the struggle of Nikita Khrushchev and his colleagues to find new methods for managing the system and society absent Stalinist terror. The decision was made to greatly increase reliance on governance through law. Soviet law, accordingly, was extensively reformed, and a commission was established to draft a new constitution to replace the Stalin Constitution of 1936. The legal reforms were carried out over two decades and a new constitution finally appeared in 1977, under Leonid Brezhnev; but nothing had fundamentally changed since Lenin's relegalization of the 1920s. The party still stood above the law as a metajuridical institution, and the law itself remained an instrument of state designed to maintain social control and drive badly needed economic modernization. From the reign of Alexander I through the death of party leader Konstantin Chernenko in early 1985, the country repeatedly failed to create a constitutional system in the spirit of the rule of law.

The USSR in Crisis: From Constitutional
Reform to Political Decline

Coming to power in 1985, Gorbachev within a year had announced his program for a major reform of the Soviet system. Called *perestroika*, or "restructuring," his program included four broad, inter-related policies: *glasnost*, or a new, more open information policy; democratization, or greater public participation in the policy process; a deep economic reform to stimulate the stagnant economy; and "new thinking," or a process of reevaluation, especially in foreign policy.

Gorbachev was not the first post-Stalin party leader to attempt to reform the economy, but two aspects distinguished Gorbachev's perestroika. First, Gorbachev proposed a systemic reform, aimed not just at the economy but at the political and social systems as well. Second was his intention to articulate and institutionalize his reforms through and in law. A lawyer by training (as was Lenin), Gorbachev manifested a greater sense of legal efficacy than any party leader before him. During his stewardship of perestroika, Gorbachev seemed to feel confident that he could fashion a legislative solution to almost any domestic problem. Predictably, then, Gorbachev presided over the most ambitious and extensive law reform process in Soviet history.[11] The output of new legislation was enormous, with over 100 major legislative acts passed in the two-year existence of the restructured union parliamentary system before the attempted coup of 1991. The only problem was that the uneven success rate of his general reforms created unanticipated problems for the law. While Gorbachev's policies of glasnost and democratization were highly successful, his related policy of economic reform repeatedly stalled. This produced a mobilized, activist public swept up in rhetoric of rising expectations amidst an economy on the verge of breakdown. The resulting combustible mix produced acute political fragmentation, intense ethnic nationalism, and profound economic frustration. Consequently, the power of the central government declined while the prestige of the union republics, caught up in the separatist fever racing across the land, rose dramatically. In terms of law, this meant that the national legislature had to compete with numerous lower legislative bodies that claimed the primacy of their laws over federal law within their republic jurisdictions (reminiscent of the Nullification controversy in the United States in the period leading up to the Civil War). The ensuing "war of laws," which some Soviet observers felt could have evolved into a civil war, created a kind of legislative gridlock as many needed new laws from all points of the compass got stuck in the implementation process.

Gorbachev's proposed solution to the general crisis of the Soviet system and the specific crisis of the legal system was a draft treaty of union (first issued in late 1990 and revised several times in 1991 until it was rendered passé by the rush to independence after the collapse of the coup) and a new constitution of the USSR which would have been based on the final version of the treaty. His hope was that the treaty would preserve and reconstitute the union as a true federal system, and that a new union constitution would salvage a restructured, more open, "law-based" Soviet system. Through both documents he hoped to secure the primacy of federal institutions and law in the reformed Soviet Union. But he was too late. Before the August coup, some union republics wanted independence while many preferred a confederal relationship at best, and virtually all demanded various degrees of "state's rights."

If all this sounds to the reader like uncanny echoes of the American constitutional convention in the late 1780s, there is indeed some resemblance. The Articles of Confederation were then in force. The young republic was weak and drifting—its ships preyed upon by Barbary pirates, foreign credit denied, its monetary system in disarray, and at least one state, New Jersey, refusing to contribute to the treasury. Violence reared its head over economic conditions in western Massachusetts, where rebellion raged on and off for nearly six months. Alexander Hamilton and other statesmen called for a constitutional convention "to render the constitution of the Federal Government adequate to the exigencies of the Union." Once summoned, the convention deadlocked over the issue of representation in the Congress until a compromise was achieved between the interests of big and small states. Then followed the struggle, state by state, for ratification of the new constitution, with one state at first rejecting it. It was a tumultuous time in American history.[12]

The situation in the USSR was similar in some respects but headed in the opposite direction. While the United States was moving from a weak confederation to a strong central government, the passage in the Soviet Union has been from an all-powerful unitary state to at best a very weak confederation. But there are other striking differences. The American states had collectively made a successful revolution against England and voluntarily entered into confederation. In contrast, the USSR was forged historically by conquest and coercion, and many of the distinct ethnic minorities are now in the process of making their own national revolutions against the imperial Russian state in its Soviet form.

Ironically, both Gorbachev and his separatist opponents have been drawing on the American constitutional experience to shape their visions of the future. Thus, while Gorbachev consciously modeled his new presidency in 1990 partially on the American office, an early draft constitution of his rival Boris Yeltsin's Russian republic originally began, "We, the multinational people of the Russian Federation. . . ."[13]

What was the progress of Soviet constitutionalism under Gorbachev? What are the prospects for constitutional process in the rump union and within the sovereign republics? To find answers we must turn first to the making, development, and implementation of the USSR Constitution of 1977, the constitution washed over by wave after wave of Gorbachevian amendments between 1988 and 1991, within which the USSR made its final voyage.

1. Brezhnev and the Soviet Constitution of 1977

Codifying De-Stalinization

In 1977—after nearly 20 years in the making—the Soviet Union finally promulgated its long-awaited new constitution. With little advance warning, impending publication of the draft document was announced at a Central Committee plenary session in late May. But the significance of this event was at once overshadowed by the simultaneously announced ouster of Nikolai Podgorny from the CPSU Politburo. Podgorny's dramatic exit from the party leadership and his "request" for retirement from chairmanship of the Presidium of the USSR Supreme Soviet paved the way for General Secretary Leonid Brezhnev to be elected to the Soviet "presidency" at the regular Supreme Soviet session in mid-June.[1]

Thus, in the space of a few weeks, Brezhnev reached the summit of his political career. Having successfully engineered the fall of his major Politburo rival, he became the first CPSU leader to serve as not only *de facto* but also *de jure* head of state. In this new capacity, he immediately embarked on a major and well-publicized state visit to France, where his reception was marked by considerable ceremony. Yet while the general secretary's new office attracted the attention abroad, the proposed constitution quickly occupied center stage at home. Indeed, the nationwide "public" discussion of the draft text during the summer and early fall, followed by revision and ratification of the new constitution in October 1977, took on the central role in the activities leading up to the celebration on November 7 of the 60th anniversary of the Bolshevik Revolution.[2]

The process of drafting a new constitution was not a smooth one. The published draft surfaced after nearly two decades of discussion and uncertainty—not just about its contents but about whether it would even appear at all. Entangled in the politics of de-Stalinization, the passage of the new Soviet constitution through the more open, factionalized, and conflict-ridden policy-making process of the post-Stalin era proved a complex undertaking, requiring numerous changes and compromises to accommodate the diverse interests involved in such a broad, overarching document.

The Path of Constitutional Reform

These circumstances contrasted considerably with those surrounding the appearance of the "Stalin Constitution" some four decades before. A constitutional commission was appointed in 1935 and charged with replacing the Constitution of 1924, which, after nearly a decade of social upheavals, no longer reflected the structure and content of the rapidly changing Soviet system. The commission produced a draft by mid-1936 and submitted it for nationwide discussion during the summer and fall. After mainly stylistic and semantic changes, it was ratified in late 1936, and December 5 was thereafter celebrated as "Constitution Day," invariably calling forth paeans of praise in the nation's media.[3]

The times then, of course, were very different. By the mid-1930s, Stalin had completed his "revolution from above," radically transforming the socioeconomic configuration of Soviet society in the process and, at the same time, ensuring his personal ascendancy over party and state. With collectivization behind him and heavy industrialization well under way, Stalin chose to consolidate these changes and stabilize the resulting *status quo.* Among other things this entailed reconstructing the legal system as a means of providing a formal framework for the planned, public economy, and of affording a larger measure of predictability to the individual citizen, who had just lived through a time of extraordinarily disruptive, indeed violent, social change. Toward this end, Soviet civil law, which had been rapidly "withering away" under the impact of radical Marxist jurisprudence, was gradually revived. A collective farm statute, legislating the peasant's right to a personal garden plot, was enacted in 1935; and new, more conservative family legislation, designed to stabilize the family as a social unit, was passed in mid-1936. The new constitution which followed served as Stalin's most public "signal" that the "revolution from above" was over and that "stabilization" was the new political and legal order of the day.[4]

The "Stalin Constitution" proclaimed that the Soviet Union had become "a socialist state of workers and peasants." It implied that the class war had ended, secured the peasant's garden plot in basic law, and constitutionally mandated the citizen's right to personal property. Although the "great purge" was reaching its crescendo at the same time, and the new constitutional guarantees of personal security were being honored in the breach for millions of Soviet citizens, the personal economic rights granted under the "Stalin Constitution" did extend to the individual some greater degree of certainty in his or her daily life.[5]

After the dictator's death and the onset of de-Stalinization, the rapid pace of reform and developmental change soon surpassed the 1936 Constitution's structural capacity to reflect it through the casual, piecemeal process of amendment and revision. Efforts to draft a new Soviet constitution formally began in 1962, but the removal of Nikita Khrushchev two years later interrupted the process.[6] Brezhnev was elected Chairman of the Constitutional Commission in place of the deposed Khrushchev; thus the project was not abandoned. Yet, while the post-Khrushchev leadership thereby maintained a commitment to replace the supposedly long outdated "Stalin Constitution," progress on a new draft slowed appreciably.[7] Nor was this surprising, since previous Soviet constitutions had reflected each succeeding phase of Soviet political development, and the Brezhnev regime in the latter half of the 1960s set about reversing many of Khrushchev's innovations while advancing new policies of its own.

Another plausible reason for the delay in constitutional change was that the project presumably did not have the same priority for the pragmatic Brezhnev that it had for his more ideological predecessor. The 1936 Constitution was easily amendable; the more serious gaps could be filled by additional statutory legislation, and the major anachronisms superseded by new legislative principles and codes. Thus, the long established practice of incremental constitutional change could continue while the post-Khrushchev leadership addressed itself to the more urgent problems of agriculture, the economy, and foreign policy.

In the late 1960s and early 1970s, however, several Western scholars learned in private talks with Soviet colleagues that the drafting process was under way once again.[8] The prospects for imminent constitutional change gradually gathered a modest momentum in the Soviet legal press and were stimulated from time to time by authoritative political hints. Speculation over the timing of the new constitution was rife among Western specialists, and anticipation from all quarters mounted as the 25th CPSU Congress approached in 1976. The most popular scenario making the rounds among Western journalists and scholars at the time predicted that Brezhnev would crown his career with a new constitution, to be presented at the Congress, which, presumably, would be Brezhnev's last in view of his age and deteriorating health. But the expected announcement failed to materialize, and Brezhnev confined himself to fresh promises on the subject in a few brief remarks at the end of his long opening-day report. His statement that work on the constitution was going forward, although "without haste," was echoed subsequently in the legal press, but without elaboration or indication of any deadline for completion.[9] Then, without the usual advance clues, there came the abrupt announcement in May 1977 that the draft of a new constitution would soon be published for nationwide discussion.[10]

Continuity and Change

In keeping with Brezhnev's political style, the new Soviet Constitution of 1977 was a moderate, middle-of-the-road document, neither anti-Stalinist nor neo-Stalinist in its thrust, but rather a generally pragmatic statement of already existing practice and principle. Despite its association with the general secretary's concurrent political triumphs, however, this document was not simply a "Brezhnev Constitution." In the first place, as stressed in its preamble, the 1977 Constitution displayed much "continuity of ideas and principles" with the three previous constitutions.[11] For example, most of the articles dealing with property and the economy (Chap. 2 of the Constitution) and with the ordinary citizen's economic rights and duties (Chap. 7) dated from the 1936 Constitution, in which they helped institutionalize and consolidate Stalin's "revolution from above." Moreover, Brezhnev himself had made constitutional "continuity" a keynote in his plenum report.[12]

Second, and of much greater importance, the 1977 Constitution codified major social and political changes which extended beyond the scope of Brezhnev's leadership alone. In the most general sense, this was demonstrated by the fact that Soviet authorities described it as the constitution of an advanced industrial society, one that, in Soviet parlance, had reached the stage of "developed socialism." In contrast, earlier constitutions were designed to serve a Soviet society at very different stages of revolutionary development or postrevolutionary consolidation.

More specifically, the new constitution took full account of the great volume of post-Stalin legislation that had affected nearly every branch and area of Soviet law. In fact, there were few points in the 1977 Constitution that had not been raised or institutionalized already in code law, statutory legislation, or the scholarly juridical commentary explicating the extensive post-Stalin legal reforms. For example, the environmental protection clauses (Arts. 18 and 67), the foreign policy section (Arts. 28–30), and the constitutional prescription (and pun) of a 41-hour maximum work week in Article 41 were all novel in comparison with the 1936 Constitution. But they broke no new ground in terms of post-Stalin policy, practice, and legal development.[13]

In broader terms, the Constitution served as a useful register of both the accomplishments and the limits of de-Stalinization. In retrospect, it was clear that Khrushchev himself had set out the boundaries of de-Stalinization in his famous "secret speech" to the 20th Party Congress in 1956. Although he indicted Stalin for the "cult of personality" and its egregious consequences for the party and "socialist legality," Khrushchev also explicitly praised his predecessor for the latter's "great services to the party" in forging the socioeconomic foundations of the Soviet system, laid out in the course of the First Five-Year Plan.[14]

One major aspect of de-Stalinization affirmed in the new document was the constitutionally enhanced status of the individual in relation to the state, especially in criminal proceedings (Arts. 151 and 160) but in civil matters as well (Art. 58).[15] No less important was the formally institutionalized "leading" role of the party (Art. 6), a change in constitutional form that culminated in the party's renaissance following the end of Stalin's personal dictatorship. At the same time, the moderate tone and obvious compromises in the Constitution illustrated the consequences of post-Stalin leadership change, political factionalism, and interest group conflict.

The limits to change, however, were no less significant. Most important, the party had constructed in the new constitution a political instrument for routinizing the governance process, but it had done so in such a manner as to leave sufficient ambiguity for a jurisprudence of political expediency to circumvent the system of "legality" when necessary. In fact, the party had merely "constitutionalized" the traditional dualism of law and extralegal coercion.[16] In this fundamental sense, the 1977 Constitution represented codification of the post-Stalin system as a party-led constitutional bureaucracy.

Still, a potentially important qualification should be considered. During the course of the lengthy constitutional drafting process, a lively theoretical debate developed among Soviet legal scholars over the concept of "constitution" in Soviet jurisprudence. In essence, two schools of thought vied in the legal press over the seemingly "academic" question of whether to call Soviet public law "state law" (*gosudarstvennoe pravo*) or "constitutional law" (*konstitutsionnoe pravo*).[17] In fact, this debate held significant implications for the 1977 Constitution's drafters. "State law" referred to the traditional view which argued that the Soviet constitution basically was intended to reflect the structure of state power prevailing in Soviet society. From this perspective, the constitution, through the continuous process of amendment, performed little more than a codification function, recording and legitimating the changes in state structure as they occurred.

The "constitutional law" school, which for years was in a decided minority within the Soviet legal profession, asserted that the traditional approach tended to reduce the constitution to a mere sociopolitical mirror while neglecting its normative potential. In contrast, this side proposed that the constitution be conceptualized as both a reflective *and* a programmatic instrument. The latter function would incorporate the Communist Party's ideological and policy goals into a more open-ended, future-oriented document. The "constitutionalists" also insisted that their perspective would better facilitate the constitutional elaboration of the citizen's increased rights and duties, which had found legislative expression in the context of the changing post-Stalin relationship between state and individual.

The "constitutional" school prevailed[18]—at least to the extent that the 1977 Constitution included greater programmatic content in comparison with the 1936 version. A further "constitutionalist" contribution was the new constitution's greater emphasis on the sociopolitical, economic, and legal status of the Soviet citizen and the explicit correlation of the state's powers with its corresponding obligations to the citizen and vice versa.

To be sure, the party leadership intended to use the post-Stalin constitution as a stable and orderly framework through which to govern the increasingly differentiated and specialized socioeconomic system, while at the same time reserving for itself the inherent power of dictatorship to bypass the "legal state" by resorting to *ad hoc,* extralegal action when it thought it appropriate. Yet, in addition to providing a general legal policy that fixed the boundaries and functions of the social regulation process in higher law, the 1977 Constitution itself contained the seeds of a major party metapolicy—that is, a set of goals and rules of behavior, given normative value and with systemwide and not merely legal ramifications.[19]

A Soviet "Systems" Approach

As expressed by Soviet political and legal commentators, a major purpose of the new Soviet constitution was to reflect the infrastructure of the Soviet system after 60 years of development. In particular, this meant recording in constitutional language the most important and enduring political, legal, socioeconomic, and doctrinal changes since promulgation of the 1936 Constitution, and especially following Stalin's death. In this connection, the more dynamic, "systems" approach to sociopolitical structure that was contained in Part I of the Constitution (Arts. 1–32) stood in decided contrast to the static, state–society formula of its predecessor.

Western-style "systems analysis" came into vogue in the Soviet social sciences in the 1970s, although its reception in jurisprudence was still in the formative stage by the end of the decade. In its legal context, the "systems" approach stemmed from post-Khrushchevian recognition of the distinction between the state (*gosudarstvo*) and the political system (*politicheskaia organizatsiia sovetskogo obshchestva*).[20]

The Constitution's description of the whole Soviet system therefore delineated a dominant political system (Chap. 1), together with economic and social subsystems (Chaps. 2 and 3). This framework implied a possible concession of at least some developmental autonomy for social and economic patterns in Soviet society. And it suggested a perceptible change in stress, from a political system that was essentially transformist to one that was more explicitly regulative.[21] The introduction of a new article which appeared to advance the notion of "political culture" (Art. 9) stood in support of this interpretation.[22] Moreover, Chapter 4, which described the functions of the Soviet system in the international environment (foreign policy), and Chapter 5, which described the functions of defending the Soviet system from possible threats in the international environment, suggested extension of the "systems" model to a global scale.

One particularly notable feature of the post-Stalin "political system" was the doctrinal evolution from "the dictatorship of the proletariat" to the "all-people's state." Although Soviet jurists had failed to conceptualize this notion clearly since its first emergence under Khrushchev, the "state of the whole people," to a large extent, remained in 1977—as earlier—a political metaphor signaling the leadership's interest in greater participation in the implementation of the party's policies by both mass organizations (Art. 7) and the public in general (Art. 5).[23] These participatory declarations were in turn operationalized in Articles 113 and 114, which provided, respectively, for legislative initiative by mass organizations and for general discussion of draft legislation by the public as a whole. With regard to both, however, the new constitution merely confirmed existing practice.

Chapter 1 also included a clause on the legal subsystem, a reference which pointed to another of the major changes in the post-Stalin period. The 1936 Constitution included a statement on the law,[24] but the new document required both the citizen (Arts. 59 and 65) and the state (Arts. 4 and 57) to observe the requirements of "socialist legality." Of course, the state's obligation to observe the law gave first priority to its function of protecting "law and order," a key slogan of the Brezhnev period.[25]

Finally, Article 6 in Chapter 1 made explicit a party-dominant political system. The Communist Party, which was mentioned twice in the 1936 Constitution (and only in connection with the rights of mass organizations),[26] was now institutionalized in the new constitution as "the leading and directing force of Soviet society, the nucleus of its political system"—finally in accord with its actual role during the past decades of Soviet history. Since the preamble declared that the Soviet system would strive to build communism in the future, the party's role was described in the more functional terms of serving as the guiding source for the domestic and foreign policy of the USSR.

The chapter on the economy described the same infrastructure of public and personal economy set forth in the 1936 Constitution, but also consolidated those structural changes associated with post-Stalin economic development.[27] Thus, Article 9 of the 1936 Constitution permitted the "small-scale private economy" of individual peasants and handicraftsmen; the corresponding Article 17 of the 1977 Constitution allowed "individual labor activity"in the delivery of "consumer services for the population."[28] Trade union property was added as a type of "socialist property" (Art. 10). This, of course, had been its *de facto* status for many years, a situation recognized formally in the 1961 Fundamental Principles of Civil Legislation. The planning clause (Art. 16) incorporated some of the features of "Libermanism" and the 1965 economic reforms with its reference to the "economic independence and initiative of enterprises, associations, and other organizations" and its explicit bow to the importance of profits, costs, and *khozraschet* (economic accountability). Article 18 declared the state's commitment to the protection and rational utilization of the environment, an injunction of both reflective and programmatic dimensions.

More purely programmatic was the consumption and labor productivity clause (Art. 15), which earmarked social production for the satisfaction of people's wants and needs and charged the state with the task of raising labor productivity in order to fulfill this commitment. The prominence accorded consumer needs in Articles 14 and 15 of the Constitution constituted a marked departure from the corresponding passage in the "Stalin Constitution" which placed relatively greater stress on economic growth.[29] Both the socialist "emulation" (i.e., competition) technique ("inspired" by the coal miner Stakhanov in the 1930s) and the post-Khrushchev "scientific-technological revolution" were invoked in quest of higher labor productivity. In view of the questionable effectiveness of the former technique and widespread doubts regarding Soviet capacity to stimulate and manage innovation, Article 15 would remain more programmatic than "reflective" for some time.[30]

Finally, the 1936 exhortation to work was softened somewhat in the new constitution (Art. 14) but nonetheless ended on a phrase which maintained the spirit of the "anti-parasite" legislation: "*Socially useful* labor and its results shall determine the status of a person in society" (emphasis added).[31] This impression was strengthened in the more exhortative "rights and duties" section (Art. 60), which described "conscientious labor in one's chosen field of socially useful activity" as both a duty and a "matter of honor."

The chapter on the social subsystem consisted largely of a set of programmatic directional signs on the road to communism, as Brezhnev acknowledged in his plenum report. Included were commitments to the enhancement of social homogeneity (Art. 19), the eventual abolition of manual labor through mechanization (Art. 21), and the development of consumer services (Art. 24)—all in connection with the long-standing commitment to encourage development of the "new man" (Art. 20). These social articles in the 1977 Constitution gave rise to a sense of *déjà vu*: the rhetoric was reminiscent of Khrushchev's 1961 Party Program, minus the detail and accompanying timetable for the realization of specified goals.[32]

The short chapters on foreign policy and defense contained a mix of reflective and programmatic elements but basically proceeded from recognition of the fact that the Soviet Union had emerged as a superpower. There was also a degree of continuity with the 1961 Party Program, particularly in the clauses on peaceful coexistence (Art. 28) and socialist (read "proletarian") internationalism (Art. 30).[33] Absent, in comparison with the earlier document, were the repeated references to world capitalism and imperialism and the spirit of competition with the West. Article 29 essentially incorporated the principles of the Helsinki Accords of 1975. At the same time, the "socialist internationalism" clause was written broadly enough to accommodate both the Brezhnev doctrine and Soviet leadership of the Council for Mutual Economic Assistance (CMEA).[34] The defense clauses offered a straightforward elaboration of the state's defense function as described in the 1936 Constitution.[35] In addition, the state's defense functions and foreign policy objectives were supplemented by the citizen's military obligation (Art. 63), the more diffuse duty "to safeguard the interests of the Soviet state and to help strengthen its might and prestige" (Art. 62), and a still vaguer "internationalist duty" (Art. 69). Of course, two years after passage of the 1977 Constitution, the meaning of Article 69 became clearer with the Soviet invasion of Afghanistan. Soviet soldiers fighting the Afghan guerrillas were described as fulfilling their "internationalist duty."

The Citizen and the State

The second main purpose of the new constitution was to define the relationship between the state and the individual. This relationship can be divided, for analytic purposes, into the citizen's economic, civil, and participatory rights and duties.

Economic Rights

The economic rights need only brief review, since these were the same rights that had been specified in the 1936 Constitution, albeit with a few additions and amplifications.[36] A constitutional guarantee of housing (Art. 44) and the right to use the achievements of culture (Art. 46) were added, while the 1936 article on economic security was expanded and divided in the 1977 Constitution into two articles on health protection (Art. 42) and old-age maintenance (Art. 43). The right to work also was enlarged to include the freedom to choose one's profession, occupation, or employment, provided the choice was consistent with society's needs (Art. 40), a constitutional "right" made possible by the higher level of economic development and the relatively general affluence of contemporary Soviet society as compared with life in the mid-1930s. Indeed, while many of the economic rights were programmatic when first included in the "Stalin Constitution," they became, for the most part, simply reflective of a highly developed welfare state.[37]

At the same time, the economic rights of the Soviet citizen were balanced by a basic economic "duty," also carried over from the 1936 Constitution. In this connection, the citizen's obligation to protect socialist property was reaffirmed, although in de-Stalinized form; that is, public property was no longer described as "sacred and inviolable," and persons who committed property crimes were not castigated as "enemies of the people." The property protection clause was already amply supported in the criminal codes of the various union republics. Yet, in view of the extent of economic crime and the scale of the "second economy" or "parallel market," countless Soviet citizens, from factory workers to enterprise directors, continued to disregard this constitutional injunction.[38]

Civil Liberties

The civil rights clauses of the new constitution, which should be judged together with the sections on the courts (Chap. 20) and the procuracy, or prosecutor's office (Chap. 21), revealed much more about the citizen's status vis-à-vis state and provided further evidence for assessing the scope and limits of de-Stalinization in the late Brezhnev years. Most important, the basic civil rights continued to be limited by the standard caveat that the rights of speech, press, association, assembly, public meetings, and demonstration were guaranteed to the citizen only in conformity with "the people's interests and for the purpose of strengthening" and developing the socialist system (Arts. 50–51).[39] The same preference for the social over the individual interest also limited the new civil right of "freedom of scientific, technical, and artistic creation" (Art. 47). In fact, the 1977 Constitution included two additional paragraphs that further emphasized the social limits on the citizen's right to exercise his or her economic rights and civil liberties. In the article introducing Chapter 7, on the "Basic Rights, Liberties, and Duties of USSR Citizens," Soviet citizens first were granted a "whole range of social, economic, political, and personal rights and liberties"—but under the condition of the closing injunction which pointed out that the "exercise of rights and liberties by citizens must not injure the interests of society and the state or the rights of other citizens" (Art. 39). The predominance of the prevailing social interests was reinforced in the duty to obey of the "rights and duties" clause (Art. 59). The spirit and some of the language of this clause incorporated most of the antecedent article from the 1936 Constitution,[40] although with an added phrase stressing the nexus between citizens' rights and their social obligations: "the exercise of rights and liberties is inseparable from the performance by citizens of their duties." Again, as with much of the Constitution's content, this concept of linkage did not represent an innovation in Soviet law. Moreover, it was relevant to all of the citizen's rights and obligations and was not addressed exclusively to the criminal justice process.[41]

Turning now to the position of the individual in the criminal justice system, we find that the most significant aspects of post-Stalin legislation on criminal law and procedure were also incorporated into the 1977 Constitution. From arrest through appeal, the position of the individual in the Soviet criminal justice process had been considerably strengthened since enactment of the all-union Fundamental Principles of Criminal Procedural Legislation in 1958.[42] A Soviet "due process of law" in ordinary (nonpolitical) criminal cases evolved and survived leadership turnover and the vicissitudes of Soviet politics.[43] For the vast majority of individual citizens, this may have been the most important and durable accomplishment of de-Stalinization.

Much of this change, of course, arose from post-Stalin reaction to the conditions of official lawlessness and terror that prevailed at the time of the adoption of the 1936 Constitution and that continued, though significantly reduced in scale, up to and even after Stalin's death in 1953. Although the 1977 personal inviolability clause (Art. 54) resembled its 1936 antecedent, the injunction against arrests without either court order or approval of a procurator was now grounded in the operative legislation and codes on criminal procedure as well as in actual post-Stalin Soviet practice.[44] After the arrest, contemporary Soviet justice was now, in fact, "administered solely by the courts" (Art. 151). The judiciary clause in the 1977 Constitution was far more explicit in this respect than its predecessor and firmly based on the Fundamental Principles of Legislation on the Court System of 1958. At the same time, neither the new clause nor the Fundamentals mentioned the existence of "special courts," which were acknowledged in the 1936 Constitution and which continued to exist.[45]

Once in court, the contemporary Soviet defendant, in theory and for the most part in practice, enjoyed equality "before the law and the court" (Art. 156). In practical terms, the class approach to justice, characteristic of revolutionary Marxist legal theory, was generally abandoned in the late 1930s. Still, it remained doubtful that all Soviet citizens did, in fact, enjoy equal standing before the court "regardless of their social" or "official status." In most legal systems there is an unacknowledged differentiation of treatment based on status, however it may be measured in a particular society.[46]

The citizen's right to defense was also strengthened in the new constitution in accordance with previous legislative development. The 1936 Constitution contained a "right to defense" clause, the language of which was nearly the same as that of the new clause (Art. 158). But the right to defense was now supported by constitutional recognition of the collegia of defense attorneys and by the right of mass organizations to assign a "social defender" to a case in support of one of their members (Arts. 161 and 162).[47] To be sure, the defense bar had existed for a long time, and the institution of citizen defenders was rooted in the earliest days of Soviet legal history.[48] At the same time, the regime evidently chose to install these well-known institutions in the new constitution as reaffirmation of the post-Stalin commitment to the Soviet version of due process. In this context, the "open court" clause (Art. 157), a carry-over from the Stalin Constitution, became more meaningful and less frequently violated.[49]

The judiciary's constitutional monopoly over the administration of justice was explicitly reinforced in a clause that reflected the post-Stalin dissolution of the notorious "special boards."[50] The constitutional declaration that "no one can be adjudged guilty of committing a crime and subjected to criminal punishment other than by the verdict of a court" and in accordance with law (Art. 160) was both a reminder of and a response to the extralegal traditions of Stalinism; it was one of several "signals" in the new document that there would be no return to what Brezhnev himself called in his May 1977 plenum report "the illegal repressions" that had "darkened" the years following ratification of the 1936 Constitution.[51] Although the clause assuring judicial independence (Art. 155) still was liable to the party's contravention, there were some indications, if difficult to document, that direct party interference in the work of the judiciary had abated since the Stalin years.[52] On the other hand, the individual's relationship to the state also had been at least somewhat clarified following de-Stalinization of the procuracy in 1955. Article 164 reflected in constitutional law the procuracy's fully restored responsibility for overseeing compliance with the law—by institutions, organizations, officials, and ordinary citizens—and thus underscored the leadership's concern for administrative legality as part of a long-range effort to raise the public's legal consciousness and build a viable "legal culture" through which the party could try to ensure that both the state and the individual observed the laws which expressed the party's policies.[53]

Collectively, these constitutional clauses appeared to codify a significant stabilization in contemporary legislation and legal practice of the relationship between the individual and the state in Soviet society, particularly in the criminal justice process. Although many of Khrushchev's reforms were repealed by the Brezhnev leadership, the legislative commitment to "due process" for the criminal defendant was maintained and even strengthened to some extent through the development of a body of "case law."[54]

With respect to the tiny minority of activist dissidents, however, both the personal security clauses and the formal rights accorded criminal defendants were sorely abused by the regime, especially since the Sinyavsky–Daniel trial in early 1966.[55] In the endless stream of dissident cases reported in samizdat, there were numerous recorded violations of the inviolability of the home (Art. 55) and of the confidentiality of correspondence and telephone conversations (Art. 56). In the 1970s, incidents of intimidation, mugging, physical assault, and, in a few instances, death under mysterious circumstances—all believed to have been provoked or even perpetrated by KGB personnel in mufti—indicated that for dissidents the right to legal protection from threats against life and health, personal freedom and property, and "honor and dignity" (Art. 57) was, for all practical purposes, a dead letter. If, as was often the case, the bureaucratic harassment and administrative actions directed against dissidents led to criminal prosecution for either a political offense or an ordinary crime, the dissident defendant routinely found his due process rights violated both in the preliminary investigation and during the subsequent trial. In fact, the constitutional due process clauses in the 1977 Constitution were frequently inverted to the disadvantage of the dissenter. Instead of executing his responsibility to legally prevent the official capriciousness experienced by dissidents (Art. 164), the procurator usually shared complicity. The dissident's right to choose a defense counsel, rather than benefiting from a strengthened right to defense (Arts. 158 and 161), generally was subject to KGB interference and frequently abridged. Finally, instead of enjoying equality before the law and the court (Art. 156), the dissident was classified as a "political case" and subjected systematically to a pattern of discrimination by the legal personnel formally involved and by the party and KGB officials who discreetly directed the administration of political justice from behind the scenes. In effect, as Harold Berman aptly pointed out, in political cases "socialist legality" broke down into its constituent parts—socialism versus legality.[56]

The dissidents' response to the regime's political justice was to put up a "legalist" defense, confronting the judges and prosecutors in an orderly fashion with a detailed and documented account of the violations of their due process rights.[57] In their "pre-trial motions," their traditional "final word" to the court, and in the post-incarceration protests, dissidents caught up in criminal process as well as their supporters "replayed" the law to their persecutors, citing the appropriate code articles, fundamental principles, and even constitutional clauses which the cadres and their mentors had violated. The legalist defense did not win any cases for dissenters. But, in using it, political defendants succeeded repeatedly in indicting the regime and putting it "on trial" in the court of Western public opinion.

The 1977 Constitution's strengthened emphasis on the "public interest" was not intended, as some Western commentators suggested, significantly to discourage the "legalist" defense. The injunction against injuring one's fellow citizens and the society in the exercise of one's rights (Art. 39) and the "rights and duties" clause (Art. 59) were neither specially designed for dissidents nor exclusively relevant to criminal law. At best, these additional caveats merely reinforced the constitutional legitimacy of bringing political prosecutions against those dissidents who chose to exercise their civil rights in contradiction to the officially defined social and political interests (Arts. 50 and 51). Still, assuming that the dissident or even an ordinary Soviet citizen failed to perform his duties and damaged the social interest (Arts. 59 and 39), there was nevertheless no constitutional mandate in either clause for denying that person the rights of personal security and due process that had been incorporated into existing Soviet law on criminal procedure. That is, commission of a political offense did not waive an individual's right to due process as provided under the 1977 Constitution. Yet what the regime did in practice in such cases was another matter. The legalist defense, focusing as it did on procedural violations, continued with similar outcomes for both the dissidents and the regime's image abroad, although the use of the defense gradually waned as the pattern of dissent and repression began to change in the late 1970s.

Participatory Rights

The Soviet citizen's economic rights and civil liberties were supplemented in the 1977 Constitution by an increased emphasis on his or her participatory rights. In theory, this was a result of the transition from a proletarian dictatorship to a "state of all the people" (Art. 1). In structural terms, a greater scope and opportunity for citizen involvement in public life was outlined in the political and economic chapters of the Constitution discussed above. The individual's specific participatory rights could be viewed as giving practical meaning to this enlargement of participatory space in the Soviet system. In general, the participatory rights were to be exercised mainly in the broad process of policy implementation, while the opportunity for greater citizen input into the policy-making process, as presented in the new constitution, was confined at most to the arena of local government.

Thus, the 1977 Constitution guaranteed to the citizen the general right of public participation (Art. 48); the right to submit proposals and to criticize with impunity the performance of governmental agencies (Art. 49); the right to lodge complaints against public officials and, in some cases, to seek judicial remedy (Art. 58); and the right to sue government agencies and public officials for tort liability incurred by illegal actions causing the citizen-plaintiff damage (Art. 58).[58] In regard to the citizens' slightly increased opportunities for participating in local policy making, Chapters 14 and 19 of the Constitution codify those post-Stalin changes in state law (*gosudarstvennoe pravo*) associated with the growth of the responsibilities of local soviets and the powers of their deputies. In the spirit of the "all-people's state," the soviets of "working people's deputies" were renamed soviets of "people's deputies" (Art. 89). And, consistent with the increased interest in participation which began under Khrushchev and continued under Brezhnev, the draft of the constitution was published in June 1977 for nationwide public discussion, as stipulated in its discussion clauses (Arts. 5 and 114).

Participation and Public Discussion

At midpoint in the nationwide public discussion, it became clear that the draft constitution was headed for ratification. Before the draft had even been published, Brezhnev in his address to the May plenum referred to the document several times in a way that seemed to forecast ratification sometime in the fall of 1977. He considered in detail some of the problems involved in "implementation of the new Constitution," and he ended his report on the reassuring note that "the adoption of the new USSR Constitution will be an important milestone in the country's political history."[59] Brezhnev's confidence about the prospects for ratification soon was echoed in lead editorials and the speeches of senior party leaders at meetings of major party organizations and at sessions of the union republic supreme soviets.[60] In a published interview with a Japanese correspondent several days after the public discussion began, Brezhnev again stressed the importance he attached to ratification, remarking that the "adoption of the new Constitution" would have great significance not only at home but abroad as well.[61]

With ratification thus a foregone conclusion, Brezhnev and the party leadership set the stage for a carefully planned, well orchestrated public "discussion" of the draft during the summer and early fall of 1977. Enjoined by Brezhnev to take the lead in drawing "the mass of the working people and representatives of all strata of the population" into discussion and to use the occasion for "the further invigoration of all social life in the country,"[62] subordinate party leaders returned to their constituencies and made the organization and leadership of the discussion a matter of highest priority for all party cadres under their jurisdiction.[63] Shortly after the draft was published, a *Pravda* editorial appropriately characterized the discussion as an "exchange of opinion on the basic questions of the development of our society and state."[64] According to well-informed sources, special arrangements were made at every level of the Soviet system for recording the subsequent comments and suggestions, and for forwarding them to the Constitutional Commission for consideration.[65]

Specifically, every party organization, state institution, and social organization was expected to discuss the draft constitution and forward its statement and/or proposals for amendment through the appropriate channels to the newly established Secretariat of the USSR Constitutional Commission (the Institute of State and Law of the USSR Academy of Sciences reportedly played a key role in the work of the Secretariat). This commission, together with its Editorial Subcommittee, was assigned the tasks of evaluating the amendments proposed in the course of the nationwide discussion and finalizing the draft for the fall ratification session of the USSR Supreme Soviet. In addition, prominent scholars, including several jurists, published in the leading newspapers lengthy individual articles presenting what appeared to be their personal views on the draft constitution. Evidently, many of those articles, especially those which appeared in June and July, had been written earlier, their authors having received advance copies of the draft constitution for this express purpose in the spring prior to the document's publication.

All commentary, both internal and published, was evaluated in generalized form by the Constitutional Commission in the process of revising the published draft for final ratification in the fall of 1977. Toward this end, the Presidium of the USSR Supreme Soviet renewed the commission in April 1977 by adding 21 new members to replace the 43 members who had "left" the commission since its last reorganization in 1966, as a result of death, demotion, retirement, or failure to gain reelection as a Supreme Soviet Deputy. The April additions increased the size of the commission to its 1966 strength of 75 members, among them various Politburo members, Central Committee secretaries, republic party first secretaries and premiers, officials of all-union state and social organizations, prominent individuals, and the leading legal officials (including Procurator General R.A. Rudenko, chairman of the USSR Supreme Court, Judge L.N. Smirnov, and USSR Minister of Justice V.I. Terebilov).[66] Each member apparently was expected to represent his particular regional or institutional interests in the politics of revision and ratification.

While an analogous "public" discussion preceded ratification of the 1936 Constitution, extensive public "commentary" on various legislative proposals had become, since Stalin's death, a much more common method of involving the average citizen in public affairs. In general, this involvement was circumstantial and very limited—usually to no more than suggesting changes in tone, wording, or emphasis in a given piece of legislation, for which the basic framework already had been set by party authorities. Public discussion thus became an oft-used leadership technique for mobilizing the population and encouraging citizen participation in policy implementation, while the party used the occasion for a mass political socialization campaign at the same time.[67]

The 1977 constitutional discussion stood apart from previous discussions of legal reform, at least in terms of its scope and duration. But it marked no obvious watershed in either the extent of mass political participation or in the quality of regime–society relations. It was extremely doubtful that the public discussion would result in significant changes in the constitution before its ratification. At most, a number of major and minor semantic revisions and shifts in stress were anticipated, although attempting to link such changes with the public discussion was problematic at best in many instances. It should be kept in mind that proposals or criticisms that appeared in the Soviet media passed through several cautious and purposive "filters" and therefore reflected the inclinations and political sensitivities of editors, censors, and various party authorities in addition to those of individual writers.

At the same time, it was almost surely the case that within general guidelines laid down by the central party leadership, editors and local government and party officials exercised a substantial amount of discretion in deciding which views were to be published. It also seems clear that the scope of what was considered permissible for public discussion in the Soviet press had grown enormously since Stalin's death, a development to which the 1977 constitutional discussion gave eloquent testimony. To be sure, commentary on certain issues remained proscribed. Thus, even passing remarks on the draft articles concerning either the party's role or Soviet foreign policy were exceedingly rare in the discussion published in the general press. On the other hand, the discussion brought forth a remarkable variety of proposals on a wide range of concerns. In a narrow sense, the discussion afforded to individuals and groups an opportunity for self-advertisement and the promotion of group or institutional interests which might be advantaged by some constitutional modification. The discussion also served, however, as a forum for individuals who were more interested in the Constitution itself and certain of its provisions. This second category of commentators seemed to take rather seriously the normative potential of the Constitution, increasingly emphasized by Soviet legal scholars.

In general, then, the discussion of the 1977 Constitution represented an important indicator, in two major respects. First, the whole of the discussion for the most part delineated the boundaries of what the party leadership regarded as legitimate for public consumption and consideration. Second, those particular issues which were raised indicated in which aspects of Soviet social, economic, and political life the party hoped to stimulate the public's interest, as well as those issues on which the party was willing to tolerate the public's comments and suggestions. This was the overarching context in the light of which the published discussion should be appraised.

In its opening weeks, this discussion was largely ceremonial in nature and produced little of substance. Major party organizations contributed laudatory statements to the pages of *Pravda* set aside for the discussion; *Izvestiia*'s special page was used to accommodate the enthusiastic declarations of different union republic supreme soviets and their presidia. In the same vein, lengthy articles by major party and government figures appeared in both newspapers during June 1977, primarily offering a recitation of various social and economic achievements within their signatories' jurisdictions.[68] At that stage of the discussion, numerous photos displaying the public's "enthusiasm" for the new document appeared in the press. And daily the major newspapers carried a page reserved for the nationwide discussion, which typically contained survey articles by correspondents reporting first impressions of ordinary citizens, a supportive statement by a worker and deputy to a local soviet, and often a more lengthy, obviously prepared essay by a scholar on a general theme of the Constitution. Occasionally, brief letters from average citizens were also included.

By the end of June, the discussion had mushroomed into a great volume of citizen activity. *Izvestiia*, for example, reported that it had received over two and a half million letters on the draft, while the municipal party organization in Kiev announced that exactly 41,787 groups were discussing the Constitution in that city alone.[69] Meanwhile, below the surface of published comment more substantive consideration of the draft already was taking place in every institution and organization throughout the nation. Those aggregated comments, suggestions, and recommendations on different constitutional articles began to flow upward through the various hierarchies and, via specially established channels, to the Constitutional Commission in Moscow. Since only a small fraction of such statements could possibly be published or broadcast, the greater part of both the ceremonial and substantive discussions inevitably took place behind the scenes and out of the public's view.

Beginning in July, however, the published commentary took on a decidedly more substantive tone. A recurring pattern of issues, reflecting themes of the leadership, group interests, and individual concerns, began to emerge in the national and regional press. Basically the nationwide discussion of the draft revolved around three sets of issues, which I will call sociopolitical, socialist legality, and "motherhood" issues. Of course, this did not prevent publication of a diverse range of individual concerns: the citizen from Sverdlovsk who suggested adding to the personal property clause (Art. 13) explicit mention of an individual's right to own a car; or the pro-women's liberation letter which advocated that a phrase promising "equal pay for equal work" be included in the document (Art. 35).[70] One "old-timer," a member of the party since 1919 and a veteran of the discussion of the 1936 Constitution, simply expressed his pleasure at again having the opportunity to take part in such a great undertaking.[71] But for the most part those were isolated comments, tangential to the main lines of the discussion.

Worker discipline and productivity and socioeconomic and political participation were the "sociopolitical" issues that generated the greatest volume of attention—from party organizations, government agencies, managers, workers, and the average citizen. Two "socialist legality" issues—"law and order" and civil liberties—stimulated somewhat less voluminous but much sharper, more intense comment. Finally, numerous letters in support of environmental protection and the promotion of science appeared. No one, of course, explicitly opposed either of these (hence my label "motherhood issues").[72] Although these particular communications were marked by greater spontaneity, they were also notably less intense. If, in fact, there were *ad hoc* "lobbies" operating from below in the course of any part of the discussion, they would appear to have been the diffuse coalitions of specialists and concerned citizens that mobilized in response to these two concerns.

Some of the issues, both within and between categories, seemed to be complementary. A stress on "law and order" dovetailed nicely with support for public participation in peer justice institutions. Between other issues, however, there was natural, and not merely implicit, conflict. Such appeared to be the relationship between the numerous and aggressive "law and order" proposals and the fewer, though more articulate, propositions for strengthened civil liberties. Finally, some of the pro-science suggestions were relevant to production questions. In contrast, advocates of environmentalism seemed to stand alone, neither antagonistic to nor supportive of the other, basic issues in the discussion.

Sociopolitical Issues

At the heart of the "work issue" was the across-the-board concern over the need for improved labor discipline. Focused primarily on the labor discipline clause (Art. 60) and, to a lesser extent, on related clauses (Arts. 14 and 40), numerous articles and letters called for recasting this theme with stronger language, greater emphasis, and, sometimes, the assistance of coercive remedies. Brezhnev touched on the general problem at the May plenum, and both *Pravda* and *Komsomolskaia pravda* cued the issue in lead editorials specifically on Article 60.[73] While the public commentary included advice, such as a factory *kollektiv*'s suggestion of awarding more medals for good work and a woman engineer's argument that the Constitution should emphasize the correlation between marriage and a positive attitude toward work,[74] the mainstream of the discussion divided between those who recommended writing into the pertinent articles (usually Art. 60) more moral stimuli, and those who favored adding more practical language—for example, the Lithuanian engineer who stressed the importance of mechanization and increased worker education "in the struggle to raise the effectiveness of production and the quality of work."[75] In general, most workers' comments inclined toward the moral approach, whereas management personnel seemed more likely to agree with the engineer's emphasis. At the same time, a number of letter writers proposed a more coercive approach to the problem. One Moscow factory worker favored holding those who violated labor or production discipline "morally and materially responsible before society." In more specific terms, various engineers and skilled workers advocated adding to Article 60 the language of legal sanction. And several writers from the Ukrainian, Lithuanian, Kazakh, and Kirghiz republics explicitly recommended including the letter and spirit of the extant anti-parasite legislation.[76]

In comparison with the "work" issue, the theme of socioeconomic and political participation evoked a much broader spectrum of interests. Concerns ranged from enhancing the individual's participatory rights of making suggestions (Art. 49) and filing complaints (Art. 58), to expanding institutional discretion in correspondence with responsibilities—of enterprises in economic decision making (Art. 16) and of local soviets with respect to local socioeconomic development (Art. 146).

Institutional participation attracted the attention of middle-level elite members in particular. Both the Irkutsk Regional Party Committee and a Moscow factory manager, for example, offered nearly identical recommendations that supplementary wording be added to Article 16 to ensure that ministries be held accountable for their economic decisions and that they comply with existing legislation permitting greater initiative on the part of the enterprise.[77] In somewhat related fashion, several letters from workers indicated interest in strengthening the section on worker participation in enterprise management, although actual suggestions consisted of minor semantic revisions that seemingly would expand the scope of such participation only slightly.[78]

The status of local soviets—especially their position vis-à-vis higher state organs—drew comment from local party and soviet officials and from prominent jurists as well. Thus, the chairman of the executive committee of a village soviet in the Kirghiz Republic recommended strengthening the language of the clause which empowered deputies to address inquiries to higher ranking officials or institutions (Art. 105). The official wanted to ensure that the deputy received a reply which would be "clear and timely." The deputies of the Moscow City Soviet, advised by a leading legal specialist, proposed enlarging the scope of the clause which defined the basic jurisdiction of a local soviet (Art. 146). In the same spirit, a party secretary from Tomsk Oblast suggested giving the standing committees of the local soviets a basis in constitutional law.[79]

At the same time, and with the apparent aim of increasing the accessibility of both the local soviets and individual deputies, a number of letters from ordinary citizens "below" concentrated on buttressing the provision of a deputy's accountability to constituents, contained in the basic clause that defined the role of a "people's deputy" (Art. 103). For example, a citizen from Odessa proposed writing into the clause a stipulation that deputies be required to appear in person before their constituents and answer questions. Another set of proposals was aimed at ensuring the responsiveness of the executive committees of local soviets by reinforcing the requirements that they report to the local soviet as a body and, in the words of one writer, "before the population and before workers' collectives," too (Art. 149). Still another citizen proposed extending the concept of accountability to the people's courts as well, by incorporating specific and demanding terminology in the last paragraph of the judicial election clause (Art. 152), which was largely *pro forma* as written in the draft.[80]

Another aspect of the broad issue of participation relates to the citizen's right of criticism (Art. 49). A prominent legal scholar emphasized the importance of this right in a major article published in *Izvestiia*, and the Chairman of the Lithuanian State Committee on Television and Radio Broadcasting proposed before the Lithuanian Supreme Soviet that Article 49 be supplemented to include a requirement that officials also be obliged to examine and reply to citizens' proposals and requests "published in the press and broadcast over television and radio."[81] The citizen's right of complaint (Art. 58) likewise received considerable attention. Two citizens wanted Article 58 to specify that "bureaucratism and red tape in the consideration of complaints" would not be permitted, while an engineer from Moscow suggested making far more explicit the paragraph outlining the citizen's right to judicial remedy.[82]

Finally, there was some interest in the press in those peer justice institutions which persisted, if on a reduced scale, since the Khrushchev period. Two writers, one a juridical scholar and the other a factory foreman, recommended that the comrades' court be mentioned specifically in the constitution. In addition, a lead editorial in *Pravda Ukrainy* elaborately praised the people's voluntary patrols (*druzhinniki*) and suggested politely that they too should be included in the new constitution. Neither institution had been mentioned in the draft.[83]

"Socialist Legality" Issues

From the time he assumed office in 1964, Brezhnev and his associates in the party leadership had consistently stressed the need for "law and order." Not surprisingly, this issue became a popular one in the nationwide discussion of the draft constitution, with the "rights and duties" and property protection clauses (Arts. 39, 59, 61) serving as special foci of attention. Several jurists and many more workers, including political activists, contributed their thoughts on both the general theme of maintaining "socialist legality" and the more specific problem of reducing economic crime. Even a few veiled, critical references to Soviet dissidents appeared. A.F. Shebanov, a distinguished legal scholar and editor of the leading Soviet law journal, *Sovetskoe gosudarstvo i pravo*, set the tone for this part of the discussion in an article in *Pravda* by characterizing "socialist law and order" as an "organic part of the Soviet way of life." One borough procurator in Moscow proposed amending Article 59 so that the citizen would be obliged "to know" as well as to observe the constitution and the laws. In addition, another Moscow lawyer suggested that the citizen should be obliged to "observe" (*sobliudat'*) rather than merely "respect" (*uvazhat'*) the norms of "socialist morality" as well. This apparently was a frequent suggestion, for *Izvestiia* noted that similar recommendations had been received "from many others."[84] Typical of the more sharply worded letters concerning economic crime was the one which suggested that Article 59 should include a requirement that the citizen adopt an implacable attitude toward "the psychology of private property." A number of individuals offered similar revision of the public property protection clause (Art. 61). Thus, an army officer proposed adding a constitutional prohibition against the use of public housing for "the acquisition of unearned income." In fact, numerous letters addressed to *Izvestiia* from various parts of the Soviet Union recommended that even the personal property clause be revised to include a general prohibition against using such property for "private gain" (Art. 13).[85] Other letters concentrated on the problem of economic crime in the factories, the prime focus of the property protection clause, with suggestions that ranged from adding more inspirational language to reworking into a more intimidating form the phrase that threatened legal sanctions against violators of the law.[86]

The polemics between General Secretary Brezhnev and President Carter over human rights and détente during the summer of 1977[87] offered several lower party and government officials the opportunity to publicly rebut Western criticism of Soviet human rights policy while scoring points on the "law and order" issue at the same time. In a prominent article in *Pravda*, the secretary of a party organization in the Academy of Sciences in Moscow asserted that the new constitution exposed the "noisy campaign in defense of the rights and freedoms of citizens of the socialist states" as mere "demagogic speculation." Moreover, he recommended greatly strengthening the linkage between rights and duties in Article 59, in language which had some clearly anti-dissident overtones. A week after this was published, *Pravda* printed a small box on its discussion page which indicated that the party secretary's article had evoked considerable interest from other readers. Two of these responses were published. One, from a metal worker in Khabarovsk, referred to the dissidents as "renegades" and strongly supported the proposal to strengthen the linkage between rights and duties. In the other, a local party secretary from the Armenian SSR observed that it was "no secret that there are still citizens who oppose their personal interest to the interests of society as a whole." He, too, supported his party comrade's recommendation that "it is necessary to strengthen Article 59." Finally, a rather singular communication from Lithuania managed to touch obliquely on all aspects of the "law and order" issue. The writer, a worker and a member of the people's voluntary patrol, urged that the latter organization be given the authority and power to deal with "not only violations of the social order" but "anti-state acts" as well.[88]

Treatment of the "civil liberties" issue differed from the "law and order" discussion in two respects. First, civil rights was a theme of both the public discussion in the press and the "underground" discussion in samizdat, while "law and order" had been a topic only in the approved public forums. Second, the civil rights issue appeared to draw its support primarily from two identifiable "interest groups," one official and institutional in nature, the other decidedly unofficial and associational. In contrast, the supporters of "law and order" seemed far more diffuse.

The public discussion of civil rights had already produced a well articulated, interrelated set of proposals by the time the "underground" discussion was just beginning to surface midway in the nationwide discussion, although in the long run the scope and depth of the latter eclipsed the former. The jurists as a group dominated the media discussion of civil rights, while various dissidents dealt with the issue in samizdat or in emigration. After only two months of constitutional discussion, the combined if independent efforts of jurists, ordinary citizens, and a handful of dissidents had produced commentary on 22 constitutional clauses and had raised more than two dozen specific proposals, questions, and criticisms concerning the status of civil liberties in the new constitution. This commentary covered a wide spectrum of questions concerning both substantive and procedural due process, and several prominent jurists reopened old debates from the criminal and civil legal reforms of the late 1950s and early 1960s.

The tone of the public discussion of civil rights was set early in the summer by Valery Savitsky, the head of the Criminal Procedure Section of the prestigious Institute of State and Law of the

USSR Academy of Sciences. He proposed emulating the East European constitutions by adding a new clause on the purpose of Soviet justice, which would include protection of the "Soviet social and state system, the rights and legal interests of citizens, as well as the rights and legal interests of state institutions and enterprises and of social organizations." More substantive concerns over due process centered first on the general socialist legality clause (Art. 4). Savitsky pointed out that its placement at the beginning of the constitution emphasized the significance now attached to "socialist legality." A lower-court judge in the Ukraine stressed the positive implications of the article for local soviets, in regard to their maintenance of law and order and the observance of socialist legality. Nevertheless, a Moscow "shock worker" argued that the draft clause was inadequate as worded and offered a substitute version which rendered the obligation of the state and its agents to obey the constitution and the laws in far more explicit terms.[89]

The public discussants refrained from criticizing the clauses on the substantive rights of speech, press, association, and religion (Arts. 50, 51, 52); but dissidents did not. On June 2, 1977, two days before the draft constitution was published, Andrei Sakharov and a group of dissidents openly appealed to the Soviet government for a "general amnesty of political prisoners" on the occasion of ratification of the forthcoming new constitution. Implicit was criticism of the regime's practice of prosecuting dissidents for exercising their civil rights in contradiction to the officially construed caveats of the main "bill of rights" clauses (Arts. 50 and 51). The day after the draft appeared, Sakharov announced that a "strong new wave of repression was under way" in Moscow and in the provinces.[90] On June 8, the "Christian Committee for the Defense of the Rights of Believers of the USSR" issued an appeal to Brezhnev as chairman of the Constitutional Commission, proposing a three-point resolution of the "legal crisis" for Christians that seemed implicit in the restricted "freedom of religion" clause (Art. 52).[91] First, the committee urged deleting from party rules the section requiring a party member to oppose "religious survivals." Next, it suggested incorporating a new statement into the party charter which would merely underscore, in principle, the incompatibility of communism and religion. Having thus proscribed religious activities and beliefs for party members, the petition continued, the party leadership should then be in a position to introduce into the text of the new constitution a provision which allowed "the possibility in principle of religion under communism."[92]

In the published discussion, suggestions for improving operationalization of the substantive aspects of due process dominated. A pensioner and old party veteran from Azerbaijan, for example, believed that the "right of criticism" clause (Art. 49) was too weak. Remarking that administrative suppression of criticism was dangerous for society and could lead to serious abuses, he argued that it should be not merely "prohibited" but classified as a punishable criminal offense. The well-known reform jurist Academician M.S. Strogovich rather eloquently elaborated the merits of the "right of complaint and redress" article (Art. 58), but also proposed additional language for further protecting the citizen's exercise of this right. He pointed out that, under provisions of the draft, not only did the citizen enjoy the constitutional right to make complaints, but that the state and its officials were constitutionally obligated to respond as well. Most important, he added, the judicial redress phrase now made it possible for a citizen to turn to the courts not only in criminal and civil matters but also to remedy purely administrative abuses by government officials. Yet, to be quite certain that this important right would not be undermined, Strogovich advised adding to the clause the stipulation that "all state and social organizations shall be categorically prohibited from referring complaints for rectification to those individuals whose actions are the object of the complaint."[93]

Certain proposals were made, too, to ensure that the structure of the legal system was compatible with the full realization by citizens of their rights. For instance, G.Z. Anashkin, a former judge of the USSR Supreme Court, suggested clarifying the judicial supervision clause (Art. 153) to better ensure that the highest court would exercise effective supervision over the work of subordinate courts. Savitsky, the criminal procedure specialist and a colleague of Strogovich, advocated substitution of a new text for the collegial decision clause (Art. 154). The revised article would include "complaints against the actions of administrative organs" within the jurisdiction of the courts. In addition, both this jurist and a "cadre inspector" from Sverdlovsk separately argued for the inclusion of more specific language in the "judicial independence" clause (Art. 155).[94] The inspector proposed increasing the responsibility of the judge and the assessors, while Savitsky offered phrasing which would subject to prosecution anyone trying to pressure the court on a decision. Finally, former judge Anashkin advocated decentralization of the power of pardon. This power, vested in the Presidium of the USSR Supreme Soviet by the draft constitution, should be extended, he argued, to the presidia of the union republic supreme soviets as well (Art. 121). But more interestingly, this jurist also urged that the clause specifying the citizen's right of complaint and redress (Art. 58) be broadened so that individuals in custody could turn to the courts when administratively deprived of their rights by investigators and procurators in the course of the preliminary investigation.[95]

There apparently was great interest in questions of procedural due process. In fact, *Pravda* found itself the target of so many questions from readers that it decided to interview the deputy procurator general of the USSR, S.I. Gusev, to obtain the appropriate answers.[96] For example, a number of citizens in various parts of the Soviet Union had written asking for clarification of the right of the inviolability of domicile (Art. 55). The procurator replied that, in comparison with the corresponding article in the 1936 Constitution, this right had been clarified and strengthened, and he added that the appropriate guarantees could be found in the criminal procedure codes of the union republics. Another letter writer's question on the privacy clause (Art. 56) received a similar response. The most interesting question, however, came from a citizen who noted that the personal inviolability clause (Art. 54) essentially was identical with the same clause in the "Stalin Constitution" and, therefore, wanted to know what current guarantees existed that this provision would not be violated. In reply, Gusev assured the readers that such guarantees were well established in the post-Stalin criminal codes of the union republics.[97]

In contrast, Anashkin suggested a few days later that the personal inviolability clause needed to be supplemented so that not only arrest but also "detention" could only be carried out subject to the law (Art. 54). On a somewhat different point, Savitsky strongly recommended combining and greatly strengthening the two clauses which reserved the administration of justice for the courts alone (Arts. 151 and 160). He advised inserting his synthesized statement at the beginning of Chapter 20 on "The Courts and Arbitration," in place of the currently worded Article 151. Finally, the clause providing "open" sessions for all court proceedings, except when exempted by law (Art. 157), elicited the criticism of a dissident who implied that this "right" had been made a mockery of in a then recent Ukrainian case and in many other cases where the trials had actually taken place *in camera*.[98]

Possibly the most important point of procedural due process was raised by Savitsky, the prominent Moscow criminal proceduralist. He ended his aforementioned article in *Izvestiia* with a strong appeal to include an explicit presumption of innocence in the right of defense clause (Art. 158), thereby reopening, no doubt, an old debate between "reformers" and "conservatives" within the Soviet legal profession. In effect, he suggested that this addition would institutionalize a meaningful right of defense in both Soviet criminal process and constitutional law. Furthermore, two letters written by jurists working as defense lawyers argued for strengthening that part of the same article that declared a defendant's right to counsel. The second letter writer, also the secretary of the party organization in a local defenders' collegium in a provincial city, proposed extending the right of defense beyond that presently provided for in Soviet criminal procedure law. He believed that the constitution should include a citizen's right to defense counsel during the "preliminary investigation" rather than at its conclusion, thereby recalling another major issue in the earlier debates on criminal procedure reform.[99]

"Motherhood" Issues

While the civil rights issue was, for the most part, the province of lawyers and dissidents—two relatively cohesive if diametrically opposed "groups"—the "motherhood" issues seemed to stimulate the interest of *ad hoc* "lobbies." Nearly everyone, especially those specialists working in these fields, was *for* science or environmentalism. Each issue attracted an extraordinary number of letters from every part of the country and at every level of the media. Article 26 in the draft committed the state to ensuring the "planned development of science and the training of scientific cadres," as well as the application of the results to the economy. Scientists and technicians from every field and discipline, from research laboratories and from teaching departments wrote to endorse this clause and propose an additional phrase or two which would tighten the "link with production," increase funding for basic research, or produce still more cadres.[100] Academicians, university presidents, and lab chiefs flooded the press with their enthusiasm for science, each one taking a few paragraphs to promote a particular specialized interest within the science community. Occasionally, a communication from a nonspecialist appeared but, even in these instances, from someone with an indirect connection with science and technology—for example, letters from a retired colonel and from a journalist polar explorer. Most of the letters, however, were written by highly educated and well-affiliated scientists.[101]

Similarly, concern for the environment proved to be an extremely popular topic in the public discussion. Specialists put forth proposals on this issue, too, but a considerable number of concerned citizens took strong environmentalist positions as well. Letters supporting the protection of nature clustered around elaborating the state's commitment (Art. 18) or strengthening the citizen's obligation (Art. 67). Many letters, such as the one from an official of the "All-Russian Society for the Protection of Nature," suggested relatively mild changes in language, although a few from average citizens advocated the inclusion of legal sanctions. While most writers promoted a general interest in environmentalism, a few seem to have had more special interests in mind, such as the forester who wanted a prohibition against poaching written into the constitution.[102]

Constitutional Revision and Ratification

Beginning in September 1977, the public discussion of the draft constitution began to wind down and gradually resumed the ceremonial character of its opening weeks in June. The quieter, more formal tone was in keeping with the then approaching ratification process, and beyond, the 60th anniversary of the Bolshevik Revolution on November 7. The final communiqué of the USSR Constitutional Commission appeared in the press on September 28, signaling the official end of the nationwide discussion, both in its public and in its internal, nonpublic forms. The brief communiqué indicated that the commission's secretariat, having coopted numerous specialists from the ranks of government and the universities, had managed to sift through the great volume of communications and that on the basis of its study the commission was recommending a number of amendments to the draft constitution.

The communiqué reported that Brezhnev, speaking as chairman of the Constitutional Commission, had outlined the major amendments which concerned such issues as "the role of labor under socialism, a solicitous attitude toward socialist property, and the further development of socialist democracy."[103] Just as he had dominated the process of bringing forth the draft in the spring, Brezhnev presided over every phase of the ratification process in the fall. In sequence, he delivered the report on the proposed revisions of the draft before the Presidium of the USSR Supreme Soviet (September 30), a plenary session of the Central Committee (October 3), and finally before the Extraordinary 7th Session of the 9th USSR Supreme Soviet which convened on October 4, four months after the appearance of the draft and on the 20th anniversary of Sputnik, which had inaugurated the space age.

In the report, published the following day throughout the USSR, Brezhnev first recited the statistics of the discussion, then outlined the major proposed amendments to the draft, and finally, before turning to the foreign reaction to the document, discussed briefly the rejected proposals. Statistically the whole undertaking was overwhelming: 140 million people had discussed the draft in several million meetings, all of which had produced approximately 400,000 proposals for amendments to the various articles of the draft constitution. Aside from purely stylistic changes, the Constitutional Commission recommended to the Supreme Soviet 150 amendments to, and textual clarifications in, 110 individual articles plus the addition of one new constitutional article. In outlining the major amendments, it was clear that Brezhnev and the leadership were responding to the sociopolitical issue of participation in the nationwide discussion as well as to the more amorphous theme of strengthening social discipline, which tended to cut across the sociopolitical, "socialist legality," and, to a lesser degree, even the "motherhood" issues of the public discussion.

Finally, Brezhnev in his report dealt swiftly with the proposals found to be "incorrect" and therefore rejected, including proposals for egalitarianism in wages and pensions, for eliminating or sharply curbing the use of the garden plot, for the abolition of the federal system and creation of a unitary state, and the "profoundly erroneous" proposals advocating the "withering away" of the state and the assumption by the party of its functions. Most of the offending proposals must have reached the Constitutional Commission through internal channels because few such proposals had been permitted to pass through the press's "filters" and surface in the public phase of the discussion. After a perfunctory and *pro forma* three-day discussion of Brezhnev's report and the revised draft, the Supreme Soviet ratified the new Soviet constitution on October 7, 1977, which henceforth became the new "Constitution Day," and the final text of the document was published in the major newspapers throughout the country the next day.[104]

The final text revealed the dozens of changes, stylistic and substantive, from the preamble throughout all nine sections and 21 chapters of the document. Although few of the amendments substantially altered the draft, the numerous changes nonetheless provided further insight into the state of Soviet "public opinion" and the points of congruence with the party's priorities. Of the major issues which arose during the public discussion, only the reform-minded jurists' proposals on civil liberties were generally ignored by the party and the constitutional drafters in the revision process. At the same time, while a number of the changes were indirectly responsive to the pro-discipline impetus behind the countervailing "law and order" issue, the many illiberal proposals for strengthening the nexus between "rights and duties" were disregarded and the "linkage" clauses remained unchanged (Arts. 39 and 59).

Nearly all of the changes contributed to the further perfecting of the constitutional "housing" designed by the party to encompass the Soviet system, but generally speaking they fell into two broad categories. One set of changes tended to enlarge the interior political space or the participatory domain within the system for both individuals and institutions; the other set of changes tended to further strengthen and reinforce the external, binding structure of the system by sealing off cracks and filling in gaps in the control and regulatory processes. The two tendencies complemented each other, the latter effecting greater system-closure, while the former pointed in the direction of "opening up" to a greater degree certain intra-system relationships and interactions.

Although some of these changes bore no observable relationship to the issue patterns discernible in the public discussion, they were apparently responsive to the internal phase of the constitutional discussion. For instance, there was little or no public commentary to foreshadow the amendments to the party hegemony clause (Art. 6), the peaceful coexistence clause (Art. 28), or the clause on state arbitration (Art. 163). In perhaps the most startling change, the party hegemony clause was supplemented by the amendment "All party organizations operate within the framework of the USSR Constitution," raising the specter of "limited government" in the Soviet Union (Art. 6). The full construal of the intended meaning of this interesting change would necessarily have to await the process of constitutional implementation. Less surprising and far less mysterious was the inclusion in the peaceful coexistence clause of the propaganda ploy of committing the USSR to "general and complete disarmament" (Art. 28). This was a familiar Soviet phrase—which raised the question of why it was left out of the draft in the first place.

While these two revisions probably came about as the result of intra-elite discussion of the draft, the third example tended to reflect Soviet-style group politics. The state arbitrators, seeing themselves primarily as specialists in settling intra-system economic disputes, apparently preferred to be in the economic rather than the legal chapter of the draft. Lobbying as a group through internal channels, they achieved at best a compromise. The arbitration clause remained where it was originally in the draft, but was amended to stipulate that the basic operation of the arbitration system would be defined by an all-union statute (Art. 163). This, in turn, opened up new vistas for future lobbying efforts by the arbitrators to amend their governing statute in the direction of changing their *de facto* status in the constitutional order.

However, more often than expected, changes in the final text of the Constitution of 1977 were traceable to the general themes which shaped the public portion of the discussion of the draft. Basically, the constitutional drafters revised and amended the draft in response to the very widely expressed desire for broader and more dependable opportunities for both individual and institutional participation in the process of implementing party policy and state legislation, as well as to the intensely felt demands for more and stricter discipline throughout the society. This two-fold response to public opinion could be seen initially in the changes and emendations to the preamble. The advocates of increased participation undoubtedly appreciated the addition of the open-ended concept of "communist social self government," a holdover from Khrushchev's days which carried with it the implication of comrades' courts, people's voluntary patrols, people's control commissions, and other vehicles of mass participation. Similarly, the social disciplinarians were no doubt pleased with the strengthened linkage concept by which citizens' "rights and liberties" were interconnected not merely with the performance of their "civic responsibility" as in the draft preamble, but with "their duties and responsibility to society" in the final text. To drive the point home, the linkage concept was also inserted in the revised conclusion of the preamble which proclaimed the linkage of rights and duties among other ideas as the core of the new constitution.[105]

The Participation Amendments

Most of the participation-oriented amendments to the draft constitution appeared to have been designed to have an effect on both mass and elite participatory structures and processes, as well as on the accountability procedures by which constituent groups at different levels in the system obtained knowledge of their elected representatives' actions. Essentially, these changes were addressed more to the quantitative aspects of participation (how much can occur) rather than the qualitative side of the issue (how effective it may be). The increased participatory emphasis was dramatically keynoted in the opening articles of the final document as the expanded labor collective clause was moved up from the economic chapter (Art. 16 of the draft) to the political chapter (Art. 8 of the Constitution). The theoretical increase of mass participation in lower-level economic decision making was paralleled by the one new article added to the draft, which constitutionally legitimated the citizen's right of indirect participation in local policy making by elevating to full constitutional status the concept of the "voters' mandates" (Art. 102). In addition, the clause on the citizen's general right of participation in national policy making was recast and strengthened, particularly with reference to the increased emphasis on the mass public's right to participate "in the discussion and adoption of laws and decisions of nationwide and local importance" (Art. 48). This tendency was complemented by the increased attention to the concept of the nationwide "referendum" (Arts. 108, 115, and 137), and the empowering of the USSR Supreme Soviet to submit for nationwide discussion not just "draft laws," but also "other very important questions of state life" (Art. 114).

Governmental bodies, as well as voters and workers, also received enhanced constitutional attention to their participatory status. The *de jure* powers of local soviets, autonomous republics, and union republics were all enlarged to include ensuring "comrehensive economic and social development" on their territories (Arts. 147, 83, and 77). In addition, each governmental stratum, respectively, gained greater supervisory authority over enterprises and other institutions of higher subordination on its territory, all of which suggested a possible commitment by the Soviet leadership to a slightly greater degree of decentralization by means of creating considerably more decision-making space for subordinate governmental levels within the system (Arts. 147, 83, 77, and 142).

Making the various representational strata of the government more accessible and accountable to their respective constituencies, at least in terms of periodic information about their activities, was the other aspect of the intensified stress on the participatory motif. As a result, a people's deputy was now obliged to report on his work not just to his constituents but "also to the collectives and social organizations that nominated him as a candidate for Deputy" (Art. 107). In turn, the executive committees of the local soviets were required not only report to their soviets at least once a year, but "to meetings of labor collectives and of citizens at their places of residence" as well (Art. 149). Another amendment enjoined the "Soviets of People's Deputies and the agencies created by them [to] systematically inform the population about their work and the decisions they adopt" (Art. 94). Even judges and people's assessors, or co-judges, were now explicitly required to "report" on their work from time to time to "the voters or the agencies that elected them" (Art. 152).

Ascending the bureaucratic hierarchy, the higher administrative bodies as well were made, theoretically at least, more accountable to the legislative branch of government. This was accomplished by amending the clause on standing committees of the USSR Supreme Soviet to read: "The committee's recommendations are subject to mandatory consideration by state and social agencies, institutions, and organizations. Reports are to be made to the committees, within established time period, on the results of such consideration or on the measures taken" (Art. 125).

Last, but hardly least, the right of criticism clause (Art. 49) was significantly amended in a way that bridged both the themes of participation and discipline in the discussion of the draft constitution. To better facilitate and protect citizen participation and to help ensure official adherence to the requirements of administrative legality, the existing prohibition against officials persecuting their critics was noticeably strengthened to read: "Persons who persecute others for criticism will be called to account" (Art. 49). If it had been faithfully executed, this amendment alone could well have proven to be the most important revision of the draft in terms of making the Soviet system somewhat more responsive to the concerns of the individual citizen. Instead, however, the "criticism" clause contained an implied "catch" to the effect that only "constructive" criticism would be afforded constitutional protection from retaliatory persecution. Under the best of circumstances, reasonable men and women will differ over what might constitute "constructive" criticism in a given situation; therefore, a safe assumption was that generally neither dissidents nor even persistent "whistleblowers" should have expected too much from the amended safeguards in this clause. In fact, dissent and nonconformity, and their constant companion, repression, grew and intensified in subsequent years under Brezhnev and his two short-lived successors, Andropov and Chernenko.

New Constitutional Duties

Considerably less ambiguous were the additional constitutional directives addressed to the Soviet citizen in his or her various roles. On top of the maze of overlapping obligations imposed on the citizen in the draft constitution, amendments provided for nine new or reinforced duties. These could be grouped together as the party's and the drafters' response to the strongly articulated and widespread demands for more discipline of all kinds cutting across the three sets of issues that had dominated the nationwide public discussion. Although largely rhetorical and frequently unenforceable, these new constitutional burdens qualified the Soviet citizen as one of the most constitutionally bound individuals of modern times.

In the final, official text of the 1977 Constitution, children were enjoined to "help" their parents (Art. 66), residents to "take good care" of their housing (Art. 44), and all ablebodied persons were expected to engage in "socially useful labor" (Art. 60). Individuals could now only use their personal property (Art. 13) or engage in "individual labor activity" in the "interests of society" (Art. 17), and those people assigned garden plots were directed "to make rational use" of them (Art. 13). All adults were cautioned against using socialist property for "selfish purposes" (Art. 10), while collective farmers "were obliged to use land effectively" (Art. 12), and workers were instructed "to take good care of the people's property" (Art. 61). In addition, everyone's civic duty to help save historical monuments was semantically reinforced and enshrined in a separate article in the final text of the new constitution (Art. 68). Finally, all citizens were put on notice that their exercise of the civil liberties of speech, press, and assembly would have to contribute not only to the "strengthening" but also to the "developing" of the socialist system as well (Art. 50). Aside from the new constitutional strictures on land use, the "motherhood" issues of science (Art. 26) and environmentalism (Arts. 18 and 67) received only nominal attention in the constitutional revision process, despite the avalanche of proposals on these issues. "Water resources" were brought under the umbrella of environmental protection (Art. 18), the citizen's "protective" duties became the sole focus of a single constitutional article (Art. 67), and the state's vast legislative and executive powers were marginally amended to include environmental and science legislation among its myriad other responsibilities (Art. 73, Sec. 5; Art. 131, Sec. 7).

Succinctly summarizing the process of revising the draft into the new Soviet Constitution of 1977, the party had skillfully exploited the existing illiberal currents of public opinion to justify the near completion of its theoretical closure of the Soviet system, while constitutionally acknowledging the participatory impulse "from below" through incremental adjustments and marginal changes, the realization of which awaited implementation.

The Constitution As "Magic Wall"

The number of individuals who participated in the constitutional discussion and the nature of many of their suggestions indicated that many Soviet citizens were attentive to—and may even have taken seriously—the potentially prescriptive aspects of their new constitution. While their perceptions would prove to be unjustified, they did serve, implicitly, as "public support" for the more normative constitution envisioned by the "constitutionalist" scholars. More important, the extent to which the 1977 Constitution functioned as a prescriptive document would provide a benchmark for measuring the scope and limits of change in the Soviet polity.

In a more fundamental sense, however, the new constitution represented the sedimentation of six decades of Soviet rule. The 1977 Constitution was a distillation of that cumulative experience, although it also served to codify the shifting emphasis from rule by force to rule by law that had emerged since Stalin's death a quarter of a century earlier. The result was a Soviet-style *Rechtsstaat*, a legal framework through which the party could govern its vast domain without irrevocably limiting its ultimate power of action. In essence, the Brezhnev regime created in constitutional form a "magic wall" which concealed the "close cohabitation between wide stretches of certainty for mass man's daily living conditions and unheard of areas of oppression [and] lawlessness."[106]

Epilogue

As the Brezhnev era underwent revision, the Constitution of 1977, in retrospect, turned out to have been one of the highwater marks of an administration extensively criticized as "stagnant." Although it was not exclusively a "Brezhnev Constitution," Brezhnev clearly left his imprint on the document, and it reflected (and, until the late 1980s, continued to reflect) the structure and functions of the Soviet system as a party-led constitutional bureaucracy. The constitutional "housing" of the Soviet system under the direction of party architects was expected to both codify de-Stalinization and to bring a conclusive, formal end to the reform impulse that de-Stalinization represented in Soviet politics and law. The success of this political endgame would depend to a large extent on the choices the party leadership would make in implementing the 1977 Constitution under Brezhnev's successors.

2. The Andropov–Chernenko Interregnum

Juridicizing the System

Was Yuri Andropov a model for Gorbachev, and his legacy the inspiration for perestroika? One school of thought would say, No, Andropov was a failed leader unable to launch needed economic reform due to lack of time, a resistant bureaucracy, the "shooting down" of the reform coalition by the South Korean airliner incident, or all of the above. Another approach might be that reform was never the issue for Andropov, that merely "perfecting" the economic mechanism was the limited undertaking which was cut short by the leader's failing health.[1] Yet another view might argue that on the eve of his death in early 1984, Andropov's protégés, including Mikhail Gorbachev, were in place in the higher party apparatus, poised to push through a major turnover of the regional Brezhnev–Chernenko old guard while a new, younger, more competent governmental team was waiting in the wings for its cue to move economic reform to center stage.[2]

Ancillary to his efforts on the economic front, whether they be deemed failed, limited, or rapidly eclipsed under Gorbachev, there was never any doubt that Andropov launched a tough "discipline" campaign. But was it "cosmetic" and doomed to fail in the face of entrenched corruption in the system and society,[3] or was it responsive to a popular yearning for "order" and hence responsible for the gains in labor productivity in 1983?[4] Even the duration of the discipline campaign has been disputed. Did it wane in the spring of 1983,[5] or was it under way throughout Andropov's brief incumbency and, if so, did it survive under his shortlived successor, Konstantin Chernenko?[6]

All of these perspectives fail to pay adequate attention to the scope of Andropov's concept of discipline, the breadth and intensity of his campaign, and, especially, the extraordinary task of reconstructing and revitalizing the legal infrastucture of the Soviet system carried out under his aegis—all within the context of the continuing implementation of the 1977 Constitution.

The USSR at the End of the Brezhnev Era: Diagnosing the Problems

What domestic problems must have caught the eye of Yuri Andropov when he succeeded Leonid Brezhnev in late 1982? Surely, as a former KGB chief and self-styled disciplinarian, the new leader realized he had inherited a pre-modern, even feudal society, one in which

> local political elites tithe collective and state farms and all other producers and vendors of consumables within their fiefs. The sale of offices and pardons is not unheard of, reminiscent of the medieval Church, and the most significant economic relations are frequently at the level of barter. The population is stratified along nearly rigid caste lines based on one's proximity to power or access to ever scarce consumer goods. This is a world of perpetual shortage in which almost everyone's energies are focused on the quest for the essentials of everyday life.[7]

Surely Andropov was in a position to know that in fact everything was for sale in the Soviet Union, even university and law school admissions and academic grades. Large parts of the higher educational system were just another branch of the vast, largely illegal "second economy" whose leading indicators included the high volume of pilferage of consumer goods from the national rail freight system and the wholesale "diversion" of foodstuffs from public catering establishments and retail food stores.

Undoubtedly, as a Politburo member, Andropov had been privy to confidential surveys which showed a surprising degree of public tolerance and even support for "second economic" behavior officially regarded as criminal, and a most "conciliatory attitude" toward petty theft of public property.[8] Less surprising to a person with Andropov's regular access to classified information, but equally dismaying, would have been the secret tabulations of crime statistics which reflected these negative public attitudes in action, for example such data as convictions for theft of public property and certain "economic crimes," constituting 21–22 percent of all crime.[9]

In the interstices of the crime data one could detect a burgeoning rate of vandalism of, say, public pay phones, and a still minor but troubling trend of burglary and armed robbery for the purpose of obtaining narcotics.[10] Both crimes testified to the rampant juvenile delinquency problem of which the average fearful and angry Soviet adult was well aware and frequently complained in letters to the press, but which was rarely noted publicly in Brezhnev's day.

Andropov, moreover, would have known that teenagers and young adults were not the sole source of concern. He and his colleagues could only have been appalled at the incidence of train crashes and boat accidents caused by drunken engineers and helmsmen, not to mention the mounting and costly accident rate among private car owners who mixed drinking with driving. And then there were the troubling reports marked "for official eyes only" on the level of violence by criminal convicts in the prisons and camps, and their comrades, the career criminals and recidivists, back on the streets of the cities and towns. Worse, as a former KGB man, Andropov had to have been cognizant of the real state of affairs in the Ministry of Internal Affairs, the courts, and the Procuracy in Brezhnev's last years. Routine law enforcement work had fallen to a low level in many local agencies, with indifference, apathy, and even incompetence increasingly becoming the norm among militia workers or ordinary policemen. For many legal officials, the administration of justice had become yet another branch of the ubiquitous second economy, and justice a cash commodity.[11]

Last but not least, in his survey of the country he was expected to lead into the 1980s, the new General Secretary's eye would most assuredly have come to rest on the most prevalent and perhaps the potentially most subversive problem of all, chronic indiscipline at work—in particular, absenteeism, tardiness, and leaving work early. Just one of the available surveys of the Moscow region (where goods and services were in greater supply and more readily available than elsewhere) would have revealed to him that in that region alone, 73 percent of the work force took time off during working hours to attend to personal business, and that in some factories and offices "no more than 10 percent of the workers were at their places during the final hour of the shift."[12] As a reportedly intelligent leader Andropov no doubt recognized the link between poor work discipline, inefficiency, low productivity, poor quality control, a declining economic growth rate, and—back once again to the beginning of the cycle—"a world of perpetual shortage."[13]

Interim Remedies: 1980–82

During his two last years in power, Brezhnev and and his associates attempted to cope with some of the USSR's myriad internal problems, but age and failing health prevented him from providing the personal leadership and sense of urgency needed for success. Although individually the proposed remedies were sound, and probably to some extent even bore the imprint of Politburo member Andropov's disciplinarian bent, they tended to fragment into isolated, *ad hoc* reactions to specific situations. Lacking any programmatic coherence and direction, the Brezhnevist remedies proved at best to be interim holding actions.

Ironically, the Brezhnev leadership's drive against corruption was stimulated by events in Poland. The Polish crisis of 1980 was naturally a major source of concern, but that story is well known. What was less widely known was the fact that the independent trade union Solidarity's success indirectly raised the issue of corruption in the USSR. On August 31, 1980, Lech Walesa, representing Solidarity, and a Polish deputy prime minister signed the Gdansk Agreement, signaling Solidarity's victory after a summer of strikes and negotiations. Two of the 21 demands agreed to by the government were intended to eliminate certain material privileges of the party elite and police personnel.

The case of Maciej Szczepanski, a member of the Polish party's Central Committee and Chairman of the State Radio and Television Committee, was particularly notorious. Dismissed from his government post on August 24, 1980, Szczepanski became the object of a special high-level investigation on September 4. What followed was the disclosure of one of the most extraordinary cases of official corruption ever made public in a communist country. Using public funds, Szczepanski had acquired seven cars, a helicopter, two executive aircraft, a luxury yacht, a mountain villa, a large collection of X-rated movies, and a 16-room palace complete with resident prostitutes. After party leader Gierek fell from power in the wake of Solidarity's success, the Polish party opened a campaign against corruption in its ranks, and Szczepanski was, predictably, arrested, tried, and convicted after a long trial.[14]

The Szczepanski case evidently caused consternation among the Soviet elite. In September 1980 the CPSU Central Committee quickly passed a resolution dealing with official corruption. It was distributed to lower party organizations in the form of a secret party circular and never made public, indicating the party's reluctance to deal with such a sensitive issue openly and by means of legal action. For the most part, the anti-corruption campaign aimed at officials was treated as an internal party matter, except for a few cases that achieved national notoriety, such as the "Great Caviar Scandal."[15]

In spite of the party's concern over corruption in its ranks, the only significant legislative response during the interim period was addressed to rank-and-file personnel in the retail trade and service organizations—clerks in stores selling consumer items, food service employees, and others who were in a position to extort under-the-counter payments for scarce goods or services,[16] or to sell or conceal, for personal gain, goods under their control.[17] Two new rules were added to the criminal law in 1981. The first, under the unwieldy title "Receipt of Illegal Remuneration from Citizens for Fulfillment of Work Connected with Servicing the Populace," was aimed at those employees who would demand an advance "tip" for selling a scarce consumer item or performing a service, and imposed as punishment "correctional work" for up to a year (usually meaning a pay reduction of 10 percent or more for the duration of the sentence, served at one's place of work), a fine, or up to three years imprisonment. The second, on "Violation of Trade Rules," was intended for warehouse or restaurant employees who sold goods or foodstuffs entrusted to them "out the back door" so to speak and pocketed the money, and related offenses, and entailed punishments ranging from up to a year of correctional work (with or without deprivation of the right to work in that particular job) to three years of imprisonment.

Until 1981, only officials were liable under the law for taking bribes and subject to harsh punishments, including even the death penalty under especially aggravating circumstances,[18] while illegal diversion of goods for personal gain was considered "abuse of authority or official position."[19] Under the new rules, subordinates as well became liable, although with commensurately milder penalties. The law on petty theft of public property was amended to include stealing the parts of automobiles in storage or in transit as freight.[20] Thus the Brezhnev regime attempted to close several loopholes through which commodities flowed into the underground second economy. A number of cases brought under the new and amended rules were publicized in the press in 1981–82 to deter others. However, the party's secret circular and legal maneuvers were disjointed and without focus, and at best were stop-gap measures as the problem of pervasive corruption continued to plague Brezhnev's final years, making a mockery of the 1977 Constitution's "socialist legality" clause (Art. 4) and the protection of "socialist property" clauses (Arts. 10 and 61).

A year later, during the summer of 1982, the all-union Fundamental Principles for Legislation on Criminal Law and on Corrective-Labor Law (penitentiary law) were amended. The changes and additions were long overdue. After the ratification of the new constitution in 1977, the Presidium of the USSR Supreme Soviet had formulated and published a five-year legislative plan for implementing the provisions of the Constitution through recodification, revision by amendment, and new legislation. Most of this work was slated for completion by 1978–79, with only six of the 34 projects scheduled for 1980–82.[21] By the end of 1979 many of the projects had not been completed, the plan was well behind schedule, and the presidium publicly admonished USSR Minister of Justice V.I. Terebilov, who was responsible for coordinating the plan.[22] A year later, in early 1981, the presidium again found it necessary to address Terebilov on the delays and on the need to improve the quality of the drafting work already done. The minister was ordered to report back to the presidium on January 1, 1982.[23]

The revision of the criminal and corrective-labor legislative principles had been two of the projects originally scheduled for completion no later than the end of 1979, but like much else during Brezhnev's latter years, things did not go as planned. Two and a half years later, in July 1982, these amendments (except for one liberalizing change) meant that convicted persons serving sentences other than imprisonment, parolees, and recidivists were to be brought under the much tighter control of the authorities while serving their sentences, or probation.[24]

The single exception involved extension of the use of deferred or "stayed" sentences for juvenile first offenders to include adult first offenders sentenced to no more than three years imprisonment.[25] Generally, the Russian Republic Ministry of Justice reported that the previous five years' experience with deferring or staying execution of sentences of juveniles had been highly encouraging in that no additional crimes were committed by the great majority of minors.[26]

The rest of the amendments involved increasing the maximum

corrective work sentence to two years, and substantially raising the ceiling on the maximum fines imposable for all crimes that incurred corrective work or fines as punishment. New provisions were also added for dealing with convicted persons who either shirked serving their corrective work sentence or failed to pay fines.[27]

In addition, the rules governing conditional (suspended) sentences and conditional release (parole) were strengthened to deter, and punish, abuses of these procedures. In the latter case, parole was denied altogether to two new categories of prisoners—double recidivists and persons committing offenses while on previous parole.[28] Finally, related changes were made in the corrective labor legislation concerning individuals serving suspended sentences or on parole with the obligation to work under specified conditions. The effect was increased police control over such individuals and an enlarged range of penalties for infractions.[29]

One last edict on criminal justice legislation bearing Brezhnev's signature as chairman of the Presidium of the Supreme Soviet was published in the official law gazette on October 15, 1982, just weeks before his death. This final edict on the subject testified eloquently to the belated, *ad hoc*, and fragmented approach to criminal justice legislation during the final two years of his administration. The edict, which was probably rushed through to appear before the November anniversary of the Bolshevik Revolution, showed signs of haste and carelessness in legislative draftsmanship.

The main purpose of the October edict was to bring the ten USSR edicts on criminal and administrative liability for various crimes and administrative violations (which provide for corrective work or fines) issued over the previous two decades (1961–82) into conformity with the summer 1982 amendments which raised the ceilings on the two penalties. Those criminal edicts covered such diverse offenses as report padding, unwarranted train stopping, hooliganism, and assault on a police officer or police auxiliary. The same realignment of penalties was accomplished for the several relevant articles of the USSR Statute on Criminal Liability for State Crimes of 1958.[30] This updating was to be expected since the summer amendments were to go into effect on January 1, 1983.

However, the fall edict was also used as a vehicle to insert omissions in the summer edict. For instance, four more articles of the all-union Criminal Legislative Principles were slightly revised by semantic changes that had already been made in related articles by the summer edict. The parole provision of the Corrective-Labor Legislation Principles, which had been amended in three different parts by the summer edict, was additionally amended in yet another part.[31]

The earlier official concern about quality control in the legislative drafting process still seemed warranted in late 1982. The manner of incremental amendment as afterthought suggested the absence of a clear policy or a consistent and systematic approach to the possible remedies for many of the problems besetting the Soviet Union under Brezhnev.

The general malaise afflicting the Soviet system was probably best epitomized by the slogans for the 65th anniversary of the Bolshevik Revolution, echoing the familiar themes of a tired administration devoid of ideas and energy, and facing a troubled future with little left to offer the public other than ideological rhetoric.[32]

Andropov Takes Charge: Campaigning for Discipline

Almost immediately following Leonid Brezhnev's death on November 10, 1982, Yuri Andropov took charge, sounding the clarion call of "discipline" as the *leitmotiv* for his administration. Not since Khrushchev's campaign for de-Stalinization had a Soviet leader so clearly enunciated a "metalegal" policy for his stewardship of the Soviet system. By this I am referring to Andropov's general political theme of discipline, a policy of systemwide scope which significantly impacted the process of regulating Soviet society as well as the system itself.[33] For him, the discipline campaign was a way of signaling that the Soviet Constitution, and especially the policies and laws underpinning it, were to be taken seriously by all involved.

While emphasizing continuity and legitimating his program with references to Marx, the 26th Party Congress (1981), and the relevant Central Committee resolutions, Andropov set a course for change.[34] His goals were ambitious: to regenerate the immobilist system, reawaken a dormant society, and reinfuse the "old" Soviet Man with a new sense of discipline. Key to all his goals, his systemic concept of discipline embraced executive, planning, labor, and diverse aspects of social discipline, including even the observance of traffic safety rules.[35] In his impromptu remarks at a Moscow factory in December 1982, Andropov made it clear that the drive to reinstitute discipline would include ministers as well as workers.[36] As the campaign unfolded during 1983, it came to include party secretaries, government officials, prosecutors, policemen, and, of course, the average citizen.

Andropov did not see his prescription for discipline as the panacea for all of the Soviet Union's ills. It was merely a first essential step which he hoped would stimulate higher labor productivity, better quality control, faster economic growth, and ultimately, a rise in the standard of living and a more efficient political and economic system.[37] This was a tall order, one he realized could not be accomplished "by slogans alone."[38] To set in motion these broad social changes, Andropov turned to Soviet law. The "implacable" law would be his instrument for social engineering and the further juridicization of the Soviet constitutional universe.[39]

In relying on law to translate his vision of a "disciplined" developed socialist society into reality, Andropov was in the mainstream of the post-Stalin period. With the abandonment of terror, Stalin's successors increasingly relied on law to govern an ever more complex and differentiated Soviet society. Khrushchev and Brezhnev each made major contributions to this post-Stalin tradition as they progressively built the Soviet-style *Rechtsstaat*, or legal state, through which the party ruled after Stalin. Andropov continued this tradition, but with some notable differences, Khrushchev had refurbished the tarnished concept of "socialist legality," giving it a connotation of anti-arbitrariness. Brezhnev shifted to a more pragmatic, anti-deviance emphasis.[40] Both men had built their legal structures gradually, and both had reasonable expectations as to what the law could accomplish after years of Stalinism on the one hand, and the persistence of an urban-industrial crime problem on the other.

By contrast, Andropov refashioned socialist legality into a pro-discipline instrument, which reflected greater confidence in the efficacy of law in general. In the short space of 15 months he carried out more legal changes than had been seen since the onset of the post-Stalin legal reforms in the late 1950s and early 1960s. Andropov's prolific legislative output and the impetus he gave to institutional revitalization encompassed criminal, labor, and administrative law as well as the police, the Procuracy, and even the law schools. The pace of constitutional implementation had quickened.

To be sure, the party-state under Andropov did not legislate in a vacuum. Some legislation flowing from the still unfulfilled legislative plan of 1977 had been in the "pipeline" when Andropov took charge in late 1982. That was certainly true for many of the extensive revisions in the criminal codes of the union republics. A number of significant changes in those codes, not foreshadowed by the 1982 summer and fall amendments to the Fundamental Principles of Criminal Legislation, suggested, however, that Andropov himself had a hand in the criminal law revisions, although he took office at a late hour in the drafting process.

In fact, the long delays in fulfilling parts of Brezhnev's 1977 post–constitutional ratification legislative plan may have been beneficial to Andropov, affording him the opportunity of putting his imprimatur on the drafting process. Such was the case with the USSR Statute on Labor Collectives, mandated by the new Constitution (Art. 8) and scheduled in the follow-up legislative plan for early 1980.[41] When it was finally passed in mid-1983, nearly three and a half years late, the statute bore the imprint of Andropov's discipline campaign, especially in its Article 9.[42] Even in those instances where legislative revision had occurred under Brezhnev, such as in the USSR Statute on Criminal Liability for State Crimes, further substantial revisions were carried out under Andropov not long afterward.[43] As final testimony to Andropov's penchant for social engineering through law, a good deal of the legislation for implementing his discipline policy had not been provided for in Brezhnev's 1982 legislative plan for the years 1983–85; it was conceived *de novo* during Andropov's tenure as party leader.[44]

Legislating for Discipline:
The Andropov Record

Andropov's first order of business in the campaign for discipline was to place trusted and tested men, disciplinarians like himself, in key positions. His major cadre changes in December 1982 were clear indications of the direction he would take. N.A. Shchelokov, the long-time USSR Minister for Internal Affairs and a Brezhnev crony, was sacked, subsequently dropped from the Central Committee, and expelled from the party on the basis of his poor management of the police ministry and rumored allegations that he was personally involved in corruption as well. V.V. Fedorchuk, Andropov's successor as KGB chairman in the spring of 1982, was named Shchelokov's replacement as head of the uniformed police.

The appointment of Fedorchuk, a career KGB professional, immediately signaled a tough new attitude toward ordinary crime. Subsequently, Fedorchuk installed his own men, former KGB associates, as his deputies.[45] V.M. Chebrikov, another seasoned KGB official, became the new chief of the secret police. In another dramatic move, G.A. Aliyev, also formerly a senior KGB official (whose reputation for managerial prowess as a party leader in the Caucasus preceded him to Moscow), was elevated from a candidate to full voting member of the Politburo. Not long after, Aliyev was appointed first deputy prime minister behind the aging N.A. Tikhonov, a Brezhnev man. Aliyev's successful assault on corruption in the Azerbaijan economy in the fall of 1982, during the last months of the Brezhnev era, would prove to be a precursor for Andropov's nationwide drive for discipline.[46] The team of Andropov, Aliyev, Fedorchuk, and Chebrikov meant that the "new puritans" were in command in Moscow, ready to wage war against crime, corruption, and indiscipline.

The general staff of the discipline campaign very quickly had in hand new weapons with which to conduct the struggle. Effective January 1, 1983, the most extensive revisions of the post-Stalin criminal codes since their inception in 1960 went into effect. In the Special Part (which defines specific crimes) of the Russian Republic code, the model for all other union republic codes, 133 of the 246 articles were amended in December 1982. The most heavily amended chapters covered the crimes against public and "personal" or private property.

In response to widespread public concern over the crime problem expressed in thousands of letters to the Politburo and the press,[47] Andropov added a half dozen new crimes and increased the punishments for dozens of other crimes. The new crimes of theft, stealing, and robbery of public or private property, accompanied by "forcible entry" into a residence, office building, or warehouse, were introduced, with penalties ranging from two to eight years' imprisonment plus the confiscation of the offender's personal property.[48]

While penalties were reduced for less than a dozen offenses including performing an illegal abortion, violations of authors' and inventors' rights, and "moonshining,"[49] the penalties for scores of other crimes were increased. Wherever the sanction of corrective work was provided for, the maximum was raised to two years, consistent with antecedent legislation. Where fines were indicated as an alternate punishment, the amounts were doubled and tripled, to some extent, presumably, in recognition of hidden inflation in the Soviet economy. In some of the articles of the code which permitted a judge to use his or her discretion on supplementary punishments such as confiscation of property, the option was deleted and the penalty made mandatory. Generally, most "official crimes," "economic crimes," and crimes against persons were assigned heavier penalties.

Special problem areas for the new law-and-order drive, such as petty theft of public property and social parasitism, received separate legislative attention, also effective with the new year 1983. A person committing petty theft at his factory, for example, could now be deprived of certain fringe benefits such as bonuses and vacation time in addition to facing criminal charges.[50] In regard to the offense of parasitism, called the "evasion of socially useful labor" in the Constitution's "duty to work" clause (Art. 60), certain key qualifying criteria for a *corpus delicti* were deleted, greatly increasing the potential applicability of this vague violation of the work ethic in Soviet society.[51]

Juvenile delinquency, a persistent problem, also came in for increased attention during 1983, with the press drawing thousands of letters from irate citizens in reaction to published accounts of especially heinous crimes by minors. The general theme was a call for tougher sanctions against juvenile lawbreakers, the public perception being that minors were treated too leniently by the authorities. By mid-year this seemed to be a party-contrived prologue to a possible forthcoming legislative revision of the use of suspended sentences and other nonconfinement measures against juveniles.[52]

In the same vein, discussions in the press called for sterner measures in the reform schools, where internal order apparently left much to be desired. Nostalgic references were heard to the methods of Anton Makarenko, a strict but effective pedagogue of discipline for delinquents during the 1920s and 1930s.[53] The Politburo also warmly praised the *druzhiny*, or volunteer police auxiliaries, on the eve of their 25th anniversary in early 1984.[54] As the year 1983 wore on, Andropov's legislative prescriptions for social ills became harsher. The effort to instill greater discipline was extended to the corrective labor camps, to arrangements for parole, to active or would-be dissidents, and to those who might pass "official secrets" to foreigners.

Beginning October 1, 1983, imprisoned convicts, who had previously been punished by being sent to a corrective labor camp's internal prisons, ran the risk of courting an additional sentence of up to three years if they were tried in the camps for the new crime of "malicious disobedience" or "any other opposition" to the lawful demands of the camp administration.[55] Similarly, after release from imprisonment the convict found the rules of administrative supervision over released prisoners completely revamped and much stricter.[56]

As for the small dissident community in the Soviet Union, their activities had been at a low ebb during the previous few years, with stern taskmasters such as Andropov, Fedorchuk, and Chebrikov consecutively at the helm of the KGB. Their position had worsened appreciably since the United States had imposed economic sanctions over Afghanistan and Poland, leaving the Soviet authorities with little to lose for cracking down on the human rights movement.[57] The extensive revision of criminal law, in force since the beginning of 1983, also encompassed the political crime articles under which dissidents had been most frequently "sentenced and tried."[58] Prosecution for defamation of the Soviet system would now cost more. The three-year maximum term of imprisonment remained, but, consistent with previous legislation, the maximum for corrective work or a fine was increased respectively from one to two years and from 100 to 300 rubles.

As a matter of course, these milder alternatives were rarely applied to dissidents (who were invariably sentenced to imprisonment), so that this change presented no serious threat to the already beleaguered dissident community. The same was true of the related article, also amended, on organizing group disorder— say, outside a courthouse where a political trial was taking place.[59] The same increases in corrective work penalties applied to the two articles of the code under which religious dissidents were most frequently brought to trial. Here the raising of the penalty was more consequential because local authorities had frequently used repeated, confiscatory fines as an alternative to imprisonment.[60]

The infamous Article 70 ("Anti-Soviet Agitation and Propaganda"), or the crime of subversion, was also amended as part of an edict decreed in January 1984, just a few weeks before Andropov's death. In a perverse way, one could say revision was overdue for this much used weapon against dissidents, since it had remained unaltered since 1961, well before the emergence of the unofficial Soviet human rights movement in the mid- to late 1960s. The thrust of the amendment was to outline more precisely the definition of what constituted subversion. The general term "literature" (one of the means of subversion) was replaced by the more differentiated "written, printed" or other forms of work of subversive content. Presumably, this was meant to reflect the realities of the 1980s, when dissent might rear its head in the form of a letter written to the leadership, to the Italian Communist Party, or even to the President of the United States, or, possibly, in the form of a printed leaflet stuffed surreptitiously in mailboxes or deliberately left on park benches. The already heavy penalties remained unchanged.[61]

The dissidents themselves expressed most concern over the new code provision on resentencing of convicts. In the late Brezhnev years, the news that a prominent dissident, on the eve of completing his term for a political offense, found himself falsely accused of an ordinary crime and reconvicted, had become all too common. The new code article on resentencing appeared to institutionalize that scandalous tendency not to release political prisoners; most of them had served time in the camp "cooler," and hence could be set up for retrial for the slightest infraction of the camp rules.[62]

Finally, a January 1984 edict further amending the USSR Statute on Criminal Liability for State Crimes defined as a new crime the transmission of an "official secret" in the form of economic, scientific or technical, or "other" information entrusted to a person at his place of work. The penalties ranged from up to two years of corrective work to eight years imprisonment. It seemed reasonable to assume Andropov was seeking to impose discipline and restraint on contacts between Soviet businessmen and their Western counterparts, and between dissidents (especially Jewish "refuseniks" fired from their jobs for applying to emigrate to Israel) and the foreign press corps in Moscow.[63] In fact, this law was not used as widely as expected, then or later; after Gorbachev came to office and sanctioned "glasnost," it became a dead letter.

Upon taking charge in late 1982, Andropov also launched a simultaneous attack on the endemic lack of labor discipline. His early speeches, accompanied by much fanfare in the press, laid out the line of advance on the labor "front" against such foes as absenteeism, tardiness, and drunkenness on the job. Managerial incompetence in forcefully dealing with these enervating problems in the production process, throughout the service sector, and at the administrative level, also received much criticism.

Andropov's dramatic, unannounced visit to a Moscow machine tool factory in January 1983 keynoted the labor phase of the discipline campaign. He expressly reminded the workers of the essential linkage between good work discipline and the yearned-for improvements in the Soviet citizen's well-being and general standard of living. Implicitly, he was adumbrating the constitutional theme of the nexus of rights and duties (Arts. 39 and 59).[64]

Andropov's factory visit was coordinated with "Operation Trawl," a spectacular countrywide dragnet to round up absentees from work during regular hours. Police went into the grocery stores, beauty shops, and even Turkish baths at midday to check documents and identify "work shirkers," people who were away from their desks and workbenches on personal errands during working hours. In one of many dramatic raids,

> police burst into a crowded theater in a provincial city near the Black Sea. Suddenly . . . the lights went on, and everyone in the twelfth row was ordered outside. Each was asked why he was at the movies rather than at work. If he didn't have a convincing explanation, the police called his boss. "We have your employee," the standard conversation went, "Why is he with us instead of with you?"[65]

Scenes such as this sent shock waves through the population, punctuating Andropov's insistent message that discipline was the order of the day. In fairness to the public's shopping problems in a scarcity society, the leadership ordered shops and consumer services to remain open in the evening, to afford people the opportunity to do their chores on their own time.[66] By late spring 1983, "Operation Trawl" began to wind down, leading some Western observers mistakenly to assume that Andropov's discipline campaign was meeting bureaucratic resistance and foundering.[67]

More likely, Andropov never intended "Trawl" as a continuing operation, but merely as a dramatic device to get people's attention for more institutionalized responses to the problem, such as the draft version of the new all-union Statute on Labor Collectives, which was published for public discussion as the dragnet was being phased out.[68]

Andropov's legislative program for tightening labor discipline consisted of the draft bill on labor collectives (published in April 1983 to elicit public comment during April and May); the amended statute passed in June; a joint implementing resolution of the CPSU Central Committee, the USSR Council of Ministers, and the centralized trade union system issued in early August; enabling legislation enacted a week later to amend existing labor law; and explanatory interviews in the press on the changes introduced —with the whole package taking effect September 1, 1983.

Soviet and East European sociologists defined the labor collective as "a group of people organizationally united for common socially useful activity on the basis of public ownership of the means of production."[69] Although the concept was introduced into Soviet jurisprudence in the 1977 Constitution, the statute, as it slowly evolved through the Brezhnevist legislative process after 1980, was probably intended at least partially as a reaction to the labor and political unrest in Poland during 1980–81. However, by the time Andropov came to power a year later, with the legislation still unfinished, General Jaruzelski had imposed martial law in Poland, abating the crisis from the Soviet perspective and giving Andropov more space to deploy the new concept in his struggle for discipline. Although the bill included 23 articles, the majority on different aspects of carefully limited worker participation in economic affairs, most of the ensuing public discussion (as filtered through the controlled press) seemed to concentrate on Article 9, the section on discipline. A number of letter writers offered suggestions to further strengthen that section, and when it appeared in the published law, it had indeed been considerably amended.[70]

The essence of Article 9 was that the state and management were no longer alone in the effort to maintain labor discipline. The individual's "collective" had now been formally enlisted in the struggle, equipped with the authority to recommend significant material deprivations for truant and slothful workers or employees, from temporary demotion to reduction of bonus and, ultimately, dismissal. In addition to the use of peer pressure, the summer also brought changes in the work brigade system, to the effect that bonuses were now to be paid on the basis of collective rather than individual performance. Thus, for example, if "one member of the brigade is absent from work, the others will suffer economically."[71]

During the summer the party, the government, and the trade union system jointly spelled out specifically the correlations between various violations of labor discipline and material penalties. For instance, in the past, absence from work without a valid reason for most but not all of a day was classified as tardiness. Under the joint proposals, absence for three or more hours was to be regarded as absenteeism, entailing reduction of vacation time on a day-for-day basis down to a minimum leave.[72] The Constitution indeed guaranteed the right to a vacation (Art. 41), but this immediately followed the "right to work" clause (Art. 40), one of several which constitutionalized the Soviet work ethic.

Several days after the joint resolution in mid-August, Andropov, in his role as chairman of the Presidium of the USSR Supreme Soviet, signed an edict legally codifying the resolution's provisions. The edict decreed a series of amendments to the relevant articles of the all-union Fundamental Principles of Labor Legislation. Under the new rules, a worker had to give longer notice (from one to two months) before leaving a job; "shirking" received a precise definition (more than three hours of unjustified absence); a worker's financial liability for damage caused on the job (usually while intoxicated) was increased; and the penalties of transfer to a lower-paying job and demotion for set terms were strengthened.[73] When asked what those changes would mean for the Soviet labor force, a government spokesman described the new regime for work as "greater differentiation between rewards for good work and penalties for violating labor obligations."[74] Absent the invisible "fist" of a free labor market, Andropov resorted to the discipline whip, using the negative reinforcement of material deprivation.

Andropov did not expect to get the country moving again by means of law alone. Recognizing the distinction between "law in the books" and "law in action," he sought to mobilize the public, began a purge of corrupt or incompetent government and lower party officials, and set in motion the revitalization of law-enforcement agencies. On an experimental basis in a few cities, citizens were invited to send the police anonymous pre-printed postcards if they wished to report social infractions, labor violations, or criminal offenses.[75] Throughout his short term in office, Andropov also presided over an extensive purge of officials in the trade, transportation, and service networks, where corruption was most rife, as well as some lower party cadres who had tolerated these situations. Thousands of government officials were dismissed, demoted, subjected to disciplinary procedures, or charged with crimes. At least three prominent officials were sentenced to death in the most egregious cases. Even corruption in the military was targeted in Andropov's broad sweep.[76]

Last but hardly least, he came down hard on those whom he was ultimately counting on to carry out his new body of law—the police, the prosecutors, the courts, and even the law schools. Corruption in the law school admissions process was exposed and corrected.[77] Very early in the Andropov incumbency, the procuracy was subjected to a withering critique. A.M. Rekunkov, the USSR procurator general, had to make a public self-criticism, acknowledging corruption in his ranks and promising to root it out.[78] The courts, in turn, were scored for long delays, easy sentences, lenient treatment of recidivists, and a host of other shortcomings.[79]

Finally, the ranks of the Internal Affairs agencies, the police themselves, came in for the harshest criticism. As a precursor of the glasnost which would flourish a few years later, the press was unleashed and extraordinary accounts of police abuses, mistakes, and venality were aired in public. The Politburo assigned political commissars to their stationhouses to oversee ideological training of the police. Fedorchuk relentlessly purged the ranks at all levels. Many landed in jail, and many others were bound over for trial as Fedorchuk strove to rebuild "the professional authority of the Soviet police."[80] By the time of his death, Andropov's revitalization of the administration of justice was in full swing, but far from complete. The question was, would it continue?

Andropov's Legacy

It is perhaps ironic to speak of a Soviet leader's legacy after so short a time in power, but as former Politburo member G.V. Romanov remarked in what was a fitting epitaph, Andropov's brief term in office was marked by "a closer unity of words and deeds."[81] By means of the "power of persuasion and the force of law,"[82] Andropov sought to bring about a sea change in attitudes and behavior of both rulers and ruled in the USSR. To accomplish his mission, with its neo-Calvinist overtones of secular salvation through honest work, Andropov presided over what to that point was one of the most prolific periods of legislative activity in recent Soviet history, advancing further in letter and spirit the ongoing implementation of the 1977 Constitution. In the space of 15 months he constructed and reconstructed a legal infrastructure designed to reenergize the Soviet system and remould the Soviet people into law-abiding, hard-working, punctual citizens. In so doing, he continued the work of his post-Stalin predecessors in leaving behind the ways of arbitrary fiat in favor of the further "juridicization" of system and society into a stable, predictable, and more efficient legal order.[83]

Although some of Andropov's methods were jarring for his hapless subordinates and too harsh for many of his constituents, his campaign for discipline struck a responsive chord with a public weary of the mediocrity of everday life and craving effective leadership to deal with the country's problems. His death in early 1984 elevated the ailing Konstantin Chernenko to leadership of the Soviet system. Whether Chernenko, who in 1983 described "discipline and order" as "inalienable aspects of socialist democracy," would match deeds with his words remained to be seen.[84]

The Chernenko Record

Despite ritual incantations of the rhetoric of continuity, much in fact changed with the arrival of Chernenko.[85] During the summer of 1984, the party piously invoked Lenin's dictum against substituting "discussion for action and talk for work."[85] Ironically, this Leninist phrase turned out to be an apt description of the record of the 13-month Chernenko regime.

Generally, Andropov's fleeting politics of revitalization gave way to his successor's politics of exhortation reminiscent of the late Brezhnev era. Chernenko, of course, had been very close to Brezhnev. Accordingly, in the party apparatus and the bureaucracy the emphasis on personnel turnover diminished, and the Brezhnevist slogan "stability of cadres" once again became the order of the day.[87] Likewise, ideological slogans, Chernenko's specialty, displaced the law, new legislation, and the enforcement of legality as the principal medium for translating high politics into the language of policy application. In turn, political socialization supplanted social regulation as the main systemic channel for policy implementation. As a consequence, Chernenko's paramount concern for correct "upbringing" replaced Andropov's singular obsession for unswerving "discipline" as the new *leitmotiv* of public discourse in the USSR. Constitutional implementation did continue to some extent, since "upbringing" was featured in two clauses of the 1977 document (Arts. 27 and 66).

This is not to say that there was no linkage from Andropov's stewardship to Chernenko's. Certainly there were a number of highly visible lines of continuity, but they were primarily cosmetic, symbolic, or, at most, the policies of a "bipartisan" consensus reaching back to the mid-1970s.

Just as Andropov had memorialized Brezhnev by emblazoning his name on a number of public places, Chernenko did no less for his predecessor, whose name was assigned to such things as cities, streets, ships, and scholarships as well as a plaque at the gates of the Lubyanka in memory of his service as KGB chief.[88] In a similarly decorative way, citation was frequently made to an Andropov plenum of the Central Committee, but reference invariably was to Chernenko's speech on ideological matters at that 1983 session.

In the realm of symbolic continuity, Chernenko did not neglect his predecessor's power base, the KGB. General Chebrikov, a former Andropov deputy who now headed the KGB, was promoted to the rank of marshal,[89] while the chairman of the Latvian KGB, Boris Pugo, was appointed first secretary of the republican party organization.[90] Similarly, Chernenko, like Andropov before him, paid a well-publicized visit to a factory, but while his predecessor used the occasion to keynote his discipline campaign, linking it to the need for raising labor productivity and thus living standards, Chernenko addressed the same problems with the standard rhetoric of the 1970s on the need for technological modernization and energy conservation.[91]

Much more ominously, Chernenko continued the bipartisan tradition in foreign affairs as well as in domestic repression policy. If Brezhnev presided over the 1979 invasion of Afghanistan and the 1981 coup in Poland, and Andropov was credited with the shooting down of the South Korean airliner in September 1983 and the Soviet walkout from the East–West arms talks a few months later; Chernenko, as their worthy successor, was no less tough in authorizing the greatest Soviet offensive in Afghanistan since the invasion, and pulling the USSR and its fraternal allies out of the 1984 Summer Olympics.

In the area of repression against dissidents and human rights activists, Chernenko carried on a draconian policy which harkened back to the late 1970s. The cynosure of his repression policy was the escalation of pressure against Andrei Sakharov, including the trial and conviction of his wife, Elena Bonner, for political defamation.[92] Predictably, Bonner was sentenced to exile in Gorky, where her husband had been administratively banished since early 1980 —effectively rendering the academician and titular leader of the Soviet human rights movement virtually incommunicado.[93] Aside from the use of police power in a few other "cases" of well known individuals, such as the dissident historian Roy Medvedev, whose apartment was placed under guard for several months,[94] Sakharov's friend Irina Kristi, who was subjected to "house arrest,"[95] the theatre director Lyubimov, who was denaturalized,[96] and the passage of new restrictive laws aimed at further reducing contacts between Jewish emigration activists and their supporters in the West,[97] the repression of many other nonconformist citizens of varied political and religious persuasions rolled on relentlessly with a dread monotony during 1984 and early 1985.

If Chernenko's health had held up, future historians might well have recorded Andropov's brief term as a mere hiatus in the Brezhnev–Chernenko era, since the new regime appeared to be in a direct line of descent from the late Brezhnev period. Depending on how one evaluated Andropov's tenure, much of the style and substance of Chernenko's even shorter incumbency was a regression to, or a continuity from, his patron and mentor, Brezhnev. Symbolic of this backward-looking stance, the Brezhnev family and other former notables who had been lying low because of political and/or legal problems with the Andropov team were once again in circulation in Moscow.[98] In the same spirit, upon hearing the news of Andropov's death, an anonymous black marketeer raised a silent toast to a more prosperous future.[99] Although spectacular cases from the depths of the "contra-system" continued to be reported in the press, with the dreaded scourge of the second economy in his grave, the economic base of the contra-system had resumed the healthy growth rates it enjoyed in Brezhnev's time.[100]

In matters of political style, the resemblance to the Brezhnev regime was striking. A Chernenko cult quickly blossomed—in marked contrast to Andropov's austerity—complete with hyperbolic references to the new leader's stint as a corporal in the border guards in the early 1930s, and larger-then-life (and bigger than his comrades') portraits bobbing up and down at the 1984 May Day parade.[101]

Chauvinism, and an accent on spectaculars, marked what passed for political substance, in a manner not dissimilar from the last years of Brezhnev, when there was little else to fill the vacuum created by paralysis of political initiative and the general immobilism of the system. Denial and displacement characterized Chernenko's approach to Soviet social problems—denial that they were indigenous to Soviet society and displacement of the blame onto foreign "imperialist" centers of intrigue conspiring to subvert Soviet values. Corruption was fobbed off on mercenary foreigners, such as the American diplomat publicly accused of selling Western consumer goods to Soviet citizens out of the trunk of his car.[102] The vibrant youth counterculture was blamed on Western radio beaming in such subversive music as "heavy metal" rock designed to encourage in Soviet youth all kinds of antisocial attitudes and sociopathological behavior.[103] What was the recommended antidote? Yet another vigilance campaign complete with a slick TV series on foreign spies.[104] Finally, the feeble attempts to use public policy to remedy the Soviet Union's long list of pressing problems were hobbled by the traditional Russian tendency toward "risk aversion,"[105] which was as pronounced under Chernenko as it was under his chief, Brezhnev. The regime, however, had to create at least a semblance of action from the clouds of rhetoric; hence, resort was made to a kind of "monumental" politics to fill the void. In Chernenko's case, it was the completion of the great construction project called the BAM, or Baikal-Amur Mainline railway, the 2,000-mile link to the natural resource treasures of distant Siberia. Public attention to pressing day-to-day problems of the quality of life was diverted (at least momentarily) to the spectacle of a rail line that "crosses 22 mountain ranges and 17 major rivers, not to speak of thousands of minor streams."[106] Truly a heroic accomplishment which recalled to mind some of the construction feats of the 1930s, but how long could that kind of surrogate for necessary political action divert the public?

Demise of a Campaign: From "Discipline" to "Upbringing"

Andropov's death triggered the demise of his campaign for discipline. Its decline was initially imperceptible in the profusion of pledges to the contrary, but gradually momentum decreased until the drive for discipline was politically moribund. As fate would have it, though, its demise turned out to be temporary once Chernenko passed from the scene.

Obviously, it would have been inexpedient for Chernenko to abruptly terminate so extensive and highly visible a program. Besides, it no doubt served his purposes to take on for a time the mantle of the fallen leader as a way of effecting the transfer of allegiance of Andropov's supporters and followers to himself. Furthermore, during the post-Stalin period, policy change from one administration to another had rarely been abrupt, least of all when a particular policy had already assumed myriad legal forms and taken on a life of its own. Aside from the occasional exception such as Brezhnev's sharp reversal of Khrushchev's bifurcation of lower party organizations, counter-reform tended to proceed incrementally and in a generally unobtrusive way which preserved the illusion of the continuity of party policy. After all, a broad-gauge policy such as discipline was usually not proprietary to the leader alone, but represented the collective wisdom of the party elite, which had a vital stake in maintaining its self-styled, corporate image as a wise, steady, and prudent legislator.

Thus, Chernenko (who like any new leader had a preferred agenda in mind) continued to carefully and gradually distance himself from Andropov's preoccupation with discipline in four identifiable but overlapping phases or shifts of emphasis. First, the campaign for discipline was continued, but in a more muted fashion, and on a more modest scale. Above all, its cutting edge was blunted, its thrust slowed, and its course of direction deflected from one of Andropov's key targets, the middle elite who constituted Chernenko's political base. Second, Andropov's major unfinished business, the purge and revitalization of the law enforcement cadres, was declaratively "completed," described as a success, and shunted off to a political siding like a train loaded with dangerous cargo. Third, legal engineering, a technique preferred by Andropov, was downscaled as a solution to chronic social problems in favor of a more "comprehensive" approach, thereby lifting from the shoulders of the police the task of nearly singlehandedly having to remedy inveterate and possibly insoluble patterns of deviance. Finally, Chernenko's regime steadily shifted the source of Russia's many difficulties from present behavior to past "upbringing," thus focusing on a sufficiently diffuse process so that any reasonable expectation of rectifying the situation could easily be deferred to the future. Deferred expectations in turn dispersed responsibility, mitigated pressures on the bureaucracy for results, and allowed one and all to slip back into the comfortable business-as-usual attitudes of the not-so-bygone days of Brezhnev in his declining years. Let us examine each of these phases in more detail.

First, under Chernenko the discipline campaign was continued, but increasingly as a shadow of its former self. A few conspicuous cases with an occasional prominent defendant still appeared in the press, but invariably these cases arose prior to Chernenko and by then concerned only second-string culprits or posthumous scapegoating.[107] Similarly, some of the newer, high profile cases were probably already under preliminary investigation when Andropov died, conveniently coming to trial under Chernenko.[108] This at least gave the appearance that some of the subtexts of the Constitution's "economic system" chapter were being taken seriously, especially the state's obligation to protect "socialist property" (Art. 10) and the implied prohibition on unearned income (Art. 13).

Likewise, the traditional post-Stalin practice of coping with deep-seated national problems by means of a "proxy" republic, or making an example out of non-Slavic ethnic groups, continued. Indeed, in the Caucasus and Central Asia, indigenous cultural factors such as extended kinship systems tended to reinforce a general Soviet tendency toward indiscipline and corruption, but aside from the familial networking, the Russians, Ukrainians, and Belorussians were no less infected by these problems. Nonetheless, given the focus of prosecutions since 1980, it appeared that epidemic corruption was confined to the southern climes of the Union, a bias which implied disregard if not contempt for the Constitution's "ethnic and racial equality" clause (Art. 36).

Under Brezhnev, Azerbaijan had been the target republic. Andropov subsequently singled out Armenia and Moldavia, although, as his general campaign accelerated, cities, towns, and districts in the RSFSR began to feel the heat as well. After Chernenko came to power, Uzbekistan became Moscow's surrogate for the erstwhile nationwide discipline campaign. In fact, the Uzbek situation was a veritable microcosm of the diverse concerns Andropov had been addressing, complete with his draconian remedies, some of which were set in motion before his death. According to a June 1984 issue of *Pravda Vostoka*, published in Tashkent, little progress had been made in raising labor discipline during the preceding year, and corruption and economic crime seemed to be growing naturally "in this soil." As a consequence, five Uzbek Republic Party Central Committee members were dropped for their abuses, other executives were recalled from the republic's Supreme Soviet as well as from local soviets, and "1,056 employees of stores, wholesale depots, pharmacies and hospitals" were dismissed and charged.[109]

What might be called the doctrinal spillover from the Andropov period was also contributing to the image of continuity. On the occasion of its 60th anniversary, during the spring of 1984, the USSR Supreme Court continued from previous plenums its line of pronouncements on the legal aspects of the discipline problem.[110] Similarly, learned articles on various legal implications of Andropov's campaign (no doubt written earlier, given the need for scholarly "lead time") continued to appear in the law journals well after Chernenko took office. Their authors advocated such proposals as a USSR statute "On Disciplinary Responsibility," the creation of coordinating councils for planning and organizing labor discipline in enterprises and institutions, and more precise legislative distinctions between legal and illegal forms of private economic activity. The latter two proposals both indirectly and directly flowed from the ongoing constitutional implementation process with regard to the "labor collective" clause (Art. 8) and the "individual labor" clause (Art. 17), respectively.[111]

Despite the impression of continuity created by various cases, the Uzbek "proxy," and the writings of legal scholars, in reality Andropov's high-visibility discipline campaign was subtly modified under Chernenko's tutelage into a much smaller-scale and far less intrusive effort. Chernenko's successor "campaign" adopted a decidedly lower profile with considerably less publicity. If anything, reportage of ordinary, garden-variety crime seemed to be increasing at the expense of coverage of economic crime.[112] For those second economy cases receiving public notice, a shift of emphasis was apparent. Earlier, under Andropov, "leading" cases highlighted in the press usually concerned systemic types of corruption, and frequently included middle-level and occasionally higher-level executives in the ranks of perpetrators. In contrast, the more dramatic cases featured in the media under Chernenko related to highly idiosyncratic capers pulled off by comparative small-fry, signifying a return to Brezhnev-style crime reporting.[113]

The relative downplaying of major economic crime and the corresponding increase in media attention to crimes against persons and personal property evoked a typical Brezhnev-era "law and order" response from the Chernenko administration. Teen crime, especially street mugging, came in for more attention, eliciting the standard calls for more police patrols and a crackdown on recidivists.[114] Internal Affairs Minister Fedorchuk promoted tougher official attitudes toward lawbreakers, stressing the need for more punishment and less admonishing.[115] New rules were issued broadening the authority of law enforcement officers, security guards, game wardens, and other armed personnel entrusted with the protection of socialist property, to use firearms.[116] Finally, confirming the law-and-order emphasis, more death sentences for especially egregious crimes seemed to be coming to light, notably in the cases of an icon thief who murdered several victims, a poacher who killed a game warden, and a woman executive convicted of large-scale extortion.[117]

What remained of the disciplinary focus under Chernenko was a much narrower orientation and a more selective approach to the types of cases being prosecuted. The former, elaborate cases involving executive responsibility and constituting *de facto* attacks on the integrity of one or another part of the system gave way to official preoccupation with petty theft and cases of speculation in scarce consumer goods. Most of those cases were brought against low-level personnel of the food supply system, the retail and wholesale trade network, and the consumer service and health delivery sectors. Thus, alongside the Politburo's announced efforts to improve the flow of consumer goods and services to the population, the public was regaled with accounts of car-stripping (right in the auto plants), freight car looting, meat gangs, gas rings, and doctors and dentists exacting illegal payments for performing their services.[118] Confirming the general impression that the Chernenko campaign was tightly circumscribed, several regional power industry executives were convicted for "expediting"—giving expensive "gifts" to ensure that their enterprise's needs were attended to by higher authorities. No personal profit motive was involved, yet none of the recipients of the bribes—senior officials in Moscow—were implicated or indicted.[119] This reflected a tendency by the new regime to fence off from legal assault the upper reaches of the bureaucracy. Therefore, except for the occasional senior official who was presumably deemed politically expendable for his abuses, such as the then recently dismissed minister of housing and municipal services in the Udmurt Autonomous Republic, it became clear that Andropov's commitment to enforce discipline against the *nomenklatura* as well as the working stiff was rapidly being forgotten.[120]

Second, just as Brezhnev had curbed but did not repeal Khrushchev's popular justice institutions in the 1960s, Chernenko correspondingly moved his predecessor's discipline campaign to the backburner, where it continued to simmer, but at much lower heat. This was no doubt a source of relief for the police and law enforcement community, which had been under maximum pressure as the spearhead of Andropov's drive. Chernenko's diversion of this drive into the more conventional law-and-order channels rendered the police's task more manageable.

Concomitant with the deemphasis on discipline, the police were a major beneficiary of Chernenko's resumption of the Brezhnevist policy favoring stability in the ranks of cadres. The sharp criticism of law enforcement cadres under Andropov, in both the general and the legal press, virtually ceased along with the unfinished purge of the corrupt cops in their ranks. To be sure, a few echoes of the past remained such as the culmination of the high-level purge of the Belorussian juridical cadres which had begun during Andropov's tenure, and the continuation of the sweeping purge of corrupt officials in Uzbekistan, including hundreds of police.[121]

Basically, though, Chernenko presided over the "rehabilitation" of the militia after the withering public criticism of Andropov's brief term. His approach was that "revitalization" had occurred and largely succeeded, despite the derailing of Andropov's purge of the police, which had been moving at full throttle at the time of his death. Some of the changes presented in support of this case included the establishment of a system of political commissars for the police, the enactment of new disciplinary rules for Internal Affairs Ministry personnel, the creation of comrades' courts within the militia, and the tightening up of police recruiting procedures.[122] It remained to be seen whether these new internal safeguards and the upbeat emphasis on "good cops" would remedy the serious deficiencies of the past.

Third, Chernenko was much less a believer in the efficacy of law to remedy social problems than his predecessor. Foremost was the crime problem, which the new regime approached in a "comprehensive" way since, as Fedorchuk has put it, "punitive measures alone" would not solve the problem of social deviance.[123] Among the nonlegal measures proposed to buttress the law enforcement process were more careful personnel selection (especially for positions in finance), better marketing techniques (to avert shortages which stimulated economic crime), tighter security over socialist property (in particular in railroad freight yards), revision of out-of-date shrinkage, spillage, and spoilage norms (which facilitated falsification of "losses"), and the dismissal of economic executives who could not deter petty theft within their jurisdictions (thus shifting the burden from enforcement to prevention).[124] In addition, special emphasis was placed on the new labor collectives, as reflected in the remarks of the Estonian Minister of Internal Affairs on the need for nonlegal preventive efforts:

> The militiá, naturally, struggles with its means and methods against petty thefts and mobilizes society against them. But it cannot surround enterprises with a chain of vigilant guards. Order must be established in the labor collectives themselves.[125]

Finally, the slack created by the reduced reliance on legal engineering and recognition of the limits of police action was taken up by what emerged as the principal theme of the Chernenko incumbency—the stress on the correct "upbringing" of all age groups and strata of the population. The term "upbringing" (*vospitanie*) was used as a synonym for political socialization (this is evident, for example, in the statement, "the upbringing effect of socialist competition and the brigade form of labor and incentives is underestimated").[126] Chernenko himself used the term in the most obvious contexts, such as the "upbringing of schoolchildren," and the "upbringing" work of the Young Communist League in the armed forces, but in their zealousness to emulate the leader, his subordinates made "upbringing" a universal tagline for nearly every situation.[127] The rollcall of usage included political, military-patriotic, internationalist, labor, atheistic, and aesthetic "upbringing."

Furthermore, upbringing work was projected as a remedy for such diverse problems as improving medical education, correcting deficiencies in institutions of higher learning, upgrading the quality of police work, shaping up political executives in Uzbekistan, overcoming "highlifeism" among the elite youth, preventing the underreporting of receipts by busdrivers, instilling "ideological immunity" in the younger generation, and combating the "psychology of consumerism" in the population at large.[128] Such a tall order was of course mostly rhetoric, or what Lenin might have referred to as talk instead of action. Attitudinal change as an outcome of political socialization or resocialization in any society is one of the more difficult, ambitious, and elusive sociopolitical objectives, generally requiring a long-term commitment. However, time ran out in early 1985 as the inexorable laws of nature took their toll of the patron of "upbringing," Konstantin Chernenko.

Epilogue

Less than two and a half years elapsed between Brezhnev's death in November 1982 and Gorbachev's selection as CPSU general secretary in March 1985. During that short space of time the USSR was governed by two leaders, Andropov and Chernenko, who promoted different political and constitutionalist approaches as panaceas for the USSR's many internal problems, including its floundering economy. Time ran out for their ailing advocates, however, before either approach could be tested. Hindsight now suggests that both efforts would have failed, so grave were Soviet problems as revealed since by the glare of glasnost. By the mid-1980s, the Soviet Union was a staggering giant beladen with an ossified governing system and a stagnant economy and society, and with the modest hopes for reform within the programmatic and normative dimensions of the 1977 Constitution significantly dimmed.

3. Gorbachev and the Soviet Constitutional Crisis

From De-Stalinization to Disintegration

Mikhail Gorbachev's succession to the Communist Party leadership in 1985 seemed to come in the nick of time for the USSR. Under the ailing Chernenko, the Soviet system had been foundering, buffeted from one internal crisis to another. The impetus for change begun by his immediate predecessor, Andropov, was rapidly losing momentum. Further constitutional and legal development had slowed and the campaign to combat corruption and restore discipline was waning.

Enter Gorbachev, the first general secretary from the post-Stalin generation. Young, dynamic, bold, and innovative, Gorbachev quickly took charge, trying to resume the forward motion begun under his mentor Andropov. Appropriately, Gorbachev's first legal moves in 1985 included legislation to step up the struggle against "unearned income" and the black market, or shadow economy,[1] and the launching of the most extensive anti-alcohol campaign in recent Soviet history, which came close to outright prohibition.[2] As in 1982–84 under Andropov, anti-corruption and pro-discipline were the themes driving Soviet internal policy. But in retrospect, these were only initial, interim policy steps as Gorbachev gathered his political forces and shaped his ideas for far-reaching change in the Soviet Union.

As in the long sweep of Russian history, change once again emanated from the top, from the Office of the General Secretary of the Communist Party of the Soviet Union. Gorbachev's ambitious reform program, called *perestroika* or "restructuring," originated as party policy and was appropriately proclaimed by Gorbachev at the 27th Party Congress early in 1986.[3] Using the past as a guide, one would have expected the party to issue a series of resolutions or policy statements that would *pro forma* be converted into legislation; thus would the reform effort be defined from the center.

This time it would be different. The component parts of domestic restructuring—*glasnost,* or more openness in information policy, and "democratization," or greater citizen involvement in politics—soon took on a life of their own, outstripping the party's ability to control the process. Only the third domestic leg of the restructuring program, economic reform, remained susceptible to party direction and tempo. Ironically, while the first two components of the program, which had been eagerly embraced by society, succeeded, economic reform under the party's cautious guidance had ground to a halt and stalled by the early 1990s.

Gorbachev's most dramatic departure from previous post-Stalin reform initiatives was not simply the scope of his program, but the change of venue for its proposed realization. As he gradually shifted the locus of his power from the party to the state, the Soviet Constitution became the principal framework for the articulation of the reform objectives. A constant refrain of Gorbachev and the reformers was the need to institutionalize the changes to ensure the "irreversibility" of restructuring. The main medium to achieve this goal became constitutional law, long just another instrument of party rule.

By 1987, the tenth anniversary year of the 1977 USSR Constitution, the document had been amended only once, a minor amendment in 1981. The following year, in late 1988, nearly one-third of the Constitution was amended.[4] A year later, many of the new and revised constitutional clauses were re-amended.[5] The year 1990 was an even more productive year for constitutional reform. As part of Gorbachev's transfer of power from the party to the state, he engineered the revision of Article 6, depriving the party of its political monopoly over the Soviet system.[6] To offset the consequential decline of his own power as party leader, Gorbachev then pushed through the legislative process the constitutional creation of the office of an executive presidency of the Soviet state.[7] In most Western constitutional systems, these systemic changes alone would represent an extraordinary development, nearly the equivalent of the constitutional transition from the Fourth to the Fifth French Republic under De Gaulle in 1958. In the Soviet Union, the process did not end there. Gorbachev constitutionally redesigned his presidency and its new, corresponding institutions twice more in 1990, and capped the year with the draft version of a proposed new Treaty of Union, which went to the heart of the federal constitutional structure of the USSR.[8]

The rate of constitutional reform and re-reform in this period was so exceptional that Elena Bonner, widow of Andrei Sakharov, quipped that perhaps Gorbachev should be in the *Guinness Book of World Records* for changing the constitution of a single country so many times in one year. What did Gorbachev hope to achieve by this cyclonic approach to constitutional reorganization?

Basically, since the 19th Party Conference in 1988, Gorbachev had sought to create a socialist *"pravovoe gosudarstvo,"* a term that can be literally translated as "a legal state" or interpretively as "a law-based state."[9] In this sense Gorbachev was building on cumulative political and legal development. The post-Stalin period had witnessed a contraction of prerogative rule, or the so-called administrative-command system, and the progressive expansion of normative means of governance, or the legal order. Khrushchev, through de-Stalinization and criminal justice reforms in the 1950s and early 1960s, and Brezhnev by continuing the law reform process and producing the new USSR Constitution of 1977, had sequentially laid the foundations for Gorbachev's proposal for a law-based state. The net result of the preceding developments, however, was a constitutionalized bureaucracy behind which the party still exercised its unlimited rule over Soviet society.

Gorbachev's idea was far more radical: to build a law-based state in the USSR as both a product of perestroika and the housing for a restructured Soviet system within which the party's rule would be limited by the boundaries of constitutional action. A source of confusion was that Gorbachev had not clearly and consistently sorted out what kind of new state he sought to develop. Would it be merely a state based on law as against unchecked party commands, or a liberal state, with laws protecting individual and group rights? Whatever the future held, Gorbachev's preferred route was via constitutional reform, which, unfortunately, led the USSR into a political labyrinth. In order to establish constitutional supremacy, Gorbachev had to concede to the public various degrees of freedom and a range of individual and collective choice. The unintended consequence was that the long hoped-for culmination of the country's quest for constitutional order degenerated into constitutional disorder in the 1990s.

The Transition to Constitutionalism

Initially, it seemed that Gorbachev would carry out his juridicization of the Soviet system within the framework of the 1977 Constitution. Beginning in mid-1986, a number of new laws were promised, and gradually enacted, which expanded but did not fundamentally alter the existing constitution.[10] Early economic reform legislation on the state enterprise and the right of individual entrepreneurship could be comfortably subsumed within the second chapter of the Constitution, on "The Economic System."[11] Similarly, while under Brezhnev, an impressive new right of judicial appeal of administrative decisions had been written into the Constitution of 1977 (Art. 58), it soon became a constitutional dead letter for lack of follow-up legislation under Brezhnev, Andropov, and Chernenko. By supporting the first law on judicial appeal, Gorbachev at last provided the necessary enabling act which converted the constitutional clause into operational legal language.[12]

Due to the success of the policies of glasnost and democratization and other legal enactments, as well as a constant flow of additions to the legislative agenda, it soon became apparent that the existing constitution could not accommodate the vast restructuring program. Without waiting for promised laws, individuals and groups had begun to appropriate to themselves implied *de facto* rights of a freer press, a wider range of permissible speech, and the virtually unprecedented acts of forming independent groups and taking causes to the streets.[13] Policy statements were outstripping legal empowerment as permitted behavior began to render numerous clauses of the Constitution, especially in the political and rights sections (Chaps. 1 and 7), unreflective of the emerging reality. Proposed new legislation on the courts and due process, not to mention a promised statute on the KGB, implied the future prospect of major constitutional surgery at the very least. In this context it was evident to Gorbachev that an entirely new constitution would be needed. Accordingly, a Constitutional Commission was appointed to draft what was supposed to have become the fifth Soviet constitution since 1918.[14]

Initially, the task of creating a new constitution, a new fundamental law of the land, appeared within reach. The division of the leadership and strategic elites into reform and conservative factions, however, greatly complicated the process of finding a consensus and slowed the drafting process.[15] The problem was compounded as some of the 15 union republics, availing themselves of the more permissive atmosphere in the country, began to carry out revision of their republic constitutions on their own initiative. The Baltic republics led the way, eventually to be followed by the Russian Republic, the country's largest, under Boris Yeltsin's leadership. Other republics followed suit. Some soon came to realize that, in the face of impending systemic change, patching an existing constitution was an exercise in futility. Thus, in addition to the federal constitutional commission, several republics empaneled their own commissions which, in turn, set off in search of constitutional formulas not necessarily consistent with the interests of the center or the integrity of the union itself.

By the end of the 1980s, Soviet law, which just a few years earlier was seen as the key to the long-term durability of restructuring, had itself become part of the problem. The outpouring of conflicting union and republic constitutional proposals was producing a gridlock. A union republic would amend its constitution in a manner at variance with the official Soviet Constitution. Moscow would react by declaring the offending clause unconstitutional and hence null and void. The republic legislature would, in turn, respond that Moscow's writ was not relevant to the matter.[16] Constitutional conflict became the norm rather than the exception as, one by one, republic legislatures began to assert their preemptive right to approve all federal legislation in order for it to have legal force on their territory. This came to be called the "war of laws."[17]

The crisis of the law itself deepened as separatism spread among a number of union republics. Lithuania led the way, and by the end of 1990 virtually all 15 republics had declared their "sovereignty" —as did most of the autonomous republics within their borders. Separatism and the assertion of sovereignty meant insistence that the language of the titular nationality within a republic take precedence over the *lingua franca,* Russian.[18] The new language demands, in turn, caused anxiety among other nationalities living within the various republics, especially among the Russians, some 25 million of whom live outside the Russian Federation. In an extreme case, a group of largely Russian-populated cities in the Moldovan union republic declared themselves a separate republic.

In this heated environment, the "war of laws" meant that republic legislatures began to routinely reject Moscow's new laws and enact their own. Sometimes these laws would be contradictory, but often they were similar, leading to Moscow's criticism that a situation of "parallel power" was being created in many parts of the country. This included dual prosecutors in some places—one appointed by Moscow as in the past, the other locally, and neither recognizing the other's authority.[19] Similar fissures opened up in republic police forces, greatly complicating the problem of coping with the ever burgeoning crime wave in the USSR. This situation set the stage for the attack of Moscow-controlled OMON special forces ("the Black Berets") on the Latvian police ministry headquarters in early 1991.[20] The years 1990 and 1991 were witness to many more such violent skirmishes between central and local forces as republic independence movements continued to gain momentum.

As these unwanted consequences of the reform program unfolded, Gorbachev became increasingly uneasy about the integrity and future of the USSR as a single, unified country. He was not alone in this concern, which was echoed by the military, the secret police and the conservative leadership of the Communist Party. In public discourse the incessant rhetoric of restructuring gradually became less salient and codewords for the restoration of "law and order" became more common. Less was heard of rights and freedoms as the emphasis shifted to civic duties and social discipline.

Gorbachev's solution was to put formal constitutional reform in abeyance and defer plans for marketization for what he perceived to be the most urgent priority, the restructuring of the union in order to maintain the USSR. For this purpose a new Treaty of the Union was hastily drafted in late 1990 to replace the 1922 treaty which had been incorporated into the first union constitution of 1924.[21] Notwithstanding changes in the number of union republics, the legal fiction of the unitary Soviet Union as a federal state had been carried forward through the 1936 Constitution and continued as an integral part of the 1977 Constitution (Chaps. 8–11).

The proposed new treaty responded to the separatist fever among the republics by conceding to them much more formal, sovereign control over their internal affairs. In effect, the decentralizing features of the treaty primarily acknowledged the *de facto* situation in many republics. The avowed aim of fashioning a more workable federal structure was, however, offset in the treaty by significant accretions of power to the central state, especially to the office of the superpresidency. In effect, the treaty (which defined far more than its predecessor) was a kind of shorthand version of a new constitution. In a kind of dress rehearsal for the introduction of the new constitution, the treaty was to be submitted to the first national referendum ever to be held in the Soviet Union.[22]

For the independence-minded republican leaderships, however, the proposed new union treaty was too little, too late. Objections were made, and some republics threatened not to permit the referendum on their territory. As Gorbachev saw it, the document would save the "renewed" union and serve as a watershed for further constitutional development. He and his aides, by now a decidedly more conservative group, campaigned vigorously for the public's endorsement of the draft treaty. The struggle took a less subtle form in the Baltic region; there, special troops and riot police carried out small-scale military assaults—presumably for their demonstration effect elsewhere in the restive union—against some of the institutional symbols of newly appropriated republic autonomy.[23] The Balts replied by holding their own referenda for independence without waiting for the all-union plebiscite, scheduled for March 17, 1990.[24]

The outcome of the national referendum was never in doubt however, given the partial, pro-union way the question was phrased. Gorbachev's vision of a restructured union was approved by a large majority, clearing the way for detailed negotiations between the center and the republics on shaping the draft treaty into a final form. Meanwhile, constitutional lawyers stood by, ready to incorporate the approved treaty into the heavily amended USSR Constitution of 1977. If the previous sweeping amendments to the document were akin to transplanting vital organs into the body politic, the anticipated constitutional surgery would have been equivalent to replacing essential parts of the skeletal structure of the USSR. But the question for the future was whether ratification of the treaty, *qua* mini-constitution, would give Gorbachev the impetus he needed to regain control of social change in the USSR, or, as can be the danger with all such operations, would society in its new plural contours ultimately reject Gorbachev's grafts and transplants?

The Dimensions of Constitutional Reform

After decades of Cold War–style Soviet polemics against "bourgeois" ideas, it has been ironic that the underlying principles for contemporary Soviet constitutionalism were drawn from the American constitutional experience.[25] As late as the mid-1980s it would have been unthinkable for a Soviet jurist to speak or write of emulating the American or any other Western constitution. An article with such a suggestion would never have passed the censor. Under Gorbachev, however, this kind of proposal became commonplace, at least among reform-minded lawyers.

The principal themes of this new Soviet realm of constitutional discourse included such familiar Western ideas as the supremacy of law, including a government subordinate to law, the separation of powers (at least of the party from the government), the precedence of the individual over the state, the emphasis on political and civil rights over the erstwhile focus on social and economic rights, and the creation of a civil society encompassing all of the above as well as the right of private ownership of property. In effect, constitutional scholars, following Gorbachev's lead, were in the process of fundamentally redrafting the "social contract" governing relations between the citizen and the party-state.[26]

The first step in reshaping the Soviet constitutional order began with the extensive wave of amendments proposed by Gorbachev and pushed through the old, compliant USSR Supreme Soviet in late 1988. The central features of these changes for further constitutional revision were new election rules and the restructuring of the Soviet legislative process. The main innovations in Soviet electoral law were the introduction of multi-candidate elections (as against the previous practice of one office, one candidate), and incumbency limitation to two consecutive five-year terms. Multiple candidacies—long permitted in some formerly communist East European countries, but a radical move by Soviet standards—gave more substance and significance to the "secret ballot" provision in the existing constitution. Previously, in standard single-candidate voting for government office, Soviet voters had the option of simply dropping the ballot with the candidate's name in the ballot box or, rather conspicuously, going into a curtained booth, crossing out the name, and then casting the ballot.[27]

While the electoral reforms were intended to introduce a degree of popular sovereignty into the operations of the Soviet system, the constitutional reform of the legislative process was intended to provide greater legitimacy to the subsequent constitutional restructuring contemplated by Gorbachev and his reformist advisors. The core of these changes was that the old Supreme Soviet, which had met in *pro forma* proceedings only a few weeks a year, was superseded by a two-tier legislature: the USSR Congress of People's Deputies and the (new) USSR Supreme Soviet.

The new Congress actually rehabilitated a similar institution which had been introduced in the 1924 Constitution, but then subsequently eliminated in the 1936 Constitution. The old Congress of Soviets had been a typical Bolshevik façade institution designed to give the appearance of popular participation in government in a party-controlled system. The new Congress of 1989, however, was set up to be an actual working supra-legislature with real policy-making powers.

But the party was still the dominant player in Soviet politics, and there was a "catch." The 2,250 deputies to the new Congress were divided into three categories, each with 750 seats. One category was to be directly elected from election districts of equal size. Another group of 750 deputies would be elected on a proportional basis corresponding to the administrative status of the unit, i.e., 32 deputies to be elected from each union republic, 11 from each autonomous republic, 5 from each autonomous region, and one from each autonomous district. Because of the complex nominating process built into the new electoral process, it could be assumed that the party would exercise considerable influence over the selection of candidates. This, indeed, proved to be the case in the first elections to the Congress of People's Deputies in 1989. The party's real political insurance, however, was the third block of 750 seats, which were reserved for deputies to be elected by so-called "social organizations." In Soviet practice, the Communist Party itself was classified as a social organization—and at that time it still controlled virtually all other economic, social, and political organizations, such as the Young Communist League and the centralized trade union system.[28]

The newly elected Congress of People's Deputies sat for the first time in the spring of 1989. Among its foremost exclusive powers were "the adoption and amendment of the USSR Constitution," decisions on the structure of the Soviet state, and election of the new Supreme Soviet and its chairman. Thus the Congress created a commission headed by Gorbachev to draft a new constitution, and elected from its membership one-fifth of the deputies (542) to convene the first session of the redesigned Supreme Soviet. The latter body was in session twice a year, for months at a time, and served as the USSR's daily, working legisla-

ture empowered to enact all necessary subconstitutional and enabling legislation. Gorbachev was, not unexpectedly, elected its first
chairman.[29]

A kind of muted Soviet separation-of-powers doctrine began to
take shape, including demonopolization of the party and the emergence of new executive and judicial institutions to complete the tri-
ad of powers. Regardless of institutional developments, the most
ardent reformers felt that no change of consequence could be implemented as long as the party—even if behind the scenes—
retained its monopoly of power over the system. Hence, in early
1990 the Constitution was amended to deprive the party of its exclusive control over policy making and implementation (Art. 6),
opening the possibility for party pluralism. Shortly thereafter, the
Constitution was again amended, this time to create the new office
of the executive presidency, modeled after the French and American presidencies.

In the 1988 amendments, modest steps had already been taken
toward a more independent judiciary and a limited constitutional
judicial review. To free judges of party and local influence, they
were no long directly elected but were appointed at the lowest
level by the next highest governing soviet. Again, to try to insure
more independence, their previous terms of five years were extended to 10.[30]

At the higher end of the judicial system, a new clause was added
to the Constitution which provided authority for a Committee for
Constitutional Supervision or oversight. In the draft version of the
amendment, this body (modeled more after corresponding communist East European institutions than any Western model) was
intended to exercise supervision over republic as well as union
legislation. However, in the public discussion of the draft amendment in late 1988, several union republics registered objections to
a Moscow-based committee overseeing their legislation, correctly
seeing this as a new version of Soviet centralism in the guise of
constitutionalism. The ratified version of the amendment weakened the committee's jurisdiction over the republics until a new
union treaty was in place (Art. 124). The committee's authority
was to be advisory, and only to the legislative branch of which it
was a part. It was not meant to be a constitutional court in the
Western sense.[31]

By early 1990, one could speak of an embryonic Soviet separation of powers. It paled in comparison with its American model,

but at least some progress had been made toward sketching out somewhat more distinct legislative, executive, and judicial domains, with even some nascent checks and balances written into the arrangement. It could be said that a viable Soviet separation-of-powers doctrine and practice had become a work in progress.

As the year progressed, however, this emerging constitutional profile became somewhat blurred by Gorbachev's substantial accretions of power as president. In the fall and winter of 1990, as internal crises intensified and his leadership tasks were compounded, President Gorbachev persuaded his legislative colleagues to grant him special emergency powers that were to be in effect until 1992, and then significant new permanent presidential powers in December. Appropriate changes were of course made in the Constitution to expand presidential decree-making power. As the year wore on, Gorbachev's decrees became increasingly arbitrary and controversial, resembling more the proclamations of a monarch than the considered executive decisions of a constitutional leader mindful of the division of power within a constitutional system.[32] By early 1991, the Soviet Union had begun to take on the appearance of a system of nearly unchecked presidential power.

Simultaneously with the grand structural changes in the Soviet constitutional universe, important subconstitutional legislation was being created to grant significant individual, group, and union republic rights. All Soviet constitutions since the 1936 version had included a heavily caveated "bill of rights." In 1936 and 1977 it was generally understood that these clauses were meant merely to give the document some democratic window-dressing for propaganda purposes. Aside from the fact that there was no enabling legislation for most of these rights, no Soviet citizen under Stalin and few in the post-Stalin years attempted seriously to exercise their individual rights of speech, assembly, demonstration, or press. Then, beginning in the 1960s, a relatively small number of bold dissidents began to act on their abstract constitutional liberties as affirmative rights, reconstruing or ignoring altogether the embedded caveats that directed the exercise of rights to the purpose of strengthening and developing the socialist system.[33] These political dissenters and ethnic activists, numbering no more than a few thousand from the mid-1960s to the mid-1980s, invariably suffered for their courage, experiencing bureaucratic deprivations, prison, psychiatric confinement, and, in a some cases, expatriation.[34]

The right of conscience was a partial exception. Official atheism was vigorously promoted, few churches, mosques, or synagogues were open, and little religious literature was available; but legally, at least, one could attend a religious service. However, even the exercise of this circumscribed right was actively discouraged through political and social pressures, particularly effective if an individual was young and ambitious, or vulnerable to job discrimination or outright dismissal. Nonetheless, hundreds of thousands worshiped publicly, millions believed secretly, and, again, a much smaller number of religious dissidents of all persuasions courted and encountered repression for such activities as seeking to worship in non–state-approved and registered congregations, trying to study the history or language of their particular religious tradition, or attempting to provide a religious education for their children.[35]

Consistent with the commitment to enhancing the status of the individual vis-à-vis the state, Gorbachev promised the public appropriate legislation to secure in actuality rights heretofore honored only in the breach. In the meantime, he allowed that they might be guided by a new axiom, "Everything that is not prohibited, is permitted." Thus, under the protective umbrella of Gorbachev's policies of glasnost and democratization, millions of people began to exercise *de facto* rights of freer speech, unofficial assembly, and a less restricted press.

Several of the empowering laws took longer to produce than initially expected. In retrospect, this was not surprising since these particular rights (as against, say, the new right of an enterprise manager to decide on the product mix) could be expected to engender long-scorned individualism and erode the party's traditional control over mass society. The drafting process for certain of these laws proved to be highly conflictual, as reform politicians and jurists struggled with conservatives over the rhetoric of legal empowerment. The long-promised statute on glasnost was a case in point. Conceived by the reformers as the cornerstone of free speech legislation, when last heard from this statute had become a virtual battleground, having gone through at least a half-dozen drafts. Similarly, in 1988, two years before the right of public association was guaranteed in law, restrictive rules on rallies and demonstrations were issued, leading a major Soviet legal scholar to suggest that the real intent of the legislators may have been to "severely limit" the citizen's constitutional right of assembly.[36]

The year 1990 also witnessed new laws on the press (eliminating pre-publication censorship) and on religious freedom (permitting private charitable activities and the right of religious education).[37] By mid-1991, the promised law on emigration, a right never before offered to Soviet citizens even *pro forma*, was finally ready, but it still included, in its enacted form, the old, ambiguous administrative canard of exposure to "state secrets" as grounds for denial of exit for a period of up to five years.[38]

This survey of the dimensions of constitutional reform in the perestroika-era USSR would not be complete without reference to the issue of secession. Posing as a federal state within a unitary system, Soviet leaders since the 1936 Constitution had conceded to the union republics the right to freely secede from the union (1936: Art. 17; 1977: Art. 72). Geographically, secession would not be an insuperable problem (except in the case of the huge Russian republic) since the union republics were located on the borders of Russia and the union. But again, the right of secession was clearly understood by all as an empty, abstract constitutional right which no Moscow-anointed union republic leader would ever presume to act upon. That was the case until in the superheated political atmosphere of perestroika, the overtly nationalist leadership of the Lithuanian republic signaled their intention to leave the Union of Soviet Socialist Republics in 1990. Since the independent country of Lithuania had been forcibly annexed to the USSR by Stalin in 1940, Lithuanian lawyers argued that their withdrawal from the union was technically not secession, but rather a resumption of independent statehood. This, of course, was not Gorbachev's perception of the situation. As Lithuania moved to proclaim independence, Gorbachev rushed through the legislative process the first Soviet law on secession, providing enabling, operative legislation to support the constitutional right of secession. Again, there were several "catches," including a five-year waiting period and the need to first settle financial obligations with the union, the latter a formidable obstacle which led Baltic leaders and many reform democrats in general to regard the new statute as an anti-secession law.[39]

Although some very good laws benefiting the individual had been put on the books, by the early 1990s Gorbachev had begun to shift to the political right, placing the implementation of some of these laws in potential jeopardy. As an example, after a confrontation between Soviet forces and Lithuanian civilians in 1991, Gorbachev, infuriated by candid and critical press accounts of the incident, called for the suspension of the law on the press which had been in force less than a year. He did not get his way, but an increasingly compliant legislature promised a fresh law to ensure "objectivity" in the press. Clearly, the pendulum was swinging rightward, and some of the more traditional Soviet methods of governance were reappearing under the mantle of constitutionalism.

Constitutional Traditionalism

Although legal restructuring had been under way for several years, a number of traditional Russian and Soviet methods of governance remained fundamentally unchanged in spirit. This should not be too surprising since many of these familiar habits were (and remain) deeply ingrained in the elite political culture. Thus we found alive and well in the early 1990s such political traditions as the concentration of power at the top, rule from above, heavy reliance on police power, manifestations of elite legal nihilism (or the circumvention of the law by officials), and the persistence of still largely unaccountable bureaucratic control over public life.

What was new, as part of the rhetoric of reform politics, was the "constitutionalization" of these heretofore unabashed expressions of power and unchecked demonstrations of political will. As the former Soviet Union moved into the modern era—into the politics of appearance as well as reality—political fashion demanded that power be draped in constitutional garb. Political power no longer lurked behind the "magic wall"[40] of party secrecy; it has metamorphosed into a form of constitutionalism. The question for the future became, could the new constitutional forms impose reasonable limits and encourage the exercise of restraint, or would these arrangements eventually become merely a more routinized and efficient means of societal domination?

The most conspicuous contemporary example of the transformation of tradition into constitutionalism was the emergence of the office of the executive presidency under Gorbachev. By the end of the 1980s, after this new Soviet institution had been the recipient of several rounds of legislative strengthening, Gorbachev had gathered in his hands formal, legal powers almost equivalent to the autocratic prerogatives of the last tsar, Nicholas II. These included nearly unlimited decree-making powers, the right to prorogue parliament under certain circumstances, and the authority to suspend the Constitution itself and impose various degrees of martial law.[41]

The main difference was that Gorbachev enjoyed these immense powers in a far more fragmented country and divided society than the Russia once ruled by the tsars. In the USSR of the early 1990s central authority was counterweighted by centrifugal forces, and the monolithic system of control and implementation had been fractured in many places. Thus, Gorbachev could issue presidential decrees on virtually any subject, but he found it nearly impossible to get them obeyed. Similarly, while he had the power to suspend parliaments at all levels of the system, if he had done so he would have had to deal with the consequences of a newly mobilized citizenry and an aroused public opinion—in effect, street politics. As for his authority to suspend constitutional rights in extreme situations, Gorbachev in the course of the late 1980s and early 1990s learned from the highly charged and violent ethnic conflicts in the Caucasian republics the limits of Moscow's political and military power in the new conditions.[42] The one factor that he did not share with his royal predecessors, and which would have changed the actual power equation in his favor, was a willingness to apply brute force. Indeed, by the 1990s, Gorbachev was openly frustrated by the intractability of the tasks of reform and appeared to be increasingly inclined to resort to legally sanctioned coercion to contain, if not eliminate, the burgeoning chaos of a country adrift.[43]

As befit a Soviet leader who sought to maintain or regain order, President Gorbachev began to deploy the enormous police power at his disposal. Since the USSR was still more a police state than the legal state it aspired to become, the state's coercive reserve was one of Gorbachev's most important political resources for holding the union together in the face of the powerful forces pulling it asunder. In effect, with his political capital dwindling along with his personal popularity, Gorbachev was left with few options to try to keep the country afloat and continue at least a semblance of economic reform.

Part of the force structure available to the Soviet president operated within the constitution writ large, but much remained, as it had been throughout the Soviet period, extraconstitutional. In the past, the nominal superior of the military and the police was the USSR Council of Ministers, through its system of ministries and state committees, while the real master of these forces was the Communist Party leadership, through the Central Committee Secretariat, with its network of oversight committees staffed by cadres of party instructors and supervisors. However, as the party's institutional authority and organizational domination gradually declined in the late 1980s, its tutelage and control over the agencies of force weakened, especially at the all-union level. Since these agencies had not yet been depoliticized (i.e., they still contained Communist Party committees before the August coup), linkage had continued, especially at the regional and local levels in many parts of the country where party organizations still exercised considerable power, including influence over the police.[44]

The net result was that the civil–military relationship that operated within the party's national institutions, as well as the civil–police relationship developed after Stalin's death to yoke the secret police to party control, had been weakened. Ideally, the supervisory slack was to be taken up by the new parliamentary committees intended to exercise oversight. These committees, however, were packed with military and KGB officer-deputies who in most cases were not inclined to carry out systematic oversight of their parent organizations. Consequently, the armed forces and the KGB had begun to operate more independently in the more open political environment of recent years, in contrast to the past, when they were confined to playing "crypto-politics"[45] within the closed party system. Hundreds of military and even KGB officers served as elected deputies throughout the hierarchy of legislatures, while the KGB routinely gave interviews, held press conferences, and operated its own public relations offices in the various republics.

To bring both of these powerful organizations fully within the emerging constitutional order, legislation was passed in 1991 defining the rights and duties, powers and obligations, and roles, generally, of the secret police, while a similar statute was being drafted on the defense establishment at the time of the coup. The first public statute governing the KGB, however, did nothing to allay liberal concern that this behemoth organization of the totalitarian era would continue to wield inordinate power in the country, except now in fully legitimate, legally sanctioned form. The process of codification seemed intended to institutionalize the KGB's extensive powers rather than subject to government regulation its myriad internal police and foreign intelligence functions. For instance, the law provided the political police considerable license to detain certain individuals "who commit actions that are harmful to the interests of state security" for up to three days. Not only was the length of detention longer than in an ordinary criminal matter, but the criterion for detention was sufficiently ambiguous to leave the door open for abuse. The leading reform lawyer Valery Savitsky commented mordantly that the law would endow the KGB with "colossal power."[46] Both the KGB and the military (at least the senior "brass"), operating as semi-independent political actors still only loosely aligned within the constitutional system, threw their political support behind Gorbachev in the multifaceted power struggles raging in the country. Whether the *quid pro quo* for their support was Gorbachev's swing to the right in the early 1990s or whether he arrived there of his own volition was irrelevant, because the president (he was still the party leader as well) and the national security bureaucracies came to share common ground.

Gorbachev, along with his appointees KGB chief Kriuchkov, MVD (police) minister Pugo, and military leaders such as Marshal Iazov (future leaders of the self-proclaimed Committee for the State of Emergency in the August 1991 coup), opposed nationalist separatism and the breakup of the union. They expressed strong support for the restoration of firm law and order in the streets where crime flourished, in the great squares where sometimes stridently critical political demonstrations took place, and in the marketplace where a freewheeling shadow economy, the black market, operated unchecked.

These uniformed services, then, appeared to constitute Gorbachev's ultimate line of defense against the possible collapse of public order and the disintegration of the USSR. Aside from the several-million-man armed forces, Gorbachev had at his disposal as president approximately 1.4 million special troops and police. These included KGB officers and armed units, the border troops, the riot troops under the USSR Ministry of Internal Affairs (MVD), the hundreds of thousands of armed militiamen or municipal police, and such smaller, specialized forces as the OMON, or paramilitary "black berets," who carried out several bloody assaults in independence-minded Lithuania and Latvia in 1991.[47] Gorbachev had used these diverse forces with relative restraint—deploying riot troops to restore peace in about a dozen violence-ridden locations throughout the union since 1988, ordering the regular army to join police patrols in the major urban areas (presumably for crime-fighting, or so he said to much skepticism), and, probably (although he would not acknowledge it), condoning airborne and OMON military forays in the Baltics.[48] It was generally assumed in the West that, should Gorbachev have decided to rely more heavily on force, the collective forces of coercion would unquestionably have provided the muscle to carry out his presidential will. In the wake of the 1991 coup which revealed deep political fissures in the military and police, the force option looked less certain in retrospect.

While the physical instrument of coercion may have been in the gray area of extraconstitutionality as the Soviet Union attempted to make the transition from the old constitution under the aegis of the party to a new self-standing constitutional order, ample legal means for invoking the use of force had already been codified. Beginning in 1988, the old Supreme Soviet enacted legislation giving the riot corps of the MVD special and exceptional powers under conditions of domestic turmoil and large-scale disorder.[49] By mid-1990, after considerable experience with communal violence and widespread unrest in several areas of the country, the new Supreme Soviet had passed an all-union state-of-emergency law, which completed the state's arsenal of legal concepts for dealing with various degrees of disorder.[50]

The minimal application of force provided by the emergency law involved imposition of a curfew, which had been used in several instances of serious urban violence. The next stage was the introduction of a condition of "special status," which permitted the authorities to ban demonstrations and meetings in the affected area. Most notably this condition was imposed in the Nagorno-Karabakh region of Azerbaijan, an area violently contested by Armenians and Azeris. In more serious circumstances, the central government could declare a state of emergency, akin to martial law, which would empower the authorities to ban cultural and sporting events and strikes, and to detain violators for up to thirty days. In early 1990, after fresh outbursts of interethnic violence in the south, the USSR Supreme Soviet, even before passage of the law on emergencies, directly ordered a state of emergency in

Baku and other areas of Azerbaijan and Armenia, and upgraded the special status in Nagorno-Karabakh to a state of emergency.

The ultimate step in the hierarchy of legally employed force would have been the declaration of "presidential rule," which could only be invoked in the event of a failure to restore order under a state of emergency. If presidential rule were imposed in an administrative jurisdiction, the president would have the right to suspend the operation of local or even republic legislatures, and to rule the area directly through a presidential representative armed with draconian powers to reestablish order. During 1991 a number of conservative politicians and the spokespersons for several besieged minorities appealed to Gorbachev to use his power of presidential rule.[51] He resisted these calls, but it seemed likely, given the turmoil in the USSR, that he would eventually be forced to invoke presidential rule. His arch-conservative appointees, however, gravely concerned about the country's disintegration and fearful that the impending signing of the new Treaty of Union in mid-August 1991 would further accelerate the process, could no longer wait for their chief's decision on force.

Political conservatives (who favored it) and reformers alike agreed that Gorbachev had the constitutional tools at his disposal for a legally declared state of emergency. The 1977 Constitution gave the Presidium of the USSR Supreme Soviet the right to proclaim martial law in all or part of the country "in the interests of the USSR's defense."[52] The 1988 amendments broadened the justification for martial law to include ensuring the domestic security of the country's citizens, while adding the requirement that the union presidium had to consult with the relevant republic supreme soviet presidium before taking action.[53] In 1990, further amendments established the executive presidency and transferred the presidium's emergency powers to the new office. In addition, the president was given the authority to proclaim presidential rule as a higher form of martial law.[54] The new law on declaring a state of emergency, passed a few months later, provided enabling legislation that gave the president the operational language, definitions, and procedures for using his extreme powers, as Article 1 states, "in accordance with the USSR Constitution."[55]

However, short of resorting to extreme measures, Gorbachev had at his direct and indirect disposal other more, pacific means for the routine tasks of order-maintenance and keeping the union intact—goals which had progressively superseded reform *per se* and drove his policies up to mid-1991. As party leader, Gorbachev controlled most of the USSR's printing facilities, which were then party-owned. This fact, and the necessity of rationing scarce newsprint stock, gave Gorbachev considerable leverage over the more critical publications of both the state press and the new independent press. In addition, he had created by decree an all-union media corporation as a kind of independent public authority in order to free it of legislative oversight. This agency institutionalized Gorbachev's control of the media, providing a bulwark for combating "informational terrorism."[56]

Similarly, given the failure of economic reform, not only virtually all productive property but also the entire infrastructure of the country, including the wholesale supply system, the production and service facilities, the transportation and communication systems, and the retail distribution network, remained largely a monopoly of the union state under control of the president and his ministers. In an early phase of the Lithuanian crisis, after the republic proclaimed its independence from the USSR in 1990, Gorbachev's control over state property enabled him to impose a crippling economic embargo on the maverick republic. Even in the area of the economic reform's single success, the emergence of the small-scale entrepreneurial sector, Gorbachev had used several measures within his authority to curb both legal and black market private business, including registration and de-registration rules, the power of taxation, Prime Minister Pavlov's sudden confiscation of large-denomination currency in early 1991, and the presidential decree on "economic sabotage." In the case of this last concept (for which lawyers found no workable definition in the law), the KGB was empowered to carry out warrantless searches of business premises.[57]

This measure, along with the currency confiscation (presumably aimed at the ill-gotten gains of organized crime and black marketeers), seemed to play well among the public at large, beset as they were by acute economic shortages, and deeply envious and resentful of those of their fellow citizens who were managing to thrive in the new entrepreneurial environment. Brushed aside were the arguments of jurists that some of these moves may not have been constitutional, for Gorbachev had increasingly appropriated to himself the right to decide what the Constitution really meant during the transition from the heavily amended but mainly obsolete 1977 document to the bright and shining constitutional future. In retrospect, this was but one of the many small and large steps taken by conservatives in the ultimate direction of the coup of 1991.

Even more chilling than the crackdown on entrepreneurs, the creation of clandestine committees of "national salvation" in the Baltics followed by the open formation of a "USSR National Salvation Committee" caused a sense of foreboding among Soviet democratic reformers. They recalled the former Polish committee of the same name, which emerged after the 1981 imposition of martial law to crush the Solidarity independent labor movement.[58] (In fact, it was said that the leader of the Soviet committee had consulted with the Poles on their experience.) No one doubted that these committees were fronts for the conservative faction of the Communist Party, openly unhappy about the direction of reform and the resulting disorder, for which they blamed the abuse of glasnost and democratization by radical democrats. From a constitutional perspective, the salvation committees seemed to represent the party's attempt to regain the authority and power it had lost in 1990 when reformers pushed through the revision of Article 6 of the Constitution (the party hegemony clause).[59]

It was events such as these, signaling the improvisation of constitutional means to achieve traditional Bolshevik ends, that led one Soviet legal observer to argue that Gorbachev had remained loyal to Lenin's cavalier approach to law, and that prompted Yeltsin, in his nationwide television remarks in early 1991, to call for Gorbachev's resignation on the grounds that he had "brought the country to dictatorship" under the constitutional guise of presidential government.[60]

The Politics of Constitutionalism

The term "constitution" and its variations had become the new codeword of Soviet politics, superseding such standbys of the bygone era of Communist Party rule as *partiinost*, or "party-mindedness." Thus, opponents who in the past were castigated as "anti-Soviet" were now routinely labeled anti-constitutional. In nearly all public discourse, the participants invoked the constitution in one meaning or another. This plurality of usage, sometimes more aptly described as a cacophony, complicated the process of decoding what Soviet politicians were actually saying.

Invoking the constitution came to mean any of at least four things in contemporary Soviet politics, depending on the speaker, the context, and the objective sought. The most familiar usage, carried over from the time of the 1977 Constitution's unchallenged hegemony in the Soviet system, was to regard the constitution as a metapolicy or a framework for subconstitutional policy making.[61] Interpreting the constitution metapolitically had been an easy task: the party secretariat, on behalf of the leadership, would provide an authoritative rendering to guide the policymaker. In conditions of perestroika, the problem was complicated by several factors. There had come into existence multiple sources of putative authoritative constitutional interpretation, and they were frequently divided among themselves in various ways, including a division familiar to American legal scholars—whether to take a narrow or a broad constructionist approach to the constitution. A major difference with the legal history of the United States is the fact of a single, undisputed constitution and a high court endowed with the power to interpret the document authoritatively.

This brings me to a more recent and novel (for the USSR) meaning of the prevailing codeword, the idea of the constitution as "supreme law." This usage came into vogue in 1988, the year of the 19th Party Conference, which formally launched the concept of a "law-based state" as a model for the Soviet future. If the existing authoritarian state were to be transformed into a government subject to law, then it was necessary to accord to the law itself in its consummate constitutional form the status of supremacy.[62] In fact, the 1977 Constitution, which in patchwork, amended fashion remained in effect, included a supremacy clause (Art. 173).[63] The statement "The USSR Constitution has supreme legal force" does not, however, have the resonance of phrase "This Constitution . . . shall be the supreme law of the land," found in the Constitution of the United States (Art. VI, sec. 2). Moreover, until the late 1980s it was generally understood by all Soviet citizens that their own supremacy clause was clearly qualified by the Communist Party's absolute monopoly on power both in fact and in law, as reflected in Article 6 of the USSR Constitution.

The issue of constitutional supremacy in the Soviet Union in the 1990s was clouded by a number of considerations. No one was quite certain what the constitution was at any moment given the fact that it had been so frequently and heavily amended. Add to this the legislative output of the USSR Supreme Soviet. In its two years of operation (1989–91), the parliament had enacted over 100 new laws and continued to produce new legislation, much of which had the effect of *de facto* amendment or revision of the constantly changing Constitution. Another difficulty had been that several union republics had set off on their own independent constitutional paths and the results were frequently in conflict with the union document.

A final consideration was the question of who, or what body, could authoritatively interpret what the Constitution said and resolve possible conflicts between its clauses and executive edicts, legislative enactments, and competing subnational constitutions. In effect, how could the doctrine of constitutional supremacy be protected in practice? The first effort in this direction was the creation by constitutional amendment in 1988 of the Committee for Constitutional Supervision (Art. 125), nominally a committee of the new USSR Congress of People's Deputies but actually subordinate only to the Constitution itself. The enabling statute setting up the committee was not passed, however, until 1990.[64] Its jurisdiction over union-republic legislation (other than acts concerning human rights) was made contingent upon the negotiation of a new union treaty. Thus, the question of the supremacy of the law would be a moot issue until a new treaty was signed.

Yet another conception of the constitution as political codeword was to treat it metaphorically as a higher symbol. In this sense, what the Constitution might say was less important than its invocation as an object of respect if not reverence. Gorbachev, in his presidential role, tended to favor this approach when making unilateral decisions or policies. In effect, he invoked the aura of the USSR Constitution to legitimate his action of the moment. Assuming a loose constructionist perspective on the Constitution, Gorbachev's critics were also known to use the symbolic constitution to legitimate their criticism of his policies or decrees. A perusal of parliamentary rhetoric also revealed legislators embellishing their speeches with magical flourishes drawn from constitutional symbolism. Clearly, the constitution as political icon was within verbal reach for any officeholder, opening up myriad possibilities for constitutional demagoguery from on high and below.

The last meaning of the constitution was to conceive of it merely as a framework or arena for civilized forms of political struggle. Gorbachev utilized the constitution in this manner as well. When he could not get his way or faced strong challenge, he would pronounce in presidential tones that the matter had to be settled constitutionally. If he was addressing a restive republic, as was often the case in this usage, Gorbachev *meant* that the conflict should be resolved according to the all-union rules of the game. This could be quite disarming for a lesser opponent, who was left with the choice of rejecting a constitutional solution, or acting extraconstitutionally and declaring independence, as did Lithuania in 1990.[65] For President Gorbachev, who usually took his stand within the temple of the Constitution, there was the further advantage of deferring a legal resolution of the conflict until he could mobilize enough political resources to prevail. Meanwhile, who could fault a leader who sought to solve political differences through legal means?

Taken together, these nuances of constitutionalism shared one common feature. All drew on the constitution, *in toto* or in its parts, as a source of vocabulary for the language of political negotiation: over center–periphery conflicts, executive–legislative differences, contradictions in legislative drafting, and the exercise of quasi-judicial oversight of decrees and laws. Just as Marxism-Leninism had once served as a vehicle for intra-elite communication, so now the Constitution in its various meanings defined the more open, public discourse of Soviet politics. Some politicians were more skilled than others in "speaking" the new language of constitutionalism. Charisma and oratorical ability were not enough for media visibility; one needed also to know the vocabulary of power in a more plural, differentiated, and open society. Gorbachev was, of course, a virtuoso of constitutional politics. In his skilled hands, the Constitution had many uses.

In Soviet public discourse one regularly heard such phrases as the "constitutionally permissible way," a "constitutionally protected right," or the need to fulfill one's "constitutional responsibility." In more extreme situations there were references to a "constitutional coup" (to describe Prime Minister Valentin Pavlov's request, without prior consultation with the president, for greater powers in June 1991), "constitutional aggression" (the Lithuanian president referring to Soviet paramilitary police actions in the republic), and the much used epithet "constitutional subversion." Subversion was claimed from various directions: a leading scholar claimed that the democratic left, by taking seriously the cosmetic civil-rights baggage of the 1977 Constitution, had disrupted society and destabilized the state;[66] a major Russian Republic politician expressed concern that the new union treaty then under negotiation (and the new union constitution which was to follow) would destabilize the Russian Federation by elevating the status of the autonomous ethnic republics within it;[67] and, finally, the leaders of the conservative faction in the USSR Supreme Soviet argued that a new constitution might subvert the intent of the pending union treaty.[68]

In the political theater of the Soviet Union in the early 1990s, constitutional rhetoric had become two-dimensional. Beneath the everyday exchanges in the press, the executive suites, and in the parliaments over tactical political issues, a constitutional convention *writ large*, addressing strategic questions on the future shape of the political system, had been under way for several years. I am not referring to a discrete, organized meeting such as the American Constitutional Convention in Philadelphia; the Soviet convention was quite different, and in fact probably unique in world constitutional annals as it was riven by ambivalences. It was both planned and spontaneous, and occurred over time in multiple venues; the quiet of constitutional deliberation was occasionally punctuated by gunfire and violence; negotiation was both continuous and episodic, operating on several levels simultaneously at different tempos and with varying degrees of intensity; and essential compromise, so vital to constitution-making, advanced and receded as circumstances constantly changed and inveterate antagonisms welled up to block the prospect of peaceful union and, in the end, the process of an orderly dissolution of the union.

What the world witnessed in the last months of the USSR was an amorphous, transitional constitutional convention not likely to produce durable agreements because that was really not its inchoate purpose. The idea had been to keep the dialogue going, to keep bringing adversaries back to the table, to continuously try new words and formulas for revitalizing old ties, forging new ones, or, if all failed, dissolving relationships amicably. Gorbachev, with his tolerance for ambiguity and reserves of optimism, had been a master of this crucial dialogue of transition. His aim was to avert the alternative, civil war, and its companions, misery and chaos.

Could the USSR have survived until the year 2000? Powerful conservative elites did not think so. Impatient for decisive action against all those who were bringing down their system, corrupting the culture, and tearing apart the union, the conservatives understood and accepted, at least for a time, that the constitutional game was the only one in town. Minimally, they wanted their party's leader, General Secretary Gorbachev, to use his immense presidential powers to curb the outrages of glasnost, quell the excesses of democratization, and restabilize the shattered economy by administrative means if necessary.[69] Meanwhile, the conservatives learned how to coopt the constitutional vocabulary for the defense of their interests, which were constantly under attack in the political process. The May Day slogans for 1991 invoked "constitutional order and duty." The leader of the Russian Federation's Communist Party declared it to be the party of "constitutional fulfillment,"[70] and when President Yeltsin of Russia banned the Communist Party from the republic's workplaces in mid-summer 1991, party leaders denounced his decree as anti-constitutional and threatened to go to court. In the end, the conservatives' maximal program would have had President Gorbachev, or the union parliamentary bodies, *constitutionally* transfer power to republican emergency committees, or "committees of national salvation."[71] If their admiration for General Pinochet of Chile was any guide, the conservatives' program would presumably have been the restoration of constitutional "order" at the expense of the inherently disorderly politics of constitutionalism.

The Limits of Constitutionalism in the USSR

The early 1990s witnessed constitutional violence as well as constitutional peacemaking in dramatic attempts to save the Soviet Union from breakup and collapse. Violence or the significant threat of violent action occurred under the canopy of constitutionalism at four different levels of the Soviet system. At the all-union level when Lithuania declared its independence, President Gorbachev called the unruly republic to order in constitutional language. Failing to achieve compliance, he then invoked his new constitutional powers as president to impose an economic embargo, a form of political coercion, on the errant republic for several months in 1990.

At the union republic level, the Armenians petitioned the center in the late 1980s for boundary relief in neighboring Azerbaijan. Gorbachev, interpreting the 1977 Constitution selectively, came down on the side of Azerbaijan and against the precedent of internal border changes. Thereafter, the contested enclave of Azerbaijan and its predominantly Armenian inhabitants were almost continuously under Moscow's or Baku's constitutional restraint, enforced by large numbers of internal troops, with much ongoing bloodshed on both sides of the intense ethnic conflict.[72]

Within a union republic, there was constitutionalized violence between Georgia and one of its autonomous regions, South Ossetia. The South Ossetians, concerned about the possible Georgification of their region under the runaway nationalist government, sought affiliation with their Northern Ossetian kinsmen within the Russian Federation. The Georgian parliament replied by stripping the South Ossetians of their autonomous status under the Georgian Constitution. Large-scale fighting broke out, with Moscow unable to effectively protect the Ossetians and their autonomous status under the still extant union constitution (Art. 87).[73]

Finally, within another union republic, Moldavia (now called Moldova), two separate minority groups, concerned over Moldavian nationalism, sought to set up separate administrative entities. The Moldovans denied these claims under the republic constitution and threatened violent action against the would-be secessionists.[74]

In all four of these examples, constitutionalism was invoked and its limits reached without resolving or eliminating the powerful underlying grievances that fueled each conflict.

On the gentler side of the ledger, President Gorbachev did attempt to maintain the integrity of the USSR peacefully, through constitutional dialogue. Beginning in 1990 and through mid-1991, he engaged all the republics who would come to the negotiating table in an extended, fluid attempt to hammer out a new Treaty of Union to supersede the original treaty of 1922, which was incorporated in the 1977 Constitution. The issues under discussion were the classic topics of constitutional concern: power-sharing, taxation powers, division of property, and ownership rights. The treaty, when finally completed in the summer of 1991, was intended to serve as the basis for drafting a new union constitution.

The problem was that for the most part five, and sometimes six, republics refused to come to the treaty table. They did not intend to participate in the new arrangement; several had stated their intentions to secede from the USSR or to reclaim lost independence. How were these republics to be treated under the new treaty, and, subsequently, under a new constitution with its emphasis on the supremacy of the law? Of the nine republics that had been negotiating, the two largest, Russia and the Ukraine, were both concerned that the new treaty might interfere with the promulgation of their own forthcoming new republic constitutions. In the case of the Russian Federation, the sixteen autonomous republics within its borders posed a profound constitutional problem, while Ukrainian political life was split between a pro-treaty group and a strong and growing independence movement. In spite of such concerns, all the signatory republics stood to gain significant legal and political authority in the formal constitutional transfer of power which was embodied in the new Treaty of Union scheduled for signature on August 20, 1991.

This brings us back to Amalrik's paradox, restated by a contemporary Western scholar as Gorbachev's dilemma: "As antistate challenges mount, totalitarian states finally confront a savage dilemma: either to do nothing and risk collapse, or to crack down and return to decay."[75]

A "Constitutional" Coup

On August 19, 1991, anticipating signature of the new Treaty of Union, a group of President Gorbachev's senior and most trusted advisors interned him and attempted a coup d'état. The failure of their coup after three days realized both sides of the totalitarian dilemma: the abortive crackdown hastened the collapse of the declining Communist Party and accelerated the demise of the disintegrating Soviet state. Declared under spurious constitutional authority, the coup thus became the ultimate act of constitutional violence.

Conservative alarm over the unintended consequences of Gorbachev's revolution had become steadily more apparent up to mid-1991. By late summer, constitutional moves by Yeltsin and Gorbachev had turned alarm into panic. Russian President Yeltsin's "departyization" decree, his dramatic implementation of Gorbachev's earlier, nominal revision of the party hegemony clause of the Constitution (Art. 6), struck at a main pillar of the party's power, its control over the economy, and signaled the party's general decline. Similarly, President Gorbachev's union treaty promised a significant constitutional transfer of power which would have substantially diminished and weakened the central state. Conservatives clearly understood the adverse implications of both moves for the locus of their authority (the party) and the instrument of their power (the state). Thus, as the historical point of no return for the Soviet state and the communist system rapidly approached, a cabal of conservative leaders set in motion a coup d'état against Gorbachev and Yeltsin.

Students of Soviet politics will no doubt long debate why the coup failed. One factor I would suggest was the plotters' striking preoccupation with the appearance of legality and even constitutional legitimation of their seizure of power. Their several proclamations and decrees during the brief coup were replete with legal references and constitutional citations. While any Latin American *junta* would unhesitatingly have cut off communications and arrested potential challengers, the Soviet conspirators were concerned to cite Article 127, Section 7 of the USSR Constitution on the transfer of power from the president to the vice president.[76] Leaving aside their false claim that Gorbachev had become incapacitated, why did the "State Committee for the State of Emergency in the USSR" not just concentrate on seizing power and deal with the rationale later?

In illustration of the peculiar "due process" aspect of the coup, the initial proclamation of "the gang of eight" emphasized the need to "guarantee legality and order" and to restore the "unconditional superiority" of the USSR Constitution throughout the Soviet Union. In their first decree the concern with constitutional order and supremacy, especially with respect to the rebellious republics, was evident. The second and third points of the decree called for disbanding "structures of power . . . acting contrary to the USSR Constitution and USSR laws," and for deeming "invalid laws and decisions of bodies of power and administration that contradict" the union Constitution and Soviet laws.[77] In effect, the coup was intended, among other things, to call a halt to the "parade of sovereignties" and the "war of laws" which had so eroded of party power and state authority.

Enter Boris Yeltsin, president of Russia, whose growing power undoubtedly contributed to the timing of the coup. Tearing away the veil of legitimacy, Yeltsin swiftly declared the coup anti-constitutional and the state of emergency invalid. The rest is history, but it should be noted that the great struggle between the authors of the coup and their principal opponents—Gorbachev, interned in the Crimea, and Yeltsin, besieged in the Russian parliament building—was played out within the metaphoric arena of Soviet constitutionalism.[78]

In the wake of the coup's collapse, political conflict—essentially between the triumphant Yeltsin and the weakened Soviet parliament and the lame duck USSR president, Gorbachev—shifted into more peaceful venues. As the republics one after another declared their independence of the center, the struggle over the foundering USSR could be defined in terms of executive power asserting its prerogative authority on one side and legislative power emphasizing normative process on the other.[79]

In effect, the tension was between Russian presidential decrees and union legislative decisions. Both during and immediately following the coup, President Yeltsin moved forcefully to assert legitimate authority, first in counterpoint to the illegal actions of the coup leaders, and then to fill the political vacuum left by their arrests and the compromised standing of union institutions. Yeltsin's decrees had temporarily closed conservative, pro-coup newspapers, suspended the Russian Communist Party and seized its property, assumed constitutional control over armed forces on Russian territory, and, as the year drew to a close, progressively taken over more and more economic and administrative functions from the dying union state. President Gorbachev's initial objections to some of these moves were brushed aside by the more powerful Yeltsin. Lawyers' legitimate concerns (e.g., about due process lapses in the suspensions of newspapers and the banning of the Russian Communist Party) were generally ignored by a Russian administrative state rising like a phoenix from the ashes of the former USSR.

Counterpoised to Yeltsin's power moves, the union parliament under Gorbachev's leadership tried to reassert control in the weeks following the coup. In this ultimately vain effort, the battered Constitution took on a riot of meanings—as a symbol of elusive stability, as a metaphor for normative process, and, in the heat of debate over the future, even as a surrogate for *Roberts Rules of Order*, as various deputies brandished their copies of the Constitution, invoking it as a procedural document.

The USSR Supreme Soviet and Congress of People's Deputies met in successive extraordinary sessions in late August and early September of 1991 in an attempt to pick up the pieces and reassemble, in at least temporary form, the shattered union. With the party in full retreat, the only game left in town was the Constitution, and the word itself was on every deputy's lips. Following parliamentary due process, the Supreme Soviet moved swiftly to de-immunize the two parliamentary deputies who were members of the Emergency Committee, so that they could be arrested in connection with the investigation of the coup. A little later, the chairman of the Supreme Soviet, Anatoly Lukyanov, was himself stripped of parliamentary immunity and arrested as the alleged ninth leader of the coup.

As the parliamentary debate moved on to the Congress, constitutional process began to fray in the political frictions of the moment. Playing to the sensitivities of the newly empowered republic leaders and the need to coopt them if the union was to be preserved, Gorbachev, as presiding officer, maneuvered in a proverbial smoke-filled room to include on the presidium of the Congress several of the most influential leaders. This was an extra-parliamentary move in violation of house rules. As one deputy pointed out rhetorically, "How can we ask the people to obey us if we don't obey our own rules?" The issue at hand was the need to reach agreement on an overarching law on a "transitional period," bridging the gap between the post-coup confusion and the unknown future. As Gorbachev cut procedural corners to engineer consent, another deputy rose to object to the attempt to "liquidate" the Constitution, saying, "When [the Constitution] suits us, we recognize it, but when we think it's outdated, we ignore it." In reply, Gorbachev invoked political necessity, arguing that the transitional document was "not simply a legal question." This in turn provoked one of the conservative floorleaders to remark, "For three days now the Constitution has been trampled."[80] Paradoxically, the Constitution reached the zenith of its symbolic life as the USSR approached the nadir of its existence.

The pre-coup Soviet system and configuration of power soon yielded—through a combination of political negotiation, parliamentary dealmaking, and legislative compromise—to a tentative and fragile framework for a transitional constitutionalism. Among the leaders, possibly only Gorbachev believed that this rickety structure could provide safe passage to a peaceful and confederative future for the USSR. The "law on the transition" redistributed all-union powers among three new institutions: a State Council made up of the union and republic presidents; yet another new version of the Supreme Soviet, whose deputies this time were largely to be appointed by the republic leaderships; and an inter-republican economic coordinating committee to guide the disparate parts of the union toward a market economy.[81]

None of these transitional institutions took hold. The State Council met in desultory fashion, more an occasion for negotiation than an effective executive body. Amidst its newly independent members, Gorbachev could not be sure of having his way. Witness the repeated failure of the body to successfully negotiate a treaty of political union, even as a paper document in the most watered-down, loose confederative form. If agreement had been reached, the result would probably have resembled the weak American Articles of Confederation rather than the more workable Swiss confederation. The new legislative setup was even less effective. Poorly attended from the outset and largely ignored by the major players, it drifted in the media shadow of the parliaments of Russia, Ukraine, and other republics. Finally, the economic commission for the transition quickly foundered, unable to navigate in the rising sea of republic and even local economic self-interest. Its futile efforts to organize anything more than a paper economic union (mainly to placate Western creditors and aid donors) belied its grand purpose of a voyage to the new world of the market.

In the face of these setbacks, Gorbachev held on to his illusion that a new union constitution could issue forth from the increasingly phantom treaties of political and economic union. He seemed alone in his constitutional faith. Other notables, from President Leonid Kravchuk of Ukraine to Elena Bonner, the widow of Andrei Sakharov, recognized that the notion of *union* constitutionalism had become irrelevant in the fragmenting, post-coup Soviet Union.[82] The ironic reality was the steady realization, at the union level, of Marx's utopian vision of the "withering away" of state and law. The ultimate task for Gorbachev's hard-won Soviet constitutionalism would be to break the free-fall, to facilitate a process of controlled dissolution of the Soviet system and the imperial USSR.

The much-amended, patchwork USSR Constitution of 1977,

along with its 1991 post-coup codicil, did not make it into 1992, which would have been its fifteenth year. It exited the stage of history as a constitution of imperial decline.

Epilogue: Constitutional Futures

As the parts of the former USSR scatter to various points of the political compass, a variety of constitutional futures can be glimpsed. Lithuania, whose independence initiative in 1990 would lead the parade of sovereignties, now looks back to its pre-Soviet, constitutional past as a path to the future. As Ukraine emerges from centuries of domination, its leaders seek Western constitutional forms to fill the void being left by rapid de-Sovietization. In Tajikistan, where the struggle between Communist and anti-Communist factions continued well after the failure of the Moscow coup, Muslim forces wait in the wings, ready to ride forth under the green flag of Islam and establish a theocratic state opposed to both "totalitarian communism and usurious Western capitalism" which they fear may come to replace it.[83]

And as the communist era of Russian history comes to a close, Great Russia struggles to redefine itself constitutionally. Characterizing the 1978 republic charter as a constitution of totalitarianism and a brake on radical reform, President Yeltsin perceives Russia to be in a profound "constitutional crisis" and proposes a new, post-Soviet draft as "a constitutional barrier . . . to chaos and disintegration."[84] The draft constitution, premised on the primacy of human rights, the indivisibility of Russia, and the supremacy of the Russian Federation constitution over the constitutions of its constituent parts, immediately collided with the ethnic ambitions of a number of Russia's autonomous formations. These include the Chechens, who seek statehood, the Volga Tatars, who have declared independence, and the Kalmyks, who composed their presidential oath without reference to the constitution or laws of the Russian Federation.[85] Faced with such contentious issues of political geography, President Yeltsin deferred to the near future parliamentary and public consideration of a new Russian constitution.

As Gorbachev, having played his historic role, was pushed to the margins of power, Yeltsin moved downstage to drive the action forward. He has become the new standard bearer in the long line of Russian constitutionalists, from Count Mikhail Speransky, of the early 19th century, through Mikhail Gorbachev, the great reformer of the late 20th century.

Along with his immense political power, Yeltsin has also inherited the enormous, intractable problems that beset Gorbachev during the nearly seven years of perestroika—ethnic fragmentation and economic decline. Will he fare any better than his predecessor? Will he be able to fashion viable constitutional solutions for problems ancient and modern? Will he be able to move beyond the rhetoric to the reality of a law-based Russian state, to stable and durable forms for legitimizing political power?[86] Or will Yeltsin's best efforts to bring about ethnic peace and economic salvation eventually meet the same fate as Gorbachev's? How will Yeltsin react to political frustration, blockage, and opposition? Will he temporize as Gorbachev did, or might he decisively mobilize his considerable forces to impose emergency order and presidential *diktat*? If Yeltsin should decide to don the familiar Russian masks of general secretary or even tsar, could force, be it arbitrary or constitutional, halt the deepening economic chaos and stem the tide of ethnic dissolution?

Finally, what does the future hold for the constellation of sovereign states emerging from the wreckage of the Soviet internal empire? Can the new Commonwealth of Independent States, cobbled together by Yeltsin and other republic presidents at the end of the tumultuous year 1991, in fact succeed and transcend the Soviet Union? Or will it turn out to be a transitional stage on the road to fully separate, independent statehoods?[87] Will the 1990s be a period of political instability and reflexive authoritarianism in the former republics of the USSR? Or, on the more hopeful side, might some of these aborning states succeed in crafting durable constitutional futures, buffering the inevitable pressures of political "majoritarianism" as they evolve toward the "law's republic"?[88]

Notes

Introduction

1. On a framework for the collapse of empires, see Joseph A. Tainter, *The Collapse of Complex Societies* (Cambridge, UK: Cambridge University Press, 1988). On Gorbachev's many uses of constitutional dialogue in political discourse, see Robert Sharlet, "The Path of Constitutional Reform in the USSR," in Robert T. Huber and Donald R. Kelley, eds., *Perestroika-era Politics* (Armonk, NY: M.E. Sharpe, 1991), ch. 2. On the conspirators' invocation of constitutional writ, see the several official pronouncements of the so-called State Committee for the State Emergency in *Izvestiia* (August 20, 1991), p. 1. (The date is a misprint and should be August 19, 1991, since all the documents are dated August 18, 1991, and the following day's issue, No. 198, also bears the date August 20, 1991.) Finally, for the summons to the soldiers, see reference to the military document entitled "An Appeal" in "The Coup Makers' Secrets," *Newsweek*, September 9, 1991, p. 24.

2. See J.P. Day, "Civil Liberty and the Rule of Law," *Political Studies*, vol. 31 (1983), esp. p. 194.

3. See Walter H. Hamilton, "Constitutionalism," *Encyclopedia of the Social Sciences*, vol. 4 (New York: Macmillan, 1931), esp. p. 255.

4. See Roscoe Pound, "Rule of Law," *Encyclopedia of the Social Sciences*, vol. 13 (1934), pp. 463–66; and Dick Thornburgh, "The Soviet Union and the Rule of Law," *Foreign Affairs*, Spring 1990, pp. 13–27.

5. Louis Fisher, *Constitutional Dialogues: Interpretation as Political Process* (Princeton: Princeton University Press, 1988), p. 11.

6. See Gabriel A. Almond and Sidney Verba, *The Civic Culture: Political Attitudes and Democracy in Five Nations* (Boston: Little, Brown, 1963).

7. Andrei Amalrik, *Will the USSR Survive Until 1984?* (New York: Perennial Library, 1970), p. 22. The author, a prominent Soviet dissident in the late 1960s and 1970s, was referring to the Soviet regime, but the paradox is equally applicable to the preceding tsarist regime as well.

8. See Marc Raeff, *Michael Speransky: Statesman of Imperial Russia, 1772–1839* (The Hague, Netherlands: Martinus Nijhoff, 1957), ch. 2.

9. See Harold J. Berman's chapter "The Spirit of Russian Law," in his *Justice in the USSR*, rev. ed. (Cambridge, MA: Harvard University Press, 1963), ch. 7; and Richard S. Wortman, *The Development of a Russian Legal Consciousness* (Chicago: University of Chicago Press, 1976), chs. 1 and 8–10.

10. Aryeh L. Unger, *Constitutional Development in the USSR: A Guide to the Soviet Constitutions* (London: Methuen, 1981), p. 9.

11. See Robert Sharlet, "Soviet Legal Reform in Historical Context," *Columbia Journal of Transnational Law*, vol. 28, no. 1 (1990), pp. 5–17.

12. Richard B. Morris, ed., *Encyclopedia of American History* (New York: Harper and Bros., 1953), p. 115. See also, Michael Kammen, ed., *The Origins of the American Constitution: A Documentary History* (New York: Penguin, 1986), Part 1; and *Notes of Debates in the Federal Convention of 1787 Reported by James Madison*, with an introduction by Adrienne Koch (New York: Norton, 1987).

13. See the draft constitution of the Russian Federation in *Sovetskaia Rossiia*, November 24, 1990, p. 1. Vladimir Kudriavtsev, a leading Soviet jurist and one of the drafters of the law on the Soviet presidency, explicitly referred to the U.S. presidency as a model. See David K. Shipler, "A Reporter at Large—Politics in the Soviet Union: Between Dictatorship and Anarchy," *The New Yorker*, July 25, 1990, p. 55.

1. Brezhnev and the Constitution of 1977

1. *Pravda*, May 25, 1977, p. 1, and ibid., June 17, 1977, p. 1. For the Constitutional Commission's brief communiqué, see ibid., May 24, 1977, p. 1. The draft was subsequently published on June 4 throughout the national and regional press. See the translation in *Current Digest of the Soviet Press* (hereafter *CDSP*), June 29, 1977, pp. 1–11, 22. Podgorny did not appear in person before the Supreme Soviet; his "resignation" was made on his behalf. The May plenum also relieved Konstantin Katushev from his post as Central Committee Secretary supervising relations with ruling Communist parties. He was replaced by K.V. Rusakov, in a change apparently unrelated to the decision to publish the new constitution.

2. The growing constitutional discussion in short order subsumed both the campaign preceding the local soviet elections, scheduled for June 19, and the socialist competitions in honor of the then forthcoming 60th anniversary celebration. See *Pravda*, June 20, 1977, for coverage of the elections. For a typical "socialist emulation" pledge by a factory in response to the constitutional discussion, see *Ekonomicheskaia gazeta*, 1977, No. 28, p. 4. On the constitutional revision and ratification process, see *Pravda* and *Izvestiia*, September 28–October 8, 1977. The final text of the new constitution appeared in the issues for October 8, 1977. For a translation of the final, official text of the new Soviet Constitution of 1977, see *CDSP*, November 9, 1977, pp. 1–13, reprinted in Robert Sharlet *The New Soviet Constitution of 1977* (Brunswick, OH: King's Court, 1978), pp. 73 ff.

3. On the drafting, discussion, and ratification of the 1936 Constitution, see S.I. Rusinova and V.A. Rianzhin, eds., *Sovetskoe konstitutsionnoe pravo* [Soviet Constitutional Law] (Leningrad: Izdatel'stvo Leningradskogo Universiteta, 1975), pp. 75–79. After December 5, 1965, "Constitution Day" became the occasion for an annual silent protest demonstration by human rights dissidents in Moscow's Pushkin Square. See *A Chronicle of Human Rights in the USSR*, No. 23–24, October–December 1976, p. 10.

4. See Robert C. Tucker, "Stalinism as Revolution from Above," and Moshe Lewin, "The Social Background of Stalinism," both in Robert C. Tucker, ed.,

Stalinism: Essays in Historical Interpretation (New York: Norton, 1977), pp. 77–108 and 111–36, respectively.

5. See the 1936 Constitution, Arts. 1, 2, 7, 9, and 10. For an English translation see Harold J. Berman and John B. Quigley, Jr., eds., *Basic Laws on the Structure of the Soviet State* (Cambridge: Harvard University Press, 1969), pp. 3–28.

6. For a summary of the constitutional revision process from World War II through 1970, see John N. Hazard, "Soviet Law and Justice," in John W. Strong, ed., *The Soviet Union Under Brezhnev and Kosygin* (New York: Van Nostrand, 1971), esp. pp. 109–14. For an authoritative account by a leading Soviet legal scholar of the constitutional proposals under discussion prior to the creation of Khrushchev's constitutional commission, see P.S. Romashkin, "New Stage in the Development of the Soviet State," *Sovetskoe gosudarstvo i pravo*, October 1960, pp. 31–40. A *CDSP* translation of this important article is reprinted in Jan F. Triska, ed., *Constitutions of the Communist Party-States* (Stanford: Hoover Institution, 1968), pp. 77–87. Several of the major ideas outlined by Romashkin in 1960 were included in the constitution ratified 17 years later. For a Western analysis of the various proposals for constitutional revision before the creation of Khrushchev's commission in 1962, see George Ginsburgs, "A Khrushchev Constitution: Projects and Prospects," *Osteuropa Recht* (Cologne), August 1962, pp. 191–214.

7. See Jerome S. Gilison, "Khrushchev, Brezhnev, and Constitutional Reform," *Problems of Communism*, September–October 1972, esp. pp. 75–78.

8. See Hazard, "Soviet Law and Justice," in Strong, op. cit., p. 111.

9. L.I. Brezhnev, "Report of the CPSU Central Committee and the Immediate Tasks of the Party in Home and Foreign Policy," *XXVth Congress of the CPSU* (Moscow: Novosti, 1976), pp. 101–02. For the "echo" in the legal press, see, e.g., the unsigned lead article, "The 25th Congress of the CPSU: Further Development of the Soviet State, Democracy, and Law," *Sovetskoe gosudarstvo i pravo*, May 1976, esp. pp.7–8.

10. Shortly after publication of the draft constitution, Politburo member G.V. Romanov, then First Secretary of the Leningrad Obkom and a member of the Constitutional Commission, reported that the draft had been discussed "repeatedly" in the Politburo, Central Committee Secretariat, Constitutional Commission, and various state institutions. To some extent, he attributed the length of the drafting process to the thoroughness with which the constitutional principles were discussed in these different forums. At the same time, he also made specific reference to Brezhnev's "initiative [in the decision] to approve this historic document in the year of the 60th anniversary of the Great October." See *Leningradskaia pravda*, June 9, 1977, p. 2. For an account of the drafting process by one of the scholars involved, see Anatoly Butenko, "How the 'Brezhnev' Constitution Was Prepared," *Moscow News*, December 10–17, 1989, p. 13.

11. For translations of the 1918 and 1924 constitutions, see Triska, *Constitutions*, pp. 2–36. For translations and commentaries on the four Soviet constitutions through 1977, see Aryeh L. Unger, *Constitutional Development in the USSR* (London: Methuen, 1981). For other analyses of the 1977 Constitution, see George Ginsburgs and Stanislaw Pomorski, "A Profile of the Soviet Constitution of 1977," in *The Constitutions of the USSR and the Union Republics ed. F.J.M. Feldbrugge* (Alphen aan den Rijn, Holland: Sijthoff and Noordhoff, 1979), pp.

3–67; and John N. Hazard, "A Constitution for 'Developed Socialism,' " in *Soviet Law After Stalin*: Vol. 2, ed. Donald D. Barry, George Ginsburgs, and Peter B. Maggs (Alphen aan den Rijn, Holland: Sijthoff and Noordhoff, 1978), pp. 1–33.

12. *Pravda*, June 5, 1977, pp. 1–2. Brezhnev's Report was published verbatim in the national and regional press on June 5, one day after publication of the draft constitution. For a translation, see *CDSP*, July 6, 1977, pp. 6–10.

13. For environmental legislation, see, e.g., *Fundamentals of Legislation of the USSR and the Union Republics* (Moscow: Progress Publishers, 1974), pp. 15–16 and 39–40. Also, see Zigurds L. Zile, "Soviet Struggle for Environmental Quality: The Limits of Environmental Law Under Central Planning," in Donald D. Barry, et al., eds., *Contemporary Soviet Law: Essays in Honor of John N. Hazard* (The Hague: Martinus Nijhoff, 1974), pp. 124–57. For Soviet perspectives on international law, see G.I. Tunkin, *Theory of International Law*, trans. by William E. Butler (Cambridge: Harvard University Press, 1974), especially chapters 2 and 3. Tunkin, a former diplomat, is a leading Soviet scholar on international law. On labor legislation, see the Fundamental Principles of Labor Legislation, in *Fundamentals of Legislation of the USSR*, p. 91. On the labor law reforms generally, see A.K.R. Kiralfy, "Soviet Labor Law Reform Since Stalin," in Barry, et al., eds., *Contemporary Soviet Law*, pp. 158–74.

14. Nikita S. Khrushchev, "The Crimes of the Stalin Era—Special Report to the 20th Congress of the Communist Party of the Soviet Union," *The New Leader*, Supplement, July 16, 1956, p. 63.

15. Although, as we shall see, this was not the case with respect to the Soviet Union's political, religious, ethnic, and cultural dissidents. See M.S. Strogovich, "On the Rights of the Individual in Soviet Criminal Procedure," *Sovetskoe gosudarstvo i pravo*, 1976, No. 10 (October), pp. 73–81, and translated in *Soviet Review*, Vol. 18, No. 2 (Summer 1977), pp. 3–17. On civil process, see Donald D. Barry, "The Specialist in Soviet Policy Making: The Adoption of a Law," *Soviet Studies*, October 1964, pp. 152–65; and Whitmore Gray, "Soviet Tort Law: The New Principles Annotated," *University of Illinois Law Forum*, Spring 1964, pp. 180–211.

16. On the duality of legality and extra-legality, see Robert Sharlet, "Stalinism and Soviet Legal Culture," in Tucker, ed., *Stalinism*, pp. 155–79.

17. The "state law" school continued to be heavily represented in the Soviet academic legal establishment, although the late Professor A.I. Lepeshkin was probably its most influential spokesman. His *Kurs Sovetskogo gosudarstvennogo prava* [A Treatise on Soviet State Law], Vol. 1 (Moscow: Iuridicheskaia literatura, 1961), was a basic reference in the debate that emerged in the early 1960s. The early leader of the "constitutionalists" was the late V.F. Kotok who had broken new ground in post-Stalin Soviet jurisprudence with his introductory essay to the book he edited with N.P. Farberov, *Konstitutsionnoe pravo sotsialisticheskikh stran* [Constitutional Law of the Socialist States] (Moscow: Akademiia Nauk SSSR, 1963). Kotok's article was sharply criticized in the legal press and at a special meeting of the faculty and graduate students of the Department of State Law and Soviet Construction at Moscow University Law School during the academic year 1963–64. The next major position statement of the "constitutional law" school was I.E. Farber and V.A. Rzhevskii's *Voprosy teorii Sovetskogo konstitutsionnogo prava*

[Theoretical Questions of Soviet Constitutional Law], No. 1 (Saratov: Saratovskii iuridicheskii institut, 1967). For a subsequent statement of the orthodox position, see B.V. Shchetinin, *Problemy teorii Sovetskogo gosudarstvennogo prava* [Theoretical Problems of Soviet State Law], Part I (Moscow: Iuridicheskaia literatura, 1969), and Part II, published in 1974. Compare this to the later authoritative statement of the "constitutionalists," Rusinova and Rianzhin, *Sovetskoe konstitutsionnoe pravo*. For an account of the unfavorable reception which this last study received at a special meeting of legal scholars, held under the auspices of the Department of State Law and Soviet Construction at Moscow University Law School in February 1976, see N.A. Mikhaleva, "The Discussion of the Book 'Soviet Constitutional Law,' " *Vestnik Moskovskogo Universiteta*, ser. Pravo (Moscow), July–August 1976, pp. 86–90. The rapporteur was a member of the "state law" school. For a Western article which pointed out the Rusinova and Rianzhin volume's implications for the process of Soviet constitutional reform, see Christopher Osakwe's review essay in *Tulane Law Review*, Vol. 51 (1977), pp. 411–22.

18. In spite of the already noted hostile reaction to the constitutionalists' 1975 statement, the author was told by a reliable source that even before publication of the new draft constitution, several leading representatives of the "old guard" had conceded privately, albeit reluctantly, that the concept of "constitutional law" had won the day in Soviet jurisprudence. The "victory" was eventually followed by changes in law school curricula.

19. For a conceptual analysis of metapolicy and *ad hoc* action as legal policy, see Robert Sharlet, "Soviet Legal Policymaking: A Preliminary Classification," in a special issue edited by Harry M. Johnson, "Social System and Legal Process," *Sociological Inquiry*, Vol. 47, Nos. 3–4 (1977), esp. pp. 212–14 and 218–19.

20. See, e.g., V.M. Chkhikvadze et al., eds., *Politicheskaia organizatsiia Sovetskogo obshchestva* [The Political Organization of Soviet Society] (Moscow: Nauka, 1967); and M.N. Marchenko, *Demokraticheskie osnovy politicheskoi organizatsii Sovetskogo obshchestva* [The Democratic Principles of the Political Organization of Soviet Society] (Moscow: Izdatel'stvo Moskovskogo Universiteta, 1977).

21. In a seminal essay, Richard Lowenthal argued that advancing socioeconomic modernization seemed to make this shift inevitable. See his "Development versus Utopia in Communist Policy," in Chalmers Johnson, ed., *Change in Communist Systems* (Stanford: Stanford University Press, 1970), pp. 33–116. For his later analysis of the dilemmas which modernization creates for one-party systems, see "The Ruling Party in a Mature Society," in Mark Field, ed., *Social Consequences of Modernization in Communist Societies* (Baltimore: Johns Hopkins University Press, 1976), pp. 81–118.

22. Article 9 read: "Further development of socialist democracy constitutes the basic direction in the evolution of the political system of Soviet society: [that is] the ever wider participation of working people in the management of the affairs of society and government; the improvement of the state apparatus; a heightening of the activeness of mass social organizations; the strengthening of the people's control; the reinforcement of the legal foundations of state and public life; the expansion of glasnost; [and] the continual regard for public opinion." (Author's translation.)

23. See Roger E. Kanet, "The Rise and Fall of the 'All-People's State': Recent Changes in the Soviet Theory of the State," *Soviet Studies*, July 1968, pp. 81–93. Years of doctrinal paring stripped the Khrushchevian concept of its emphasis on the "withering away" of the state through the transfer of selected state functions to mass organizations of "social self-government." The then contemporary concept merely envisioned limited democratization of the Soviet political system through a somewhat greater participation of mass social organizations as collective entities. See, e.g., B.N. Topornin, "The All-People's State and Socialist Democracy," *Pravovedenie*, March–April 1975, pp. 7–17,

24. See Stalin Constitution, Art. 130.

25. See Peter H. Juviler, *Revolutionary Law and Order: Politics and Social Change in the USSR* (New York: Free Press, 1976), pp. 85–116.

26. See Stalin Constitution, Arts, 126 and 141.

27. Cf. ibid., Arts. 4–12.

28. I am indebted to Professor John N. Hazard of Columbia Law School, who alerted me to this change of wording.

29. Cf. Stalin Constitution, Art. 11.

30. See *Sotsialisticheskoe sorevnovanie v SSSR 1918–1964* [Socialist Competition in the USSR, 1918–1964] (Moscow: Profizdat, 1965), pp. 127–40 and Part Three. Also see Erik P. Hoffmann, "The 'Scientific Management' of Soviet Society," *Problems of Communism*, May–June 1977, pp. 59–67; and Robert F. Miller, "The Scientific-Technical Revolution and the Soviet Administrative Debate," in Paul Cocks, Robert V. Daniels, and Nancy Whittier Heer, eds., *The Dynamics of Soviet Politics* (Cambridge: Harvard University Press, 1976), pp. 137–55.

31. Cf. Stalin Constitution, Art. 12. See also R. Beermann, "The Parasite Law in the Soviet Union," *British Journal of Criminology*, Vol. 3 (1962), pp. 71–80.

32. See "The 1961 Programme of the Communist Party of the Soviet Union," in Jan F. Triska, ed., *Soviet Communism: Programs and Rules* (San Francisco: Chandler, 1962), esp. Part 2, pp. 68–122.

33. Ibid., pp. 35–39 and 63–67.

34. Article 29 included "Basket Three," or the human rights principles, of the Helsinki document. Cf. "Conference on Security and Cooperation in Europe: Final Act," *The Department of State Bulletin* (Washington, DC: Government Printing Office, September 1, 1975), pp. 323–50. From the Soviet perspective, these principles needed to be viewed within the context of Part II of the Constitution, on "The State and the Individual." The "Brezhnev doctrine" was covered in Article 30 in the guise of "comradely mutual assistance."

35. Cf. Stalin Constitution, Art. 14.

36. Cf. ibid,, Arts. 118–22.

37. In a June 1977 session at the Kennan Institute (Washington, DC) devoted to a discussion of the Draft Constitution, Professor Moshe Lewin characterized the cluster of economic and other rights as descriptive of a "super welfare state," based on an obligation to work. For the details of Soviet health care legislation, see the Fundamental Principles of Health Legislation of 1969 in *Fundamentals of Legislation of the USSR*, pp. 62–88. The new article on old-age maintenance was elaborated in practice by a developing body of pension law. See, for example, M.L. Zakharov, ed., *Sovetskoe pensionnoe pravo* [Soviet Pension Law] (Moscow: Iuridicheskaia literatura, 1974).

38. See Stalin Constitution, Art. 131. On the problem of economic crime, see, e.g., Gregory Grossman, "The 'Second Economy' of the USSR," *Problems of Communism*, September-October, 1977, pp. 25–40; and Valery Chalidze, *Criminal Russia: Essays on Crime in the Soviet Union* (New York: Random House, 1977), chs. 8–10.

39. Cf. ibid., Arts. 125–26.

40. Cf. ibid,, Art. 130.

41. It was misleading to describe the "linkage" of rights and duties as the regime's "answer" to the dissidents. For an argument in this direction, see "New USSR Draft Constitution," *International Commission of Jurists Review*, June 1977, p. 30. Rather, the nexus of rights and duties was a general principle in contemporary Soviet legislation. See, e.g., the Land Fundamentals, Art. 11, and the Civil Fundamentals, Art. 5, in *Fundamentals of Legislation of the USSR*, pp. 15–16 and 153–54, respectively.

42. Ibid,, pp. 271–99. See also, John Gorgone, "Soviet Jurists in the Legislative Arena: The Reform of Criminal Procedure, 1956–1958," *Soviet Union*, Vol. 3, Part I (1976), pp. 1–35; and Harold J. Berman's Introduction to Berman and James W. Spindler, eds., *Soviet Criminal Law and Procedure: The RSFSR Codes*, 2nd ed. (Cambridge: Harvard University Press, 1972), esp. pp. 47–70 and 84–89.

43. See Christopher Osakwe, "Due Process of Law Under Contemporary Soviet Criminal Procedure," *Tulane Law Review*, Vol. 50, pp. 266–317. Nine such "cases" were translated by Harold Berman in *Soviet Statutes and Decisions*, Summer 1965, pp. 5–41. Numerous others were translated in John N. Hazard, William E. Butler, and Peter B. Maggs, eds., *The Soviet Legal System: Fundamental Principles and Historical Commentary*, 3rd ed. (Dobbs Ferry, NY: Oceana, 1977), Ch. 7.

44. Cf. Stalin Constitution, Art. 127, See also the Criminal Procedural Fundamentals, Art. 6, in *Fundamentals of Legislation of the USSR*, p. 274; the RSFSR Criminal Procedure Code, Art. 11, in Berman, *Soviet Criminal Law and Procedure*, p. 209; Berman's analysis of the personal inviolability articles in ibid., pp. 48–50; and the Bortkevich case in Hazard et al., *The Soviet Legal System*, pp. 112–13.

45. See Stalin Constitution, Art. 102. The "special courts" were transportation courts with jurisdiction over criminal offenses that took place on the railway and water transport systems. These were abolished in the post-Stalin era and were not mentioned in the Fundamental Principles of Legislation on the Court System. See *Fundamentals of Legislation of the USSR*, Art. 1, p. 137. However, on "special courts" of the Brezhnev period which had special legal personnel and jurisdiction over individuals engaged in classified work, see Yury Luryi, "The Right to Counsel in Ordinary Criminal Cases in the USSR, in Donald D. Barry, George Ginsburgs, and Peter B. Maggs, eds., *The Citizen and the State in Contemporary Soviet Law* (Leiden, Holland: A.W. Sijthoff, 1977), esp. pp. 106-8. The author was a former Soviet defense counsel.

46. On the class approach to justice and its abandonment, see John N. Hazard, "Reforming Soviet Criminal Law," *Journal of Criminal Law and Criminology*, July–August 1938, pp. 157–69. In the USSR, members of the nomenklatura enjoyed privileged status before the law.

47. Cf. Stalin Constitution, Art. 111. For analysis of the changing status of the Soviet defense counsel, see Jean C. Love, "The Role of Defense Counsel in Soviet

Criminal Proceedings," *Wisconsin Law Review*, 1968, No. 3, pp. 806–900; and Lawrence M. Friedman and Zigurds L. Zile, "Soviet Legal Profession: Recent Developments in Law and Practice," ibid., 1964, No. 1, pp. 32–77. The mass organizations could also assign a "social accuser" to assist a procurator in a criminal case. For a brief analysis of both social accusers and defenders, see Berman, *Soviet Criminal Law and Procedure*, pp. 69–70.

48. See John N. Hazard, *Settling Disputes in Soviet Society: The Formative Years of Legal Institutions* (New York: Columbia University Press, 1960), pp. 34–35, 47–49, 159–62.

49. The "open court" clause specifies: "The examination of cases in all courts is open. The hearing of cases in closed court is permitted only in instances provided for by law, and then with the observance of all the rules of judicial procedure." (Author's translation.)

50. Harold J. Berman, *Justice in the USSR*, rev. ed. (Cambridge: Harvard University Press, 1963), p. 70.

51. *Pravda*, June 5, 1977, p. 1.

52. Except for "political" cases, in which *partiinost'* (party-mindedness) routinely supersedes *zakonnost'* (legality), the following statement by a Soviet university lecturer seemed to characterize the administration of justice in the post-Stalin period: "The Party organs oversee the selection, placement, and ideological education of juridical cadres. But, at the same time, any kind of interference in the administration of justice in specific cases is absolutely ruled out." *Pravda*, August 19, 1977, p. 3. See also Robert Sharlet, "The Communist Party and the Administration of Justice in the USSR," in *Soviet Law After Stalin*: Vol. 3, ed. Donald D. Barry, George Ginsburgs, and Peter B. Maggs (Alphen aan den Rijn, Holland: Sigthoff and Noordhoff, 1979); and Peter H. Solomon, Jr., "Soviet Politicians and Criminal Prosecutions: The Logic of Party Intervention," in James R. Millar, ed., *Cracks in the Monolith: Party Power in the Brezhnev Era* (Armonk, NY: M.E. Sharpe, Inc., 1992).

53. See Stalin Constitution, Art. 113. The corresponding passage in the 1977 Constitution is more specific and emphatic and appears at the beginning of a separate chapter on the Procuracy (Ch. 21). For a history of the Procuracy's functions under Stalin, see Glen G. Morgan, *Soviet Administrative Legality: The Role of the Attorney General's Office* (Stanford: Stanford University Press, 1962), pp. 76–126.

54. See the 13 cases analyzed in Christopher Osakwe, "Due Process of Law and Civil Rights Cases in the Soviet Union," in Donald D. Barry, George Ginsburgs, and Peter B. Maggs, eds., *Law Reform Under Khrushchev and Brezhnev* (Leiden: A.W. Sijthoff, 1978). Even in ordinary (nonpolitical) cases, however, a "major retreat of the due process function in favor of the crime control function" took place at least temporarily during the various anti-crime campaigns under Khrushchev and Brezhnev. See Stanislaw Pomorski, "Criminal Law Protection of Socialist Property in the USSR," in ibid.

55. See Max Hayward, ed., *On Trial: The Soviet State versus "Abram Tertz" and "Nikolai Arzhak,"* rev. and enlarged ed. (New York: Harper and Row, 1967). See also Robert Sharlet, "Dissent and Repression in the Soviet Union," *Current History*, October 1977, pp. 112–17 and 130.

56. Harold J. Berman, "The Educational Role of Soviet Criminal Law and Civil Procedure," in Barry et al., *Contemporary Soviet Law*, pp. 14–16. The literature on

violations of dissidents' rights is voluminous. See, e.g., Christopher Osakwe, "Due Process of Law and Civil Rights Cases in the Soviet Union," loc. cit., for a detailed and systematic analysis of the due process violations reported in political cases; and the journal *A Chronicle of Human Rights in the USSR*, and *A Chronicle of Current Events* for continuous unofficial documentation of Soviet political "justice" during the Brezhnev period.

57. For examples of the "legalist" strategy, see Valery Chalidze, *To Defend These Rights: Human Rights and the Soviet Union* (New York: Random House, 1974); and the "legalist" analyses of Soviet constitutional law, prior to publication of the draft constitution, by Henn-Juri Uibopuu and Alexander Volpin in Leon Lipson and Valery Chalidze, eds., *Papers on Soviet Law* (New York: Institute on Socialist Law, 1977), pp. 14–51 and 52–107, respectively. For a "legalist" analysis of the Draft Constitution, see Sofia Kallistratova, "Comments on the Draft Constitution," *A Chronicle of Human Rights in the USSR*, No. 27, July/September 1977, pp. 56–64. This critique appeared in the West via samizdat just after the 1977 Constitution was ratified.

58. For the pertinent post-Stalin legislation on tort liability, see the Civil Fundamentals, Ch. 12, in *Fundamentals of Legislation in the USSR*, pp. 188–90; enactment of the Civil Fundamentals in the RSFSR Civil Code of 1964, Ch. 40, in Whitmore Gray and Raymond Stults, eds., *Civil Code of the Russian Soviet Federal Socialist Republic* (Ann Arbor: University of Michigan Law School, 1965), pp. 117–24; and the analysis of the Fundamental Principles, code law, and selected cases in Donald D. Barry, "The Soviet Union," in Donald D. Barry, ed., *Governmental Tort Liability in the Soviet Union, Bulgaria, . . . and Yugoslavia* (Leiden: A.W. Sijthoff, 1970), pp. 54–70.

59. *Pravda*, June 5, 1977, p. 2. The following account of the constitutional discussion was based on a survey of articles and letters about the Draft Constitution published from June 4 through mid-September 1977, in the following newspapers: *Pravda, Izvestiia, Vecherniaia Moskva, Literaturnaia gazeta,* and *Ekonomicheskaia gazeta,* In addition, six other national and republican newspapers were surveyed intermittently during the same period: *Komsomol'skaia pravda* (Moscow), *Krasnaia zvezda* (Moscow), *Sovetskaia Litva* (Vilnius), *Pravda Ukrainy* (Kiev), *Bakinskii rabochii* (Baku), and *Leningradskaia pravda.*

60. See, e.g., G.V. Romanov's report to the *aktiv* of the Leningrad party organization, *Leningradskaia pravda*, June 9, 1977, p. 2; *Pravda*'s lead editorial, June 9, 1977, p. 1; and P.P. Griškjavicius's report to the Lithuanian Supreme Soviet, in *Sovetskaia Litva*, July 3, 1977, p. 1. Griškjavicius was then First Secretary of the Central Committee of the Lithuanian Communist Party and, like Romanov, was elected a member of the Constitutional Commission in April 1977.

61. *Pravda*, June 7, 1977, p. 1.

62. Ibid., June 5, 1977, p. 2.

63. See, e.g., *Pravda*'s lead editorial, June 6, 1977, p. 1; Romanov's remarks of June 9, 1977, loc. cit.; and Sh. R. Rashidov's report to the *aktiv* of the Uzbek republic Party organization, *Pravda*, June 10, 1977, p. 3. Rashidov was then First Secretary of the Central Committee of the Uzbek Communist Party and a member of the CPSU Politburo.

64. June 9, 1977, p. 1. For a quantitative study of the "discussion," see E. Schneider's article in *Soviet Studies*, vol. 31, no. 4 (1979).

65. The following description was based in part on several conversations the author had with well-informed persons.

66. See Christian Duevel, "A Secretive Reorganization of the Constitutional Commission," *Radio Liberty Research*, RL 141/77, June 7, 1977, especially pp. 2, 4, and 6–8; and *Vedomosti Verkhovnogo Soveta SSSR*, No. 18 (1884), May 4, 1977, Item 274.

67. See Robert Sharlet, "Concept Formation in Political Science and Communist Studies: Conceptualizing Political Participation," in Frederic J. Fleron, Jr., ed., *Communist Studies and the Social Sciences* (Chicago: Rand McNally, 1969), pp. 244–53,

68. See, e.g., *Pravda*, June 11, 1977, p. 3; ibid,, June 13, p. 3; and V.V. Grishin's article in ibid., June 14, pp. 2–3. Grishin was then First Secretary of the Moscow City Party Committee and a member of the Politburo. See also the article by the Chairman of the Presidium of the Ukrainian Supreme Soviet in *Izvestiia*, June 14, 1977, p. 2. For Gorbachev's contribution to the discussion, see M.S. Gorbachev, *Izbrannye rechi i stat'i* (Moscow: Izdatel'stvo politicheskoi literatury, 1987), Vol. 1, pp. 149–53. Gorbachev was then a regional party first secretary. He was speaking as a Deputy to the USSR Supreme Soviet.

69. *Izvestiia* July 8, 1977, p. 2; and *Pravda Ukrainy*, July 3, 1977, p. 2. Subsequently, the Constitutional Commission reported that through July 20, 1977, more than 650,000 meetings of working collectives had been held, involving 57 million people. See *Izvestiia*, July 30, 1977, p. 1.

70. See *Izvestiia* July 10, 1977, p. 2; and ibid., July 15, 1977, p.2.

71. *Pravda*, July 9, 1977, p. 3.

72. In the context of electoral politics, these have been called "valence issues." See Donald E. Stokes, "Spatial Models of Party Competition," in Angus Campbell et al., *Elections and the Political Order* (New York: Wiley, 1966), pp. 161–79.

73. *Pravda*, July 13, 1977, p. 1; and *Komsomol'skaia pravda*, July 14, 1977, p. 1.

74. *Pravda*, July 18, 1977, p. 3; *Izvestiia*, July 19, 1977, p. 2.

75. *Sovetskaia Litva*, June 29, 1977, p. 1. For other letters agreeing with the engineer's emphasis, see also *Bakinski rabochii*, June 28, 1977, p. 2.; *Izvestiia* July 7, 1977, p. 2; and *Pravda*, July 17, 1977, p. 3. For letters advocating increased "moral" incentives, see, e.g., *Sovetskaia Litva*, June 28, 1977, p. 2; *Izvestiia*, July 12, 1977, p. 2; and *Krasnaia zvezda*, August 16, 1977, p. 2.

76. For the comment of the Moscow factory worker, see *Vecherniaia Moskva*, July 16, 1977, p. 2. For letters proposing legal sanctions, see, e.g., *Literaturnaia gazeta*, 1977, No. 27 (July 6), p. 2; *Komsomol'skaia pravda*, July 23, 1977, p. 2; and *Pravda*, August 1, 1977, p. 3. See the proposal on anti-parasitism by Deputy A.V. Ivanov at the first session of the newly elected Leningrad City Soviet, *Izvestiia*, June 25, 1977, p. 3, See also *Pravda Ukrainy*, July 1, 1977, p. 2; *Sovetskaia Litva*, July 7, 1977, p. 2; *Pravda*, July 12, 1977, p. 3; ibid., July 13, 1977, p. 3; ibid,, August 3, 1977, p. 3; *Vecherniaia Moskva*, August 10, 1977, p. 2; and *Pravda*, September 9, 1977, p. 3.

77. *Pravda*, July 8, 1977, p. 3; and *Vecherniaia Moskva*, July 9, 1977, p. 2. See also, *Pravda*, September 8, 1977, p. 3.

78. *Vecherniaia Moskva*, July 7, 1977, p. 2; *Izvestiia*, July 9, 1977, p. 2; and *Komsomol'skaia pravda*, July 22, 1977, p. 1. See also, *Vecherniaia Moskva*, August 17, 1977, p. 2; and *Pravda*, August 21, 1977, p. 3.

79. *Izvestiia*, July 7, 1977, p. 2; ibid., June 30, 1977, p. 2; and ibid., July 2, 1977, p. 2. See also, *Pravda*, September 14, 1977, p. 3.

80. *Izvestiia*, June 28, 1977, p. 2; ibid., July 9, 1977, p. 2; and *Pravda*, July 9, 1977, p. 3. See also, *Izvestiia*, July 14, 1977, p. 2; *Pravda*, August 14, 1977, p. 3; and ibid., September 9, 1977, p. 3. A related participatory clause, Art. 96 which conferred the "right . . . to be elected" deputies on 18–year-olds, stirred considerable discussion pro and con. See, e.g., *Pravda*, September 18, 1977, p. 3. The result in the final, amended text was a compromise.

81. *Izvestiia*, July 15, 1977, p. 2; *Sovetskaia Litva*, July 3, 1977, p. 2.

82. *Izvestiia*, July 16, 1977, p. 2; *Komsomol'skaia pravda*, July 22, 1977, p. 1; and *Vecherniaia Moskva*, July 22, 1977, p. 2. See also *Pravda Ukrainy*, July 3, 1977, p. 2; and *Pravda*, August 1, 1977, p. 3.

83. *Izvestiia*, July 7, 1977, p. 2; *Pravda*, July 3, 1977, p. 3; *Pravda Ukrainy*, June 29, 1977, p. 1. See also *Pravda*, June 27, 1977, p. 3; *Pravda*'s lead editorial, July 3, 1977, p. 1; *Izvestiia*, August 6, 1977, p. 2; *Pravda*, August 23, 1977, p. 3; and *Izvestiia*, September 9, 1977, p. 2. The absence of reference to these two institutions in the draft constitution was apparently not meant to signal their gradual "withering away." In a May 1977 speech, the then USSR Minister of Justice V.I. Terebilov indicated that both institutions had been given increased authority and responsibility in order to fulfill their assigned roles in the implementation of the new legislation on juvenile delinquency, enacted in February 1977. See *Pravda*, May 20, 1977, p. 3, as translated in *CDSP* June 15, 1977, pp. 1–2. For basic studies on these institutions, see Harold J. Berman and James Spindler, "Soviet Comrades' Courts," *Washington Law Review*, Vol. 38 (1963), pp. 842–910; and Dennis M. O'Connor, "Soviet People's Guards: An Experiment with Civic Police," *New York University Law Review*, Vol. 39 (1964), pp. 579–614.

84. *Pravda*, July 15, 1977, pp. 2–3; *Vecherniaia Moskva*, June 28, 1977, p. 2; and *Izvestiia*, July 13, 1977, p. 2. See also ibid., August 6, 1977, p. 2; and *Vecherniaia Moskva*, August 10, 1977, p. 2.

85. *Pravda*, July 8, 1977, p. 3; *Krasnaia zvezda*, July 23, 1977, p. 2; and *Izvestiia*, July 24, 1977, p. 2. See also *Pravda*, July 28, 1977, p. 3. For a readers' "debate" on the personal property clause (Art. 13), see ibid., July 30, 1977, p. 3.

86. *Vecherniaia Moskva*, June 21, 1977, p. 2; ibid., July 1, 1977, p. 2 (two letters); ibid., August 22, 1977, p. 2; *Komsomol'skaia pravda*, July 31, 1977, p. 1; and *Izvestiia*, August 6, 1977, p. 2.

87. See, e.g., the attacks on Zbigniew Brzezinski, then U.S. National Security Advisor, in *Komsomol'skaia pravda*, May 25, 1977, p. 3, as translated in *CDSP*, June 22, 1977, pp. 6–7, and on President Carter in *Izvestiia*, June 9, 1977, p. 5. Later in the summer, the polemics shifted from personalities and policies to the U.S. system as a whole. See, e.g., the extended comparative critique of the U.S. Constitution in *Literaturnaia gazeta*, 1977, No. 35 (August 31), p. 13.

88. *Pravda*, July 8, 1977, p. 3; ibid., July 16, 1977, p. 3; and *Sovetskaia Litva*, July 8, 1977, p. 2. See also *Pravda Ukrainy*, July 1, 1977, p. 2. Brezhnev had given some emphasis in his report to the linkage of rights and duties, and the press cued the public on this issue rather heavily in lead editorials. See *Vecherniaia Moskva*, June 6, 1977, p. 1; *Izvestiia*, June 8, 1977, p. 1; and *Krasnaia zvezda*, June 21, 1977, p. 1.

89. *Izvestiia*, July 3, 1977, p. 2; *Pravda Ukrainy*, July 8, 1977, p. 2; and *Pravda*, July 14, 1977, p. 3. See also *Izvestiia*, August 18, 1977, p. 2.

90. On Sakharov's appeal, see *Le Monde* (Paris), June 4, 1977, p. 5. For his subsequent statement, see *The New York Times*, June 6, 1977, p. 4, See also G. Snigerev's "Open Letter to the Soviet Government," *Russkaia mysl'* (Paris), July 7, 1977, p. 2. He argued that the "linkage" of rights with duties (Art. 39), combined with the caveat of Art. 50, effectively "canceled" his rights as a citizen. Snigerev is a writer and documentary film maker who had been active in Ukrainian dissident circles since 1966. In 1974 he was expelled from membership in the Communist Party and the professional organization necessary for him to work in films, apparently for refusing to renounce publicly his friendship with the dissident writer Viktor Nekrasov, then an émigré. For information on dissidents' reactions to the Soviet Draft Constitution, I am indebted to Dr. Gene Sosin, formerly of Radio Free Europe/Radio Liberty, New York. For post-ratification émigré dissident criticism of the new Soviet Constitution in general and its civil rights clauses in particular, see Vladimir Bukovsky, "An Appeal to the Heads of State and Government of the Thirty-five Countries that Signed the Helsinki Agreements," *New York Review of Books*, October 13, 1977, p. 44; and Valery Chalidze, "Human Rights in the New Soviet Constitution," *A Chronicle of Human Rights in the USSR*, No. 28, October–December 1977.

91. Article 52 reads in part: "The incitement of hostility and hatred in connection with religious beliefs is prohibited."

92. Information on the religious appeal is from Radio Free Europe/Radio Liberty. For the party rule referred to in the religious petition, see John N. Hazard, *The Soviet System of Government*, 4th ed. (Chicago: University of Chicago Press, 1968), Appendix, p. 244. In contrast to the religious dissidents, a colonel in the military law office of the Soviet Army urged a far more restrictive religious freedom clause (Art. 52). See *Krasnaia zvezda*, July 31, 1977, p. 2. See also, *Pravda*, September 1, 1977, p. 3.

93. *Bakinskii rabochii*, July 2, 1977, p. 2; and *Literaturnaia gazeta*, 1977, No. 29 (July 20), p. 2. See also *Izvestiia*, August 17, 1977, p. 2.

94. Article 155 specified that both "Judges and people's assessors are independent and subordinate only to the law."

95. Doctor of Jurisprudence G.Z. Anashkin was a former Chairman of the Criminal Division of the USSR Supreme Court. His article appeared in *Pravda*, July 11, 1977, p. 3. Also see *Izvestiia*, July 3, 1977, p. 2; *Pravda*, July 8, 1977, p. 3; and the joint letter from two well-known jurists urging reinforcement of the independence of the procurator from the local soviet in his jurisdiction, as a safeguard for ensuring the observance of legality, *Izvestiia*, August 3, 1977, p. 2. Earlier, in samizdat, Roy Medvedev had advanced similar proposals. He, too, suggested broadening the court's jurisdiction so that citizens could seek judicial remedies against administrative abuses. See his *On Socialist Democracy* (New York: Knopf, 1975), esp. pp. 162–63. On the policy and law of pardon, see Zigurds L. Zile, "Amnesty and Pardon in the Soviet Union," *Soviet Union*, Vol. 3, Part 1 (1976), pp. 37–49.

96. *Pravda*, July 6, 1977, p. 3.

97. Deputy Procurator Gusev was far less persuasive in his previous "exchange" with Sakharov and Chalidze on the Op-Ed Page of *The New York Times*. See *The New York Times*, February 23, 1977, p. A23; Valery Chalidze's rebuttal,

March 5, 1977, p. 19; and Sakharov's reply, March 29, 1977, p. 27.

98. *Pravda*, July 11, 1977, p. 3; *Izvestiia*, July 3, 1977, p. 2; and Snigerev, "Open Letter." Snigerev was referring to the conviction of two Ukrainian dissidents in June 1977 for their leadership of an unofficial human rights "watch group" in Kiev whose purpose was to monitor Soviet compliance with the Helsinki accords. The trial had taken place in an out-of-the-way small town instead of in Kiev, thus making it very difficult for the defendants' relatives and supporters to attend and in effect rendering it *de facto* a "closed trial." A few months later, in September 1977, Snigerev was arrested in Kiev. See *A Chronicie of Human Rights in the USSR*, No. 27, July–September 1977, p. 21.

99. *Izvestiia*, July 3, 1977, p. 2; ibid., June 26, 1977, p. 2; and *Pravda*, August 3, 1977, p. 3. On the earlier debates over the right to counsel and the presumption of innocence, see Gorgone, "Soviet Jurists in the Legislative Arena: The Reform of Criminal Procedure, 1956–1958"; and Kazimierz Grzybowski, "Soviet Criminal Law," *Problems of Communism*, March–April 1965, especially pp. 60–62. See also Eugene Huskey, "The Politics of the Soviet Criminal Process: Expanding the Right to Counsel in Pre-Trial Proceedings," *American Journal of Comparative Law*, Winter, 1986, pp. 93–112.

100. While everyone was "for" science, this did not preclude possibly serious disputes over the allocation of science-targeted funds. In particular, those who would tighten the "link with production" by directing a still larger share of the science budget into "applied research" would no doubt come into conflict with the interests supporting "basic research."

101. For a sample of such letters, see *Pravda*, June 27, 1977, p. 3; ibid., July 20, 1977, p. 3; ibid., August 3, 1977, p. 3; ibid., August 14, 1977, p. 3; *Izvestiia*, July 1, 1977, p. 2; ibid., August 3, 1977, p. 2; *Vecherniaia Moskva*, July 7, 1977, p. 2; and *Bakinskii rabochii*, July 1, 1977, p. 2. See also, *Pravda*, September 14, 1977, p. 3.

102. *Pravda*, July 10, 1977, p. 3; *Izvestiia*, July 8, 1977, p. 2; *Pravda*, July 21, 1977, p. 3; and *Vecherniaia Moskva*, June 27, 1977, p. 2. The enactment in June 1977 by the USSR Supreme Soviet of the all-union Fundamental Principles of Forest Legislation, which was accompanied by a number of pro-environmentalist speeches by various deputies, gave additional impetus, no doubt, to the ad hoc lobby on environmentalism. See *Izvestiia*, June 18, 1977, pp. 1–7. For other letters on the general issue, see, e.g., *Bakinskii rabochii*, July 1, 1977, p. 2; *Ekonomicheskaia gazeta*, 1977, No. 27 (July),p. 8; ibid., 1977, No. 30 (July), p. 6; *Izvestiia*, July 24, 1977, p. 2; *Krasnaia zvezda*, July 30, 1977, p. 2; *Pravda*, August 22, 1977, p. 3; and ibid., September 11, 1977, p. 3.

103. See *CDSP*, October 26, 1977, p. 4. According to well-informed sources with whom the author had discussions, the enlarged Secretariat numbered approximately 500 people and the two articles which drew the most communications were reportedly the housing clause (Art. 44) and the clause on "individual labor activity" (Art. 17). Apparently, tens of thousands of people took advantage of the public discussion on the new right of housing to write to higher authorities complaining about and seeking improvements in their housing arrangements.

104. For a translation of Brezhnev's fall report on the proposed constitutional revisions, see *CDSP*, October 26, 1977, pp. 1–7 and 13, esp. pp. 1 and 5. The final text of the 1977 Constitution was published in *Pravda* and other major newspapers

on October 8, 1977. For an English translation, see *CDSP*, November 9, 1977, pp. 1–13. Beginning in 1977, October 7 replaced December 5 as Soviet "Constitution Day."

105. See *CDSP*, ibid., p. 2.

106. Otto Kirchheimer, "The Rechtsstaat as Magic Wall," in Kurt H. Wolff and Barrington Moore, Jr., eds. *The Critical Spirit: Essays in Honor of Herbert Marcuse* (Boston: Beacon Press, 1967), p. 312.

2. The Andropov–Chernenko Interregnum

1. Kevin Devlin, "Andropov's First Year: Italian Communist's Judgment," *Radio Free Europe Research*, Vol. 8, No. 48, Background Report 267 (November 23, 1983), p. 2.

2. "Zhores Medvedev Assesses Andropov's Power and Priorities," *Labour Focus on Eastern Europe*, Vol. 7, No. 1 (Winter 1984), pp. 2–3.

3. Konstantin Simis, "Andropov's Anticorruption Campaign," *Washington Quarterly*, Vol. 6, No. 3 (Summer 1983), pp. 121.

4. Marshall I. Goldman, "Chernenko's Inheritance: A Low-Tech Economy at Home . . . ," *New York Times*, February 19, 1984, Section F, p. 2.

5. John F. Burns, "Andropov's Changes: Early Pace Bogs Down," *New York Times*, May 5, 1984, p. A-14.

6. Serge Schmemann, "Policy After Andropov: No Drastic Changes Expected in Moscow," *New York Times*, February 11, 1984, pp. 1, 8.

7. Robert Sharlet, reviewing *USSR: The Corrupt Society* by Konstantin Simis, *Worldview* Vol. 26 (January 1983), p. 25.

8. "Poll Finds People Don't Care About Petty Thefts of Public Property," *Current Digest of the Soviet Press* (hereafter *CDSP*), Vol. 35, No. 26 (1983), p. 3.

9. This statistic is drawn from Soviet crime data on the late 1960s in Peter H. Juviler, *Revolutionary Law and Order* (New York: Free Press, 1977), pp. 138, 238; and crime data on the late 1970s in Fridrikh Neznansky, "New Information on Soviet Criminal Statistics: An Inside Report," *Soviet Union*, Vol. 6, Part 2 (1979), pp. 208–11.

10. On phone vandalism in Latvia, see *Soviet Nationality Survey*, Vol. 1, No. 1 (January 1984), p. 3.

11. Konstantin Simis, *USSR: The Corrupt Society* (New York: Simon and Schuster, 1982), chapters 4, 7.

12. "Campaign for Labor Discipline Continues," *CDSP*, Vol. 34, No. 52 (1983), p. 6.

13. Requoted from Sharlet, note 7, above.

14. "Maciej Szczepanski and Associates Sentenced by Warsaw Court," *Radio Free Europe Research*, Vol. 9, No. 5, Poland Situation Report, January 23, 1984, pp. 8–12. On the Polish Crisis in 1980, see Radio Free Europe, *August 1980: Strikes in Poland* (Munich: Radio Free Europe, October 1980), and on the corruption campaign in particular, pp. 209–12. See also Timothy Garton Ash, *The Polish Revolution: Solidarity* (New York: Vintage, 1985).

15. Zhores Medvedev, *Andropov* (New York: Norton, 1983), chapter 14. See also Jonathan Steele and Eric Abraham, *Andropov in Power* (Garden City, NY: Doubleday, 1984).

16. See Article 156–2 of the RSFSR Criminal Code in *Basic Documents on the Soviet Legal System*, W. E. Butler, ed. (Dobbs Ferry, NY: Oceana, 1983), p. 354. The new rule was introduced first in all-union legislation and then in the RSFSR and other union republic criminal codes.

17. See Article 156–3, ibid.

18. See Article 173, ibid., pp. 359–60.

19. See Article 170, ibid., p. 359.

20. See Article 96, paragraph 2, ibid., p. 338.

21. "Ob organizatsii raboty po privedeniiu zakonodatel'stva Soiuza SSR v sootvetstvie s Konstitutsiei SSSR," *Vedomosti verkhovnogo soveta SSSR*, No. 51, December 21, 1977, item 764, pp. 849–54.

22. "O khode podgotovki zakonoproektov, predusmotrennykh Planom organizatsii raboty po privedeniiu zakonodatel'stva Soiuza SSR v sootvetstvie s Konstitutsiei SSSR," *Vedomosti verkhovnogo soveta SSSR*, No. 1, January 2, 1980, item 3, pp. 20–21.

23. "O khode vypolneniia Plana organizatsii raboty po privedenniu zakonodatel'stva Soiuza SSR v sootvetstvie s Konstitutsiei SSSR i o podgotovke Svoda zakonov SSSR," *Vedomosti verkhovnogo soveta SSSR*, No. 2, January 14, 1981, item 49, pp. 37–39.

24. "O dal'neishem sovershenstvovanii ugolovnogo i ispravitel'no-trudovogo zakonodatel'stva," *Vedomosti verkhovnogo soveta SSSR*, No. 30, July 28, 1982, item 572, pp. 505–508. The edict was scheduled to go into effect January 1, 1983 (hereafter July Edict).

25. See Article 39–1 of the Fundamental Principles of Criminal Legislation of the USSR and the Union Republic, in *Legislative Acts of the USSR*, Vol. 3 (Moscow: Progress, 1983), pp. 202–204.

26. "Tougher Penalties for Criminals Set," *CDSP*, Vol. 35, No. 5 (1983), p. 8.

27. See the July Edict, parts I-2 and I-3, p. 507, and the corresponding Articles 25 and 27 of the Fundamental Principles of Criminal Legislation . . . , in *Legislative Acts of the USSR*, Vol. 3, pp. 194–96.

28. See the July Edict, parts I-4 and I-6, pp. 506–508, and the corresponding Articles 38, 44-, and 44-2 of the Fundamental Principles of Criminal Legislation . . . , ibid., pp. 200–202, 209–11.

29. See the July Edict, part II, p. 508, and the corresponding Article 39–2 of Fundamental Principles of Corrective Labor Legislation of the USSR and the Union Republics, ibid., pp. 268–70.

30. "O vnesenii izmenenii i dopolnenii v nekotorye zakonodatel'nye akty SSSR," *Vedomosti verkhovnogo soveta SSSR*, No. 42, October 20, 1982, item 793, parts III-4, III-5, and V, pp. 714–15. The edict was scheduled to go into effect January 1, 1983, hereafter October Edict.

31. Ibid., parts I and II, pp. 712–13.

32. "Slogans of the Revolutionary Anniversary," *CDSP*, Vol. 34, No. 42 (1982), pp. 17–18. The 1982 slogans were published on October 17, two days after the October Edict. See especially slogans nos. 23–26, 42, 43, 46, and 47.

33. For a typology of legal policy, see Robert Sharlet, "Soviet Legal Policy Making," in *Social System and Legal Process*, Harry M. Johnson, ed. (San Francisco: Jossey-Bass, 1978), pp. 209–29.

34. "Andropov on Marx and the Soviet Economy," *CDSP*, Vol. 35, No. 33 (1983), pp. 1–3, 23.

35. "Andropov Speaks to Party Veterans," *CDSP*, Vol. 35, No. 33 (1983), p. 3, and "Stiffer Penalties for Breaking Traffic Rules, *CDSP*, Vol. 35, No. 18 (1983), pp. 12–14.

36. Serge Schmemann, "Andropov, on Plant Tour, Tells Workers to Produce," *New York Times*, February 1, 1983, p. A-4.

37. See USSR Minister of Justice Terebilov's formulation of this linkage in "New Laws on Labor, Management Scanned," *CDSP*, Vol. 35, No. 33 (1983), p. 6.

38. Quoted in the *New York Times* from Andropov's first major speech as leader on November 22, 1982. See Serge Schmemann, "Andropov Lights Fire Under a Slumbering Nation," *New York Times*, February 7, 1983, p. A-14.

39. "Andropov Outlines Party Program Changes," *CDSP*, Vol. 35, No. 25 (1983), p. 6.

40. See Robert Sharlet, "Legal Policy Under Khrushchev and Brezhnev: Continuity and Change," in *Soviet Law After Stalin*, Vol. 2: *Social Engineering Through Law*, D. D. Barry, G. Ginsburgs, and P. B. Maggs, eds. (Alphen aan den Rijn, Holland: Sijthoff and Noordhoff, 1978), pp. 319–30.

41. *Vedomosti verkhovnogo soveta SSSR*, No. 51, December 21, 1977, item 764, part I-15, p. 852. On the Constitution, see Robert Sharlet, *The New Soviet Constitution of 1977* (Brunswick, OH: King's Court, 1978).

42. "The Law on Labor Collectives," *CDSP*, Vol. 35, No. 28 (1983), pp. 9–10.

43. Revised under Brezhnev in the October Edict of 1982, and again, more extensively, under Andropov in early 1984. See "O vnesenii izmenii i dopolnenii v nekotorye zakonodatel'nye akty SSSR ob ugolovnoi otvetstvennosti i ugolovnom sudoproizvodstve," *Vedomosti verkhovnogo soveta SSSR*, No. 3, January 18, 1984, item 58, pp. 91–93.

44. "O proekte plana podgotovki zakonodatel'nykh aktov SSSR i postanovlenii Pravitel'stva SSSR na 1983–1985 gody," *Vedomosti verkhovnogo soveta SSSR*, No. 39, September 29, 1982, item 743, pp. 667–71.

45. "2 Ex-KGB Officials Given New Soviet Posts," *New York Times*, September 14, 1983, p. A-9. Under investigation for corruption, Shchelokov later committed suicide.

46. "Aliyev on Azerbaidzhan's Economy, Crime," *CDSP*, Vol. 34, No. 47 (1982), pp. 19–23.

47. See the Politburo's concern for "law and order in cities and rural communities, bearing in mind that these questions seriously disturb working people and are urgently raised in their letters." "First Reports on Politburo Meetings Appear," *CDSP*, Vol. 34, No. 50 (1983), p. 13.

48. See Articles 89–91 and 144–146 of the RSFSR Criminal Code in Butler, ed., *Basic Documents on the Soviet Legal System* (1983), pp. 335–36 and 144–146. In a related move, for the first time (after four major previous amnesties), Article 162, the economic crime of "Engaging in Prohibited Trade," was excluded from the amnesty on the occasion of the 60th anniversary of the formation of the USSR. See "Amnesty Decree Frees Some Criminals, Cuts Terms," *CDSP*, Vol. 34, No. 52 (1983), pp. 8–9.

49. The reductions were from possible imprisonment for up to a year, to corrective work for up to two years.

50. "Penalties for Petty Theft Stiffened," *CDSP*, Vol. 35, No. 14 (1983), pp. 14.

51. "A Crackdown on Parasites Begins," *CDSP*, Vol. 35, No. 2 (1983), pp. 5–6. The new legislation went into effect on January 1, 1983. The previous criteria that parasitism had to be practiced systematically and over a protracted period of time were dropped.

52. "Leniency for Young Criminals Protested," *CDSP*, Vol. 35, No. 22 (1983), pp. 11–12.

53. "Life in a Juvenile Delinquent's Colony," *CDSP*, Vol. 35, No. 34 (1983), pp. 8–10.

54. "Communist Party: In the Politburo of the CPSU Central Committee," *CDSP*, Vol. 36, No. 2 (1984), p. 20.

55. "Disobedient Convicts' Terms Can Be Extended," *CDSP*, Vol. 35, No. 47 (1983), p. 9. The new law became Article 188–3 of the RSFSR Criminal Code.

56. "More Surveillance for Released Convicts," *CDSP*, Vol. 35, No. 50 (1984), pp. 12, 23.

57. See Peter Reddaway, "Dissent in the Soviet Union," *Problems of Communism*, Vol. 32, No. 6 (November–December 1983), pp. 1–15.

58. The phrase suggests the actual order in which political prosecutions proceed. It is taken from a book by Eugene Loebl, *Sentenced and Tried* (London: Elek, 1969), based on his experience with Czechoslovak political justice.

59. See Articles 190–1 and 190–3 of the RSFSR Criminal Code in Butler, ed., *Basic Documents*, p. 365.

60. See Articles 227 and 142, ibid., pp. 382, 248–49.

61. *Vedomosti verkhovnogo soveta SSSR*, No. 3, January 18, 1984, item 58, part I-3, pp. 91–92. Article 7 of the USSR Statute on Criminal Liability for State Crimes was the antecedent legislation for Article 70 of the RSFSR Criminal Code and its equivalent in other union republic codes.

62. See *Help and Action Newsletter*, Vol. 6, No. 28 (November–December 1983), A, A-1.

63. *Vedomosti verkhovnogo soveta SSSR*, No. 3, January 18, 1984, item 58, part I-4, p. 92. The new Article 13–1 of the statute was reflected in code law and went into effect on February 1, 1984. For an analysis of the new law, see Robert Sharlet, "Andropov's Legacy: Law, Discipline and the New Crime on Official Secrecy'," U.S. Information Agency, *Addendum*, No. 30 (1984), pp. 1–10.

64. Schmemann, "Andropov, on Plant Tour, Tells Workers to Produce," *New York Times*, February 1, 1983, pp. A-1, A-4.

65. Karen Elliott House and David Satter, "In the Andropov Era, Soviet System Reverts Quickly to Old Ways," *Wall Street Journal*, July 21, 1983, p. 1.

66. "Politburo Discusses Store Hours . . . ," *CDSP*, Vol. 35, No. 2 (1983), p. 18.

67. John F. Burns, "Andropov's Changes: Early Pace Bogs Down," *New York Times*, May 5, 1983, p. A-1.

68. "Draft Law on Labor Collectives," *CDSP*, Vol. 35, No. 15 (1983), pp. 14-18.

69. A. S. Pashkov, "Pravovoi status trudovogo kollektiva," *Pravovedenie*, No. 6 (1983), p. 13.

70. "Debating the Draft Law on Labor Collectives," *CDSP*, Vol. 35, No. 18 (1983), pp. 10–11.

71. *Labour Focus on Eastern Europe*, Vol. 7, No. 1 (Winter 1984), p. 5.

72. "Steps Taken to Tighten Labor Discipline," *CDSP*, Vol. 35, No. 32 (1983), pp. 4–7.

73. *Vedomosti verkhovnogo soveta SSSR*, No. 33, August 17, 1983, item 507, pp. 555–58.

74. "Explaining the Changes in Labor Laws," *CDSP*, Vol. 35, No. 33 (1983), p. 7.

75. "Soviets Introduce System of Denunciation by Mail," *Samizdat Bulletin*, No. 127 (November 1983), pp. 1–5.

76. See *New York Times*, November 25, 1983, p. A-16; and January 14, 1984, p. 4 on the death sentences. On military corruption, see Konstantin Simis, "An Officer and a Crook: Ripping Off the Red Army," *Washington Post*, January 8, 1984, pp. C-1, C-2.

77. "Legal System Under Fire for Abuses," *CDSP*, Vol. 35, No. 44 (1983), pp. 1–3.

78. For the criticism and self-criticism, see *Sotsialisticheskaia zakonnost'*, No. 3 (March 1983), pp. 3–4, 5–10.

79. V. Terebilov, "Immediate Tasks before the Organs of Justice and the Courts in Light of the Decisions of the November 1982 Plenum of the CPSU Central Committee, translated from *Sotsialisticheskaia zakonnost'* in *Soviet Law & Government*, Vol. 22, No. 1 (Summer 1983), pp. 27–38.

80. "Fedorchuk Reviews Law Enforcement,"*CDSP*, Vol. 35, No. 32 (1983), p. 4.

81. "Romanov Keynotes Nov. 7 Celebration," *CDSP*, Vol. 35, No. 45 (1983), p. 2. Romanov stood in for Andropov, who by that time could no longer appear in public because of his health.

82. Paraphrased from *Pravda*, December 27, 1982, in *Labour Focus on Eastern Europe*, Vol. 6, Nos. 1–2 (Summer 1983), p. 45.

83. See Robert Sharlet, "Constitutional Implementation and Juridicization of the Soviet System," in *Soviet Politics in the Brezhnev Era*, Donald R. Kelley, ed. (New York: Praeger, 1980), pp. 200–34.

84. See "Chernenko Keynotes CC Session," *CDSP*, Vol. 35, No. 24 (1983), p. 5. However, for Chernenko's previous, pre-Andropov views on the "discipline" approach to the USSR's problems, see Archie Brown, "Andropov: Discipline and Reform," *Problems of Communism*, Vol. 32 (January–February 1983), p. 19.

85. Shortly after Andropov's death, Chernenko first referred to the late leader's discipline campaign as "a line which will be pursued permanently and undeviatingly." "Excerpts from Chernenko's Speech in Moscow," *New York Times*, March 3, 1984. For similar reaffirmations by other senior leaders, see Serge Schmemann, "Gorbachev's High Rank in Soviet Is Affirmed," *New York Times*, March 1, 1984, p. A-15, and "Chebrikov Reviews State Security Work," *CDSP*, Vol. 36, No. 9 (1984), p. 13.

86. Quoted in "Estonia: Ideological Work Found Wanting: In the CPSU Central Committee," *CDSP*, Vol. 36, No. 31 (1984), p. 3.

87. On high turnover under Andropov, see Archie Brown, "Brief Authority," *Times Literary Supplement*, July 6, 1984, p. 750.

88. John F. Burns, "City Named Andropov Makes Maps Obsolete," *New York Times*, March 15, 1984, p. A-6.

89. "Military Affairs," *CDSP*, Vol. 36, No. 16 (1984), p. 27.

90. "Latvia's KGB Chief Becomes Party Leader," *New York Times*, April 16, 1984, p. A-10.

91. See Allan Kroncher, "Chernenko's Speech at the 'Hammer and Sickle'

Works and the Party's Economic Policy," *Radio Liberty Research Bulletin*, 1984, No. 19, pp. 1–3.

92. Bonner was tried in Gorky on August 17, 1984 under Art. 190–1 (defamation) of the RSFSR Criminal Code, convicted, and sentenced to a five-year term of internal exile. See "Trial of Ye. Bonner and Situation of A. Sakharov," *USSR News Briefs*, No. 16–1 (August 31, 1984), pp. 1–2. See also ibid., No. 9–1 (May 15, 1984), pp. 1–2.

93. Commenting on Bonner's exile, a well-connected Soviet journalist observed "The whole point of isolating Dr. Sakharov in Gorky was negated when she was running back and forth to Moscow carrying messages from him." Quoted in Seth Mydans, "Friends Tell of Trial of Sakharov's Wife," *New York Times*, September 14, 1984, p. A-3.

94. See Serge Schmemann, "Moscow in May: Icy Toward the U.S.," *New York Times*, May 18, 1984, p. A-3.

95. See *USSR News Brief*, No. 17/18–24 (September 30, 1984), pp. 7–8.

96. See "State and Law," *CDSP*, Vol. 36, No. 37 (1984), p. 19.

97. On the new decree (effective July 1, 1984) restricting contacts with foreigners, and on the change in customs policy (effective August 1, 1984) on parcels sent from abroad, see the U.S. State Department's discussion reprinted in "New Soviet Legislation Restricts Rights, Strengthens Internal Security," *Samizdat Bulletin*, No. 135 (July 1984), esp. pp. 1 and 4. On the new decree in action, see "Soviet Campaign to Limit Contacts with Foreigners," *CSCE Digest* (July 18, 1984), pp. 7–8. On the new parcel rule, see Kevin Klose, "What Are the Soviets Afraid Of?" *Washington Post*, May 2, 1984, p. B-5.

98. See John F. Burns, "Chernenko Is Star at Moscow's May Day Parade," *New York Times*, May 2, 1984, p. A-12.

99. See generally Medvedev in *New York Times*, February 15, 1984, p. A27.

100. See Robert Sharlet, "Dissent and the 'Contra-System' in the Soviet Union," in *The Soviet Union in the 1980s*, ed. Erik P. Hoffmann (New York: Academy of Political Science, 1984), pp. 135–46.

101. See Burns in *New York Times*, May 2, 1984, p. A-12, and Serge Schmemann, "Military Past of Chernenko Embroidered," *New York Times*, May 11, 1984, p. A-13.

102. See "Soviet Paper Reports Expulsion of American," *New York Times*, June 17, 1984, p. 6.

103. See "Heavy Metal Rock on Western Radio Assailed as Anti-Soviet Propaganda," *CDSP*, Vol. 36, No. 37 (1984), pp. 4–5.

104. On the series "Tass Is Authorized to State . . . ," *New York Times*, August 14, 1984, p. C-18.

105. On this concept, see John M. Joyce's perceptive essay "The Old Russian Legacy," *Foreign Policy*, Summer 1984, esp. pp. 133 and 144.

106. Seth Mydans, "Final Rails Laid on Key Line to Open Up Siberian Riches," *New York Times*, September 30, 1984, p. 16.

107. On the continuation of the Moscow Circus case which began under Andropov as KGB chief in early 1982, see Serge Schmemann, "Moscow Gossip," *New York Times*, September 25, 1984, p. A-17. On the continuation of the purges and prosecutions of Krasnodar officials, which also bore Andropov's imprint beginning in the summer of 1982, see "Influence—Thoughts on Some Cases," *CDSP*,

Vol. 36, No. 27 (1984), pp. 16–17. On the execution and posthumous scapegoating of Sokolov, former manager of Moscow's Store No. 1 who received the death sentence in late 1983, see "The Birth and Death of a Food Scam," *CDSP*, Vol. 36, No. 32 (1984), p. 19; and Seth Mydans, "A Russian Epicure's Path to the Firing Squad," *New York Times*, August 5, 1984, p. 8.

108. For instance, on March 8, 1984, *Pravda* announced that a deputy minister of the farm equipment industry had been dismissed and was being brought up on charges along with his accomplices. See "In the CPSU Central Committee's Party Control Committee," *CDSP*, Vol. 37, No. 10 (1984), p. 30.

109. Quoted from "More Uzbek Party, State Officials Replaced," *CDSP*, Vol. 36, No. 33 (1984), p. 9. See generally "Corruption, Mismanagement in Uzbekistan," *CDSP*, Vol. 36, No. 26 (1984), pp. 1–6, 13–14, and 24.

110. See S. I. Gusev, "Povyshat' uroven' sudebnoi deiatel'nosti," *Sovetskoe gosudarstvo i pravo* (hereafter *SGP*), 1984, No. 5, esp. pp. 4 and 7. For Supreme Court commentary on discipline under Andropov, see Peter H. Juviler, "The Drive for Discipline: Andropov Makes His Mark," in "Symposium on Soviet Law After Brezhnev," ed. Robert Sharlet, *Soviet Union*, Vol. 11, No. 3 (1984).

111. See Iu. S. Adushkin, "Voprosy sovershenstvovaniia distsiplinarnogo zakonodatel'stva," *Pravovedenie*, 1984, No. 3, pp. 54–60; A. A. Shugaev, "Ispol'zovanie pravovykh sredstv v ukreplenie trudovoi distsipliny," *SGP*, 1984, No. 8, pp. 125–29; T. A. Abakarov, "Ugolovnaia otvetstvennost' za chastnopredprinimatel'skuiu deiatel'nost'," *SGP*, pp. 135–39. The journals *Sotsialisticheskaia zakonnost'* and *Sovetskaia iustitsiia* also continued to devote some space to the discipline question, but these articles, most of which were very brief, mainly explicated changes which had already occurred in criminal and labor law.

112. Serge Schmemann, "Moscow Gossip," *New York Times*, September 25, 1984, p. A-17.

113. For instance, see the cases on the underground "drugstore," the foreign student connection in Rostov-on-Don, and the "tape pirate" in, respectively, "Face to Face with the Law: CACHE," *CDSP*, Vol. 36, No. 34 (1984), pp. 18–19; "State and Law: Follow-Up," *CDSP*, Vol. 36, No. 35 (1984), p. 16; and "Russian Tape Pirate Jailed," *New York Times*, May 4, 1984, p. A-9.

114. See "Fighting Teenage Crime in Estonia," *CDSP*, Vol. 36, No. 31 (1984), pp. 4–5 and 24.

115. See "Fedorchuk Reviews the War on Crime," *CDSP*, Vol. 36, No. 34 (1984), p. 4.

116. "O zaderzhanie pravonarushitelei rabotnikami voenizirovannoi okhrany, primenenii imi v iskliuchtel'skykh sluchaiakh oruzhiia," *Vedomosti verkhovnogo soveta SSSR*, No. 26, June 27, 1984, item 457, pp. 564–65.

117. See "Courtroom Sketch: Not Subject to Appeal," *CDSP*, Vol. 36, No. 38 (1984), pp. 23–24; "State and Law: Gunshot on the Path," *CDSP*, Vol. 36, No. 22 (1984), p. 20; and "From the Courtroom: Verdict Rendered," *CDSP*, Vol. 36, No. 17 (1984), p. 26.

118. See "Mismanagement, Theft at Volga Auto Plant," *CDSP*, Vol. 36, No. 35 (1984), p. 6; "Fedorchuk Reviews the War on Crime," pp. 3–4; "Increase Exact-ingness Toward Cadres," *CDSP*, Vol. 36, No. 33 (1984), p. 10; and "With Tacit Consent," *CDSP*, Vol. 36, No. 37 (1984), p. 20.

119. See "Bratsk Officials Jailed for 'Gift-Giving,' " *CDSP*, Vol. 36, No. 34 (1984), pp. 7, 13.

120. See "Party Life . . . ," *CDSP*, Vol. 36, No. 29 (1984), pp. 21–22.

121. On the Belorussian purge, see John F. Burns, "Fraudulent Trial Sets Off Purge in Soviet Republic," *New York Times*, March 16, 1984, p. A-8, and "State and Law: What Was Done After *Izvestia* Spoke Out?" *CDSP*, Vol. 36, No. 10 (1984), pp. 29–30. On the Uzbek police purge, see "Bukhara: Police Corruption . . . with Crimes," *CDSP*, Vol. 36, No. 33 (1984), p. 10.

122. See "O distsiplinarnom ustave organov vnutrennykh del," and "O Polozhenie o tovarishcheskikh sudakh . . . organov vnutrennykh del," *Vedomosti verkhovnogo sovetov SSSR*, No. 19, May 9, 1984, items 342 and 343, p. 446. On the other changes, see "Fedorchuk Reviews the War on Crime," p. 1.

123. "Fedorchuk Reviews the War on Crime," pp. 2, 5.

124. Ibid., pp. 3–4. See also on managerial accountability "State and Law: Barrier to Theft," *CDSP*, Vol. 36, No. 23 (1984), p. 20. On executives who have either been dismissed or censured for not effectively deterring economic crime among their employees, see *CDSP*, Vol. 36, No. 20 (1984), p. 24, and *CDSP*, Vol. 36, No. 27 (1984), pp. 18–19.

125. Quoted from "Estonia," *Soviet Nationality Survey*, Vol. 1, No. 9–10 (September–October 1984), p. 3.

126. "Estonia . . . ," *CDSP*, Vol. 36, No. 31 (1984), p. 2.

127. See "Chernenko Speaks to the Central Committee," *CDSP*, Vol. 36, No. 15 (1984), p. 4, and "Chernenko Speaks to Military YCL Officials," *CDSP*, Vol. 36, No. 22 (1984), p. 1.

128. Numerous articles appeared in the Soviet press on the *leitmotiv* of upbringing. See, e.g., "Fighting Attempts to Subvert Soviet Youth," *CDSP*, Vol. 36, No. 37 (1984), pp. 1–3; and "The Problem Teenager," *CDSP*, Vol. 36, No. 31 (1984), pp. 21–22. On the upbringing struggle in medical school and the bus fleet, see, respectively, "Medicine/Public Health: Passing Grade," *CDSP*, Vol. 36, No. 16 (1984), p. 27; and "State and Law: What Was Done After *Izvestia* Spoke Out?" *CDSP*, Vol. 36, No. 13 (1984), pp. 22–23. See also Vladimir Tolz, "'Highlifeism,'" *Radio Liberty Research Bulletin*, May 16, 1984, pp. 1–6.

3. Gorbachev and the Soviet Constitutional Crisis

1. See generally Ben Eklof, *Soviet Briefing* (Boulder, CO: Westview, 1989), ch. 5, and specifically *Pravovye sredstva bor'by s netrudovymi dokhodami* (Moscow: Nauka, 1989).

2. See Stephen White, *Gorbachev and After* (Cambridge, UK: Cambridge University Press, 1991), pp. 120–21; and L. Smirnov, "Primenenie zakonodatel'stva o bor'be s p'ianstvom i alkogolizmom, *Sovetskaia iustitsiia*, 1986, no. 22, pp. 6–8.

3. See Gorbachev's "Political Report" to the 27th Party Congress in Robert Ehlers, ed., *Current Soviet Policies IX* (Columbus, OH: Current Digest of the Soviet Press, 1986), pp. 10–46.

4. For a foreshadowing of the sweeping constitutional changes, see "Demokratizatsiia i zakonodatel'stvo," *Sovetskaia iustitsiia*, 1988, no. 18, pp. 2–4; for the 1988 amendments in translation, see *Review of Socialist Law*, vol. 15, no. 1 (1989), pp. 75–118.

5. For a translation of the USSR Constitution of 1977 as it appeared after the second major wave of amendments in late 1989, see F.J.M. Feldbrugge, "The Constitution of the USSR," *Review of Socialist Law*, vol. 16, no. 2 (1990), pp. 163–224.

6. For the revised Article 6, see Gordon B. Smith, *Soviet Politics*, 2d ed. (New York: St. Martin's, 1992), p. 350.

7. See B.M. Lazarev, "The President of the USSR," *Soviet Law and Government*, vol. 30, no. 1 (1991), pp. 7–26; and M.N. Marchenko, "Institut Prezidenta v SSSR" (forthcoming).

8. See John N. Hazard, "The Evolution of the Soviet Constitution," in Donald D. Barry, ed., *Toward the Rule of Law in Russia? Political and Legal Reform in the Transition Period* (Armonk, NY: M.E. Sharpe, 1992). It should also be noted that the late physicist and human rights champion Andrei Sakharov's draft constitution entitled "Constitution of the Union of Soviet Republics of Europe and Asia" had some influence on constitutional drafting in both the USSR and the RSFSR during the Gorbachev period. For a translation of the draft, see FBIS, *JPRS Report—Soviet Union: Political Affairs* (January 19, 1990), pp. 1–5. In initial discussions of the original Soviet Treaty of Union of 1922, Lenin had proposed an almost identical title for the new federal Soviet state, "Union of Soviet Republics of Europe and Asia," which was of course revised. See Iu.S. Kukushkin and O.I. Chistiakov, *Ocherk istorii Sovetskoi Konstitutsii* (Moscow: Izd. politicheskoi literatury, 1980), p. 64. For an excellent commentary on the Sakharov constitution, see A.A. Mishin, "Nekotorye mysli o Konstitutsii A.D. Sakharova," in *Pravo i vlast'* (Moscow: Progress, 1990), pp. 231–40.

9. Bonner made the observation on "The MacNeil-Lehrer News Hour," PBS, on December 12, 1990. For the most insightful commentary on the idea of the law-based state, see Harold J. Berman, "The Law-Based State," *Harriman Institute Forum*, vol. 4, no. 5 (1991) as well as his fuller treatment of the subject in Barry, ed., *Toward the Rule of Law in Russia?* For an historical analysis, see Gianmaria Ajani, "The Rise and Fall of the Law-Governed State in the Experience of Russian Legal Scholarship," in the same volume. For Soviet juridical commentary on the idea, see N.N. Khoroshii, "Konstitutsionalizm v pravovom gosudarstve," in V.F. Volovich, ed., *Problemy pravovedeniia v sovremennyi period* (Tomsk: Izd. Tomskogo universiteta, 1990), pp. 25–27; and R.Z. Livshits, "Jus and Lex: The Evolution of Views," in W.E. Butler, ed., *Perestroika and the Rule of Law: Anglo-American and Soviet Perspectives* (London: I.B. Tauris, 1991), esp. pp. 27–28.

10. For the legislative agenda in translation, see Mervyn Matthews, ed., *Party, State and Citizen in the Soviet Union: A Collection of Documents* (Armonk, NY: M.E. Sharpe, 1989), ch. 1, sec. 1.7. Gorbachev's very heavy reliance on law as the framework for systemic reform confirmed Hazard's prescient thesis, presented in The Goodhart Lectures at Cambridge University in 1982, that Soviet jurisprudence was becoming a policy science for managing change in the USSR, with its concomitant that lawyers would increasingly play an enhanced role in the Soviet system. See John N. Hazard, *Managing Change in the USSR: The Politico-Legal Role of the Soviet Jurist* (Cambridge, UK: Cambridge University Press, 1983).

11. For the economic clauses of the Constitution in translation, see Robert Sharlet, *The New Soviet Constitution of 1977* (Brunswick, OH: King's Court, 1978), pp. 79–82. For learned commentary on the new economic legislation, see O.S. Ioffe,

" 'Non-Labor' Income and Individual Labor Activity in the USSR," in William E. Butler, Peter B. Maggs, and John B. Quigley, Jr., eds., *Law After the Revolution* (New York: Oceana, 1988), pp. 47–67; Stanislaw Pomorski, "Notes on the 1986 Law 'On Individual Labor Activity,' " in Albert J. Schmidt, ed., *The Impact of Perestroika on Soviet Law* (Dordrecht, The Netherlands: Martinus Nijhoff, 1990), pp. 143–56; Peter B. Maggs, "Constitutional Implications of Changes in Property Rights in the USSR," *Cornell International Law Journal*, vol. 23, no. 2 (1990), pp. 363–76; and Paul B. Stephan III, *Soviet Economic Law: The Paradox of Perestroyka* (Pittsburgh: Carl Beck Papers in Russian and East European Studies, no. 805, 1991). Two other scholars discuss major impediments to the full implementation of the new laws: Vladimir Entin, a Soviet jurist, points out that much of the perestroika-era legislation was characterized by "low normative saturation," by which he means that implementation mechanisms were not created. Added to this was the continuing problem of "departmental instructions" as discussed by Eugene Huskey whose focus is agency rulemaking designed to blunt the reformist thrust of new economic legislation. See, respectively, V.L. Entin, "Law and Glasnost," in Butler, ed., *Perestroika and the Rule of Law*, esp. p. 102; and Huskey, "Governmental Rulemaking as a Brake on *Perestroika*," *Law and Social Inquiry*, vol. 15, no. 3 (1990), esp. pp. 426–27.

12. For the law in translation, see W.E. Butler, ed., *Basic Documents on the Soviet Legal System*, 2d ed. (New York: Oceana, 1991), pp. 229–32. For Western commentary, see Hiroshi Oda, "Judicial Review of Administration in the USSR," in Schmidt, ed., *The Impact of Perestroika on Soviet Law*, pp. 157–71; Gordon B. Smith, "The Procuracy, Citizens' Rights and Legal Reform," *Columbia Journal of Transnational Law*, vol. 28, no. 1 (1990), esp. pp. 85–89; and Donald D. Barry, "The Quest for Judicial Independence: Soviet Courts in a *Pravovoe Gosudarstvo*," in Barry, ed., *Toward the Rule of Law in Russia?* For Soviet reformist criticism of the first, more restrictive version of the law, see Valery Savitsky, quoted in "Demokratizatsiia i zakonodatel'stvo," op. cit. at n. 4, p. 4.

13. See Robert Sharlet, "Party and Public Ideals in Conflict: Constitutionalism and Civil Rights in the Soviet Union," *Cornell International Law Journal*, vol. 23, no. 2 (1990), pp. 343–62.

14. See the reference in *Current Digest of the Soviet Press*, vol. 41, no. 33 (1989), pp. 25–26. Andrei D. Sakharov, a newly elected People's Deputy, was appointed to the Gorbachev Constitutional Commission. In the posthumous second volume of his memoirs, he describes briefly the role of the Communist Party in both the formation and planned operation of the commission. See Andrei Sakharov, *Moscow and Beyond: 1986–1989* (New York: Knopf, 1991), pp. 129–30 and 156–57.

15. See generally, Cohen's framework in "The Friends and Foes of Change: Reformism and Conservatism in the Soviet Union," in Stephen F. Cohen, Alexander Rabinowitch, and Robert Sharlet, eds., *The Soviet Union Since Stalin* (Bloomington, IN: Indiana University Press, 1980), pp. 11–31, and his more recent "Introduction: Gorbachev and the Soviet Reformation," in Stephen F. Cohen and Katrina vanden Heuvel, *Voices of Glasnost* (New York: Norton, 1989), pp. 13–32. On the reformist-conservative tension in Gorbachev's legal reform process, see George Ginsburgs, "Perestroika in the Soviet Union and the Common Law of Mankind," *Review of Socialist Law*, vol. 17, no. 1 (1991), esp. sec. 6, pp. 38–43.

16. The first example of many was Estonia in late 1988. See Richard Sakwa, *Gorbachev and His Reforms, 1985–1990* (New York: Prentice Hall, 1991), p. 238.

17. As Leon Lipson points out, the reformers attempted "to keep control of the law in order that the law will control the centrifugal tendencies in the country." See Lipson's comments in "Roundtable Discussion: Crises in the USSR," *Cornell International Law Journal*, vol. 23, no. 2 (1990), pp. 382–83. The reformers did not succeed and the law itself became an arena of political and ethnic conflict. On the "war of laws," see Iu. Kalmykov, "Piat' prichin 'voiny zakonov': O pravovoi situatsii v strane," *Izvestiia*, April 4, 1991, p. 4.

18. Eventually, every republic, with the exception of the Russian Republic, passed legislation establishing the primacy of the language of its titular nationality. See FBIS, *JPRS Report—Soviet Union: Political Affairs—Republic Language Legislation*, December 5, 1989.

19. E.g., Latvia in 1990–91. See "Two Prosecutor's Offices, Two Laws?" *Current Digest of the Soviet Press*, vol. 42, no. 52 (1991), pp. 28–29.

20. A criminal investigation into this incident was opened by the Procuracy of newly independent Latvia in 1991 with the intention of bringing to trial those responsible.

21. See the commentary to ch. 2 in Aryeh L. Unger, *Constitutional Development in the USSR* (London: Methuen, 1981).

22. The new law on referendum was published in *Izvestiia*, March 7, 1991, pp. 2–3.

23. The assaults included communication centers and customs posts.

24. See Walter C. Clemens, Jr., *Baltic Independence and Russian Empire* (New York: St. Martin's, 1991), chs. 6–13, for the background and leadup to the restoration of the independence of the three Baltic states in 1991.

25. The *Federalist Papers* has now been published in Russian reflecting the enormous doctrinal distance travelled in Soviet constitutional theory in little more than a decade. In 1978, a well-known Soviet constitutional scholar wrote that the ideas of "scientific communism" were embodied in the Soviet Constitution of 1977. See I.M. Stepanov quoted in L.A. Morozova, *Konstitutsionnoe regulirovanie v SSSR* (Moscow: Iuridicheskaia literatura, 1985), p. 123. In 1990, the leading Soviet historian of American history argued that the U.S. Constitution, "far from reflecting the outlook of the eighteenth-century bourgeoisie, as previous Soviet scholars would have it, embodied 'universal human ideals,' especially the concept of a 'law-based state.'" See Eric Foner, "Restructuring Yesterday's News: The Russians Write a New History," *Harper's*, December 1990, p.71.

26. In policy and in law, a fundamental shift was taking place from guaranteed economic rights to the granting of political and civil liberties. See Peter Hauslohner, "Gorbachev's Social Contract," *Soviet Economy*, vol. 3, no. 1 (1987), pp. 56–65; and Valery Chalidze, *The Dawn of Legal Reform (April 1985 to June 1989)*, ed. by Lisa Chalidze (Benson, VT: Chalidze Publications, 1990), Appendix A and pp. 65–115.

27. See Viktor Danilenko, "Electoral Reform," in Robert T. Huber and Donald R. Kelley, eds., *Perestroika-era Politics* (Armonk, NY: M.E. Sharpe, 1991), ch. 3.

28. See D.A. Kerimov, G.B. Mal'tsev, and I.P. Il'inskii, *Demokratizatsiia sovetskogo obshchestva* (Moscow: Mysl', 1989), ch. 7.

29. See Michael E. Urban, *More Power to the Soviets: The Democratic Revolution in the USSR* (Aldershot, UK: Edward Elgar, 1990); and Huber and Kelley, eds., *Perestroika-era Politics* , chs. 4 (Goldman), 8 (Huskey), and 9 (Remington).

30. See V. Savitsky, "Democratization in the USSR," *Criminal Law Forum*, vol. 2, no. 1 (1990), esp. pp. 100–110; John Quigley, "Law Reform and the Soviet Courts," *Columbia Journal of Transnational Law*, vol. 28, no. 1 (1990), pp. 59–76; and Barry, "The Quest for Judicial Independence," in Barry, ed., *Toward the Rule of Law in Russia?* On the impact of court reform on the municipal police, and on both old and new forms of "telephone" law, see, respectively, Louise I. Shelley, "Policing Soviet Society," *Law and Social Inquiry*, vol. 15, no. 3 (1990), esp. pp. 516–18; Peter H. Solomon, "Soviet Politicians and Criminal Prosecutions: The Logic of Party Intervention," in James R. Millar, ed., *Cracks in the Monolith: Party Power in the Brezhnev Era* (Armonk, NY: M.E. Sharpe, 1992); and Iu.D. Severin, "Nezavisimost' pravosudiia—Problemy vremeni," *Sovetskoe gosudarstvo i pravo*, 1991, no. 9, esp. pp. 47–49 on the new "telephone" law (on meddling by parliamentary deputies in the judicial process).

31. See Herbert Hausmaninger, "The Committee of Constitutional Supervision of the USSR," *Cornell International Law Journal*, vol. 23, no. 2 (1990), pp. 287–322; and the interview with S.S. Alekseev, the first and only chairman of the committee before it expired along with the USSR, in *Pravovedenie*, 1991, no. 3, pp. 3–7. Even while the USSR committee was still sitting, the Russian Federation parliament in 1991 established a Russian Constitutional Court which eclipsed its USSR predecessor in jurisdiction and in the scope of its review authority within the Russian Federation.

32. For the most part, Gorbachev's decrees were not implemented. They were generally ignored due to the progressive breakdown of the implementation process as well as bureaucratic opposition to particular decrees.

33. See Sharlet, *The New Soviet Constitution of 1977*, p. 93.

34. For a framework for the analysis of dissent and repression, see Robert Sharlet, "Dissent and Repression in the Soviet Union and Eastern Europe: Changing Patterns Since Khrushchev," *International Journal*, vol. 33, no. 4 (1978), pp. 763–95. For more comprehensive studies of Soviet dissent, see works by Alexeyeva and by Reddaway in section VII-B, on "Political and Civil Rights," in the reading list at the back of this volume.

35. Religious groups across the spectrum were harassed by the bureaucracy and the police. See, e.g., works by Bourdeaux and by Hill in section VII-B-2, on "Religion: General Studies," in the reading list at the back of this volume.

36. Aleksandr Iakovlev, "Constitutional Socialist Democracy: Dream or Reality," *Columbia Journal of Transnational Law*, vol. 28, no. 1 (1990), p. 125.

37. See Robert Sharlet, "The Fate of Individual Rights in the Age of *Perestroika*," in Barry, ed., *Toward the Rule of Law in Russia?* On the press law, see also Thomas Remington, "Parliamentary Government in the USSR," in Huber and Kelley, eds., *Perestroika-era Politics*, esp. pp. 186–94; and on the freedom of conscience law, see A.S. Loviniukov's analysis in *Sovetskoe gosudarstvo i pravo*, 1991, no. 4, pp. 23–35.

38. Soviet legal rules on entering and leaving the country were always restrictive. Early in *perestroika*, these rules were slightly revised, leading a prominent Western

specialist on Soviet law to cautiously conclude "The government still holds all the trump cards but at least the citizen has a few other cards to play too." See F.J.M. Feldbrugge, "The New Soviet Law on Emigration," *Soviet Jewish Affairs*, vol. 17, no. 1 (1987), pp. 11–24. For the new entry–exit law of 1991 in translation, see FBIS, *Daily Report: Soviet Union* (June 7, 1991), pp. 32–35.

39. For the law on secession, see Butler, ed., *Basic Documents on the Soviet Legal System*, pp. 57–63.

40. See the discussion of "The Constitution as 'Magic Wall' " in chapter 1 of this volume, pp. 53–54.

41. The presidency and the considerable powers of the office became a new separate chapter (15 (1)) of the heavily amended 1977 Constitution. For a translation, see Smith, *Soviet Politics* (2d ed.), pp. 370–73. Article 127 (3), sec. 16 empowered the Soviet president to declare a state of emergency subject to an enabling statute. For the 1990 statute on the emergency regime, see Butler, ed., *Basic Documents on the Soviet Legal System*, pp. 51–55. For Western and Soviet commentary on the law, see, respectively, Paul Goble, "Draconian State of Emergency Law," RFE/RL, *Report on the USSR*, vol. 2, no. 18 (1990), pp. 8–9; and V.N. Grigor'ev, "Pravovoi rezhim chrezvychainogo polozheniia," *Pravovedenie*, 1991, no. 2, pp. 87–91. After the August coup, it was revealed that one of the conspirators, former KGB chief Vladimir Kriuchkov, had been one of the most vigorous advocates pressing for passage of the emergency law.

42. The ongoing Nagorno-Karabakh conflict between Armenians and Azerbaijanis, one of the most intractable and bloodiest ethnic conflicts which confronted Gorbachev during his tenure, has the potential for becoming a post-Soviet Beirut or Belfast. On the conflict, see Ronald G. Suny, "Nationalities and Nationalism," in Abraham Brumberg, ed., *Chronicle of a Revolution: A Western-Soviet Inquiry into Perestroika* (New York: Pantheon, 1990), esp. pp. 112–13 and 123–24.

43. E.g., Gorbachev's attempt to block a pro-Yeltsin rally with 50,000 troops and police, was frustrated and ended in stalemate. On this episode and the events leading up to it, see John Morrison, *Yeltsin: From Bolshevik to Democrat* (New York: Dutton, 1991), ch. 18. For a Western eyewitness account of the March 28, 1991 confrontation between the rival presidents' "forces," see Mark Galeotti's article in RFE/RL, *Report on the USSR*, vol. 3, no. 16 (1991), pp. 9–10. The author's conclusion that the event showed that the Kremlin could "still rely on its coercive apparatus" would in a matter of months prove to be premature.

44. As a result, the implementation of the new human rights legislation was very uneven throughout the USSR, depending on the strength of local conservative elites armed with the state's police power. On the police power, see N. Gevorkyan et al., "Props of Power," *Moscow News*, no. 30 (July 28–August 4, 1991), p. 15, an article in a liberal paper on the eve of the unsuccessful August coup of 1991. On the human rights situation, see Sharlet, "The Fate of Individual Rights in the Age of *Perestroika*," in Barry, ed., *Toward the Rule of Law in Russia?*; and Peter Juviler, "Human Rights After Perestroika: Progress and Perils," *Harriman Institute Forum*, vol. 4, no. 6 (1991).

45. This is Rigby's concept. See T.H. Rigby, "Stalinism and the Mono-Organizational Society," in Robert C. Tucker, ed., *Stalinism* (New York: Norton, 1977), esp. pp. 58–59.

46. Quoted in Amy W. Knight, "The Future of the KGB," *Problems of Communism*, vol. 39, no. 6 (1990), p. 33. The newly enacted law on the KGB was published in *Izvestiia*, May 24, 1991, pp. 4–5, and then, after the August coup, suspended with the exception of a few of its provisions. See Carla Thorson, "Weekly Record of Events," RFE/RL, *Report on the USSR*, vol.3, no. 44 (1991), pp. 28–29.

47. After the collapse of the August coup, the Procuracy of independent Lithuania intensified its investigation, in collaboration with the USSR and Russian procuracies, into the Soviet military assault in Vilnius in January 1991 and the mysterious killing of several Lithuanian customs officers in July. Arrests and trials were anticipated.

48. Colonel Viktor Alksnis, a USSR People's Deputy and avowed conservative, who was involved in the secret planning for KGB–military–police operations against the independence-minded Baltic republics which began in mid-1990, indicated in a post-coup interview that Gorbachev was fully involved. See Robert Cullen, "Report from Moscow: The Coup," *The New Yorker*, November 4, 1991, p. 74.

49. See "Ob obiazannostiakh i pravakh voisk Ministerstva vnutrennikh del SSSR pri okhrane obshchestvennogo poriadka," *Vedomosti Verkhovnogo Soveta SSSR*, 1988, no. 44, item 684.

50. See op. cit. at n. 41.

51. While most of the August coup leaders had urged President Gorbachev, behind the scenes, to use his emergency powers, Deputy Alksnis, who was not implicated in the coup, did so publicly and consistently in parliament and the press before and even after the coup. For one of Alksnis's pre-coup interviews (with a Swedish paper), see FBIS, *Daily Report: Soviet Union*, March 27, 1991, pp. 26–28. For one of his post-coup appeals, see ibid., November 1, 1991, pp. 21–22. He argued that the USSR was sliding into chaos and that only the temporary imposition of emergency power could restore order. Throughout the last few years of Gorbachev's tenure, many reform democrats were convinced he would respond to the conservative appeal for "order." See, e.g., Yuri Afanasyev, "The Coming Dictatorship," *New York Review of Books*, January 31, 1991, pp. 36–39.

52. See Article 121, sec. 16 in Sharlet, *The New Soviet Constitution of 1977*, pp. 112–14.

53. As a result of the 1988 constitutional amendments, the revised and expanded martial law powers were found in Article 119, sec. 14. For a translation, see *Review of Socialist Law*, vol. 15, no. 1 (1989), p. 97. After the 1989–90 amendments, these powers migrated to the new Article 127 (3), sec. 16, becoming a presidential power. For a translation, see Smith, *Soviet Politics* (2d ed.), pp. 370–72.

54. On "presidential rule," see Article 127 (3), sec. 16 in Smith, ibid. For a commentary, see Elizabeth Fuller and Stephen Foye, " 'Special Status,' 'State of Emergency,' and Presidential Rule," RFE/RL, *Report on the USSR*, vol. 3, no. 5 (1991), pp. 33–35. For a broader Soviet commentary on the new executive presidency, see B.M. Lazarev, "Ob izmeneniiakh v pravovom statuse Prezidenta SSSR," *Sovetskoe gosudarstvo i pravo*, 1991, no. 8, pp. 32–44.

55. See Butler op. cit. at n. 41, p. 51. Aptly, a Soviet jurist has characterized a state of emergency declaration as "the extreme legal form for ensuring the safety

of citizens and normalizing conditions." Grigor'ev, "Pravovoi rezhim chrezvy-chainogo polozheniia," *Pravovedenie*, 1991, no. 2, p. 87.

56. From a speech by I.K. Polozkov, an archconservative and then First Secretary of the RSFSR Communist Party, in *Sovetskaia Rossiia*, February 6, 1991, p. 2.

57. See V.N. Kudriavtsev, "Demokratiia i pravovoi poriadok," *Izvestiia*, February 5, 1991, p. 3. The author, the leading Academician in law and a USSR People's Deputy, pointedly suggested that the economic sabotage decree was in violation of the Constitution and derivative laws.

58. In a candid interview in the Polish press, Vladimir Voronin, head of the USSR salvation committee formed in early 1991, expressed the hope that power would be transferred to his committee constitutionally either by presidential or parliamentary decree. A month later, *Pravda* wrote in praise of the Polish martial law model, closing with the observation that "political shock therapy" was the only way to "rouse a society disoriented by the hysteria of mass rallies." See, respectively, FBIS, *Daily Report: Soviet Union*, February 22, 1991, p. 67, and March 12, 1991, pp. 52–53, esp. 53. On the Polish martial law model, see Lawrence Weschler, *The Passion of Poland: From Solidarity through the State of War* (New York: Pantheon, 1984); and Robert Sharlet, "The Road to Gdansk and Beyond," Amnesty International, *Labor News*, April 1982, pp. 5–8.

59. For the text of the revised Article 6, see op. cit. at n. 6.
For a participant's account of the political and parliamentary struggle to amend Article 6, see Anatoly Sobchak, *For A New Russia: The Mayor of St. Petersburg's Own Story of the Struggle for Justice and Democracy* (New York: Free Press, 1992), ch. 7 (which is appropriately entitled "Deputy Sakharov's Amendment").

60. The legal observer, writing in a liberal, pro-reform paper, described Gorbachev as a schizophrenic who as president strove for a law-based state, while as party leader he remained loyal to Lenin's precept that "Laws, at a time of transition, are of provisional significance. And if a law hampers the revolution's development, it is repealed or corrected." FBIS, *Daily Report: Soviet Union*, February 20, 1991, pp. 49–50, esp. 50. Yeltsin is quoted in Morrison, *Boris Yeltsin*, p. 232.

61. See Robert Sharlet, "Soviet Legal Policy Making," in Harry M. Johnson, ed., *Social System and Legal Process* (San Francisco: Jossey-Bass, 1978), ch. 7.

62. As Gorbachev put it in his report to the conference, "the main characteristic of a law-based state is that the supremacy of law is in fact secured." M.S. Gorbachev, *Izbrannye rechi i stat'i* (Moscow: Izd. politicheskoi literatury, 1989), vol. 6, p. 374.

63. The Soviet supremacy clause begins "The USSR Constitution has supreme legal force." See Sharlet, *The New Soviet Constitution of 1977*, p. 130. The last version of the 1977 Constitution (before the collapse of the USSR in 1991) had undergone further revision and renumbering, with the result that the supremacy clause became Article 172. See Smith, *Soviet Politics* (2d ed.), p. 379.

64. For the text of the statute, see Butler, ed., *Basic Documents on the Soviet Legal System*, pp. 185–94. In the 1988 amendments, the new constitutional supervision clause was numbered Article 125, but after the 1989 amendments, it became Article 124. In the process, the content of the clause was also revised. For the last 1991 version see Smith, *Soviet Politics* (2d ed.), pp. 369–70. For Soviet commentary on the constitutional clause and the statute, see D.A. Kerimov and A.I.

Ekimov, "Konstitutsionnyi nadzor v SSSR," *Sovetskoe gosudarstvo i pravo*, 1990, no. 9, pp. 3–13.

65. On Lithuania's declaration of independence in 1990 and Gorbachev's temporary economic embargo, see Clemens, Jr., *Baltic Independence and Russian Empire*, pp. 193–204. After the failure of the August coup in 1991, the USSR formally recognized Lithuania's independence.

66. See Aleksandr Tsipko's complaint in the Spanish press, translated in FBIS, *Daily Report: Soviet Union*, March 11, 1991, pp. 74–75.

67. See interview with Sergei Shakhrai in *Rossiiskaia gazeta*, July 2, 1991, pp. 1–2. Shakhrai saw the revised union treaty as a "breeding ground for 'Karabakhs' deep inside Russia." His reference was to the Armenian–Azeri conflict (see op. cit. at n. 42).

68. In the spring and summer of 1991, parliamentary conservatives took various positions on the prospect of a new union treaty and a subsequent new constitution. Basically, conservatives seemed uneasy with both projects—in the longer term because of their perceived subversive potential for the Soviet system, and in the short term due to the likelihood of renewed legislative restructuring, the consequent loss of safe seats under the original 1988 electoral rules, and the necessity of having to face reelection in fully open contests.

69. The party became a center of conservative opposition to Gorbachev and his reforms. This was reflected in the election of Gorbachev's outspoken critic, Ivan Polozkov, as leader of the Russian Communist Party as well as Gorbachev's reelection as all-union party leader at the 28th Party Congress in 1990 with over a thousand delegates voting against him. See Robert G. Kaiser, *Why Gorbachev Happened: His Triumphs and His Failure* (New York: Simon and Schuster, 1991), ch. 9.

70. See Polozkov's speech printed in *Sovetskaia Rossiia*, March 1, 1991, p. 2.

71. See op. cit. at nn. 51 and 58.

72. Gorbachev rested his constitutional case for disallowing the annexation of the predominantly Armenian enclave within Azerbaijan by Armenia, on Article 78 which stated that "The territory of a union republic cannot be changed without its consent." See Sharlet, *The New Soviet Constitution of 1977*, p. 100. In the wake of the defeated August coup in late 1991, a pullout of union (mostly Russian) peacekeeping troops from the Nagorno-Karabakh began, eliminating the buffer between Azeris and Armenians and setting the stage for heavier casualties in the post-Soviet period.

73. For the background of the Georgian-South Ossetian conflict, see Ronald Grigor Suny, *The Making of the Georgian Nation* (Bloomington, IN: Indiana University Press, 1988), chs. 11–13 passim.

74. The two restless minorities in Moldova are Slavic and Turkic groups, concentrated respectively in different parts of the republic. The Moldovans used the occasion of the August 1991 coup to arrest several of their leading Russian opponents. See "The Situation in the Dnestr Region," *Current Digest of the Soviet Press*, vol. 43, no. 38 (1991), p. 35.

75. Alexander J. Motyl, *Sovietology, Rationality, Nationality: Coming to Grips with Nationalism in the USSR* (New York: Columbia University Press, 1990), p. 67.

76. On departization and the new draft union treaty, against both of which the conspirators were reacting, see, respectively, Alexei Ulyukayev, "Departization without decrees," *Moscow News*, August 4–11, 1991, p. 9; and "Treaty on the Union of Sovereign States," *Current Digest of the Soviet Press*, vol. 43, no. 31 (1991), pp. 21–24. For the text of Article 127(7), see Smith, *Soviet Politics* (2d ed.), p. 373. As a Soviet journalist put it, the coup leaders were "fascinated by the idea of doing everything 'constitutionally.'" Vladimir Dashkevich, "Plot and Counter-Plot," *Independent Newspaper from Russia*, vol. 2, no. 12–13 (1991), p. 12. In fact, of course, the junta "flouted" the Constitution as the editors of the principal Soviet law journal indignantly wrote right after the coup. See "Avgustovskii putch: Posledstviia i uroki," *Soviet gosudarstvo i pravo*, 1991, no. 10, p. 14.

77. FBIS, *Daily Report: Soviet Union*, August 19, 1991, pp. 9 and 12.

78. For a discussion of Soviet constitutionalism as an arena for political conflict, see Robert Sharlet, "The Path of Constitutional Reform in the USSR," in Huber and Kelley, eds., *Perestroika-era Politics*, esp. pp. 22–26.

79. On prerogativism and normativism in Soviet politics and law, see Robert Sharlet, "Stalinism and Soviet Legal Culture," in Tucker, ed., *Stalinism*, esp. pp. 155–57.

80. Quotes are from CNN live television coverage of the post-coup, extraordinary session of the USSR Congress of People's Deputies on September 3 and 4, 1991. In the same spirit, another deputy declared that it was "time to stop treating the Constitution like a prostitute, adapting it every time to please a new courtier." FBIS translation from Soviet Central Television for September 2, 1991, in *Daily Report: Soviet Union*, September 4, 1991, p. 26–27, esp. 27. Citing the above deputy, a *Pravda* journalist several weeks later condemned the practice of treating the Constitution "as a mere office instruction." See ibid., October 9, 1991, pp. 31–33, esp. 33.

81. For the post-coup transition law, see *Soviet Business Law Report*, vol. 2, no. 5 (1991), pp. 8–9. This represented the last major revision of the 1977 Constitution. As Article 8 of the law stated: "The provisions of the USSR Constitution are still valid except those sections which contradict this law." For the "Declaration of Human Rights and Freedoms," also adopted by the extraordinary session of the USSR Congress of People's Deputies, see *New York Times*, September 7, 1991, p. 5.

82. The Soviet press was also skeptical at this late hour about either the prospects for a new union constitution or even the survival of the USSR itself. Since the late Brezhnev years, October Seventh had been designated as "Constitution Day" in honor of the adoption of the 1977 Constitution on October 7, 1977. On October 5, 1991, *Komsomol'skaia pravda*, in anticipation of the anniversary, published a lead article appropriately entitled "Poslednii Den' Konstitutsii" (The Final Constitution Day). Similarly, *Nezavisimaia gazeta*, correctly predicting an overwhelming vote for independence in Ukraine's upcoming December 1 referendum, ran as its headline on Saturday, November 30, 1991, "Konets imperii" (The End of Empire). On Gorbachev's resignation from the Presidency marking the "end of the Lenin dynasty and the Soviet period in Russian history," see Robert C. Tucker, "The Last Leninist," *New York Times*, sec. 4 (December 29, 1991), Op-Ed p. 9.

83. Quoted from an interview with the leaders of the National Islam Party for Revival of Tajikistan in *Independent Newspaper from Russia*, vol. 2, no. 3 (1991), p. 8.

84. TASS account of Yeltsin's parliamentary report on the draft Russian Constitution in FBIS, *Daily Report: Soviet Union*, November 4, 1991, pp, 56–59. For a translation of the late 1991 draft Russian Federation Constitution, see FBIS, *Soviet Union: Republic Affairs*, October 25, 1991, pp. 1–31.

85. On Russian criticism of the Kalmyk oath, see FBIS, *Daily Report: Soviet Union*, October 9, 1991, p. 45. On the tension between Volga Tatars and Russians, see "Tatar Nationalists Stir Secession Fever," *Current Digest of the Soviet Press*, vol. 43, no. 47 (1991), pp. 1–6. The rhetorical crossfire has included Tatar references to Genghis Khan, conqueror of Russia, and Russian allusions to the "second taking of Kazan," when the Russians threw off the Tatar yoke. On the Stalinist background of the current Chechen-Ingushi conflict with Russia, see Aleksandr M. Nekrich, *The Punished Peoples: The Deportation and Fate of Soviet Minorities at the End of the Second World War*, trans. by George Saunders (New York: Norton, 1978), which also includes material on the repression of the Kalmyks. For a contemporary account of the rising tensions between North Caucasians, including Chechens, and Russians in the Tver region of Russia, see L. Leontyeva, "Landslide: Ethnic Conflict in Russian Heartland," *Moscow News*, 1991, no. 29, p. 6.

86. On the need to move from rhetoric to reality, see Nick Lampert, "The Socialist Legal State," in Martin McCauley, ed., *Gorbachev and Perestroika* (New York: St. Martin's, 1990), ch. 7. Elena Bonner believes that Russia will have to travel the road to a civil society "for a long time." See Elena Bonner, "We Didn't Defend Gorbachev," *Uncaptive Minds*, Fall 1991, pp. 35–38, esp. 37.

87. For the founding documents of the new Commonwealth of Independent States, see *New York Times*, December 9, 1991, p. A8, and December 10, 1991, p. A19. The founding fathers of the CIS, especially Yeltsin, took great care to legitimate their new commonwealth by underscoring the constitutional continuity of their actions in the preamble of the main document. This constitutionalist concern was especially apparent in President Yeltsin's speech before the Russian parliament, seeking ratification of Russia's participation in the CIS, as televised live by CNN on December 12, 1991. As I see it, the resulting accord on the CIS by most of the successor states of the former USSR, appears to resemble ideas and institutional arrangements found in the American Articles of Confederation of 1781 as well as in the Sakharov draft constitution of 1989 (see op. cit. at n. 8).

88. See Frank Michelman, "Law's Republic," *Yale Law Journal*, vol. 97, no. 8 (1988), pp. 1493–1537. In their many learned discussions of the journey to a civil society and the rule of law during the last years of Gorbachev and the USSR, Soviet jurists harbored no illusions that the passage would be an easy or even a certain one. A leading scholar hopefully laid out the arduous route for the future: "The journey to a law-based state system must become for our society as a whole a school for legal culture, a school for understanding the meaning, purpose and value of law, [and] a state governed by law [as well as] the rules of law ." V.S. Nersesiants from his presentation at a Moscow roundtable discussion of the law-based state as published in V.S. Nersesiants and E.A. Chirkin, eds., *Sotsialisticheskoe pravovoe gosudarstvo: Kontseptsiia i puti realizatsii* (Moscow: Iuridicheskaia literatura, 1990), pp. 44–45.

Readings for Further Study

I. Background Studies and General Textbooks on the Constitutions, History, and Politics of the USSR

A. Constitutional Studies and Texts

1. Feldbrugge, F.J.M., ed. *The Constitutions of the USSR and the Union Republics: Analysis, Texts,Reports*. 1979. Sijthoff and Noordhoff. [Texts of the 1936 and 1977 USSR constitutions and the 1978 union republic constitutions, and analysis of the 1977 document.]

2. Kudryavtsev, V.N., et al., eds. *The Soviet Constitution: A Dictionary*. 1982. Progress Publishers.

3. Sharlet, Robert. *The New Soviet Constitution of 1977: Analysis and Text*. 1978. King's Court.

4. Topornin, Boris. *The New Constitution of the USSR*. 1980. Progress Publishers. [Analysis and text.]

5. Unger, Aryeh L. *Constitutional Development in the USSR: A Guide to the Soviet Constitutions*. 1981. Methuen. [Texts of 1918, 1924, 1936 and 1977 constitutions and analysis.]

B. Historical Surveys

1. Daniels, Robert V. *Russia: The Roots of Confrontation*. 1985. Harvard University Press.

2. Dziewanowski, M. K. *A History of Soviet Russia*. 3rd ed. 1989. Prentice-Hall.

3. Heller, Mikhail, and Aleksandr M. Nekrich. *Utopia in Power: The History of the Soviet Union from 1917 to the Present*. 1986. Simon and Schuster.

4. Kort, Michael G. *The Soviet Colossus: A History of the USSR*. 2nd ed. 1990. Unwin Hyman.

5. MacKenzie, David, and Michael W. Curran. *A History of Russia and the Soviet Union*. 3rd ed. 1987. Dorsey.

6. MacKenzie, David. *A History of the Soviet Union*. 2nd ed. 1991. Wadsworth Publishing Co.

7. Pipes, Richard. *A History of the Russian Revolution*. 1990. Knopf.

8. Thompson, John M. *Russia and the Soviet Union: An Historical Introduction*. 2nd ed. 1990. Westview.

9. Treadgold, Donald W. *Twentieth Century Russia*. 7th ed. 1989. Westview.

C. Textbooks on Soviet Politics

1. Baradat, Leon P. *Soviet Political Society*. 3rd ed. 1992. Prentice-Hall.

2. Barghoorn, Frederick C. and Thomas Remington. *Politics in the USSR*. 3rd ed. 1986. Harper Collins.

3. Barry, Donald D. and Carol Barner-Barry. *Contemporary Soviet Politics: An Introduction*. 4th ed. 1991. Prentice-Hall.

4. Bertsch, Gary K. *Power and Policy in Communist Systems*. 3rd ed. 1985. John Wiley and Sons.

5. Hammer, Darrell P. *The USSR: The Politics of Oligarchy*. 3rd ed. 1990. Westview.

6. Hazard, John N. *The Soviet System of Government*. 5th ed. 1980. University of Chicago Press.

7. Hill, Ronald J. *Soviet Union*, 2nd ed. 1989. Pinter Publishers.

8. Jacobs, Dan N., David P. Conradt, B. Guy Peters and William Safran, *Comparative Politics: Introduction to the Politics of the United Kingdom, France, Germany, and the Soviet Union*. 1983. Chatham House.

9. Lane, David. *State and Politics in the USSR*. 1985. New York University Press.

10. Little, D. Richard. *Governing the Soviet Union*. 1989. Longman.

11. Medish, Vadim. *The Soviet Union*. 4th ed. 1991. Prentice-Hall.

12. Reshetar, John S., Jr. *The Soviet Polity: Government and Politics in the USSR*. 3rd ed. 1989. Harper Collins.

13. Roeder, Phillip G. *Soviet Political Dynamics: Development of the First Leninist Polity*. 1988. Harper Collins.

14. Sakwa, Richard. *Soviet Politics: An Introduction*. 1989. Routledge.

15. Rothman, Stanley and George Breslauer. *Soviet Politics and Society*. 1978. West Publishing Company.

16. Schapiro, Leonard. *The Government and Politics of the Soviet Union*. 6th ed. 1984. Longwood Publishing Group.

17. Smith, Gordon B. *Soviet Politics: Struggling With Change*, 2nd ed. 1992. St. Martin's.

18. Theen, Rolf H.W. and Frank L. Wilson. *Comparative Politics: An Introduction to Six Countries*. 1986. Prentice-Hall. [USSR, Sec. 4]

19. Wesson, Robert. *Russian Dilemma*. 2nd rev. ed. 1985. Praeger.

II. The Political System

1. Bialer, Seweryn. *The Soviet Paradox: External Expansion, Internal Decline*. 1986. Random House.

2. Bialer, Seweryn and Michael Mandelbaum, eds. *Gorbachev's Russia and American Foreign Policy*. 1988. Westview.

3. Brzezinski, Zbigniew. *The Grand Failure: The Birth and Death of Communism in the Twentieth Century*. 1990. Collier Books.

4. Colton, Timothy J. *The Dilemma of Reform in the Soviet Union*. Rev. ed. 1986. Council on Foreign Relations.

4. Colton, Timothy J. *The Dilemma of Reform in the Soviet Union*. Rev. ed. 1986. Council on Foreign Relations.

5. Cohen, Stephen F. *Rethinking the Soviet Experience: Politics and History since 1917*. 2nd ed. 1992. Oxford University Press.

6. Hough, Jerry F. *Russia and the West: Gorbachev and the Politics of Reform*. 1988. Simon and Schuster.

7. Lewin, Moshe. *The Gorbachev Phenomenon: A Historical Interpretation*. Expanded ed. 1991. University of California Press.

8. Tatu, Michel. *Mikhail Gorbachev: The Origins of Perestroika*. 1991. Columbia University Press.

9. Thom, Francoise. *The Gorbachev Phenomenon: The History of Perestroika*. 1990. Pinter Publishers.

10. *Russian Politics: A Journal of Translations* (formerly *Soviet Law & Government*). Published since 1964 by M.E. Sharpe.

11. Tucker, Robert C. *Political Culture and Leadership in Soviet Russia*. 1988. Norton.

12. Yanov, Alexander. *The Russian Challenge and the Year 2000*. 1987. Blackwell.

A. Communist Party and the Soviet System

1. Bialer, Seweryn and Thane Gustafson, eds. *Russia at the Crossroads: The Twenty-Sixth Congress of the CPSU*. 1982. Allen & Unwin.

2. Breslauer, George W. *Khrushchev and Brezhnev as Leaders: Building Authority in Soviet Politics*. 1982. Allen & Unwin.

3. *Current Digest of the Soviet Press* (See translations of the proceedings of the 27th (1986) and 28th (1990) Party Congresses, and the 19th Party Conference (1988).

4. Dallin, Alexander, ed. *The Twenty-fifth Congress of the CPSU: Assessment and Context*. 1977. Hoover Institution Press.

5. Gorbachev, Mikhail. *Perestroika: New Thinking for Our Country and the World*. 1987. Harper and Row.

6. Hill, Ronald J. and Peter Frank. *The Soviet Communist Party*. 3rd ed. 1987. Unwin Hyman.

7. Hough, Jerry F. *The Soviet Prefects: The Local Party Organs in Industrial Decision-Making*. 1969. Harvard University Press.

8. Laird, Roy D. *The Politburo: Demographic Trends, Gorbachev and the Future*. 1986. Westview.

9. Loeber, Dietrich André (editor-in-chief), D.D. Barry, F.J.M. Feldbrugge, G. Ginsburgs and P. B. Maggs, eds. *Ruling Communist Parties and Their Status Under Law*. 1986. Martinus Nijhoff.

10. Medvedev, Zhores. *Gorbachev*. 1986. Norton.

11. Medvedev, Zhores. *Andropov*. 1983. Norton.

12. Ryavec, Karl W. ed. *Soviet Society and the Communist Party*. 1978. University of Massachusetts Press.

13. Schwartz, Donald V. ed. *Resolutions and Decisions of the Communist Party of the Soviet Union*: Vol. 5: *The Brezhnev Years, 1964–1981*. 1982. University of Toronto Press.

14. Voslensky, Michael S. *Nomenklatura: The Soviet Ruling Class*. 1984. Doubleday.

B. Soviet Politics from Brezhnev to Gorbachev: Interpretive Studies

1. Bialer, Seweryn. *Stalin's Successors: Leadership, Stability and Change in the Soviet Union*. 1980. Cambridge University Press.
2. Brucan, Silviu. *The Post-Brezhnev Era*. 1983. Praeger.
3. Cohen, Stephen F., and Katrina vanden Heuvel, *Voices of Glasnost: Interviews with Gorbachev's Reformers*. 1989. Norton.
4. Daniels, Robert V. *Is Russia Reformable?: Change and Resistance from Stalin to Gorbachev*. 1988. Westview.
5. Doder, Dusko. *Shadows and Whispers: Power Politics Inside the Kremlin from Brezhnev to Gorbachev*. 1986. Random House.
6. Doder, Dusko, and Louise Branson. *Gorbachev: Heretic in the Kremlin*. 1990. Viking Penguin.
7. Eklof, Ben. *Soviet Briefing: Gorbachev and the Reform Period*. 1989. Westview.
8. Frankland, Mark. *The Sixth Continent: Mikhail Gorbachev and the Soviet Union*. 1987. Harper and Row.
9. Goldman, Marshall I. *What Went Wrong with Perestroika*. 1991. Norton.
10. Hoffmann, Erik P., and Robbin F. Laird. *Technocratic Socialism: The Soviet Union in the Advanced Industrial Era*. 1985. Duke University Press.
11. Hosking, Geoffrey A. *The Awakening of the Soviet Union*. 1990. Harvard University Press.
12. Hough, Jerry F., and Merle Fainsod. *How the Soviet Union is Governed: An Extensively Revised and Enlarged Edition by Jerry F. Hough of Merle Fainsod's "How Russia is Ruled."* 1979. Harvard University Press.
13. Kaiser, Robert G. *Why Gorbachev Happened: His Triumph and His Failure*. 1991. Simon and Schuster.
14. Kagarlitsky, Boris. *Farewell Perestroika*. 1990. Verso.
15. Kelley, Donald R. *Soviet Politics from Brezhnev to Gorbachev*. 1987. Praeger.
16. Laqueur, Walter. *Long Road to Freedom: Russia and Glasnost*. 1989. Scribner.
17. Linden, Carl A. *The Soviet Party-State: Aspects of Ideocratic Despotism*. 1983. Praeger.
18. Mandel, Ernest. *Beyond Perestoika: The Future of Gorbachev's USSR*. Trans. by Gus Fagan. Rev. ed. 1991. Verso.
19. Medvedev, Roy A. *On Socialist Democracy*. Trans. by Ellen de Kadt. 1977. Norton.
20. Medvedev, Roy, and Giulietto Chiesa. *Time of Change: An Insider's View of Russia's Transformation*. Trans. by Michael Moore. 1989. Pantheon.
21. Melville, Andrew, and Gail W. Lapidus, eds. *The Glasnost Papers: Voices on Reform from Moscow*. 1990. Westview.
22. Naylor, Thomas H. *The Gorbachev Strategy: Opening the Closed Society*. 1987. Lexington Books.
23. Sakwa, Richard. *Gorbachev and His Reforms, 1985–1990*. 1990. Prentice Hall.
24. Sobchak, Anatoly. *For a New Russia*. 1991. Free Press.
25. Soros, George. *Underwriting Democracy*. 1991. Free Press.

26. Walker, Martin. *The Waking Giant: Gorbachev's Russia*. 1988. Pantheon.

27. White, Stephen. *Gorbachev and After*. Rev. ed. 1991. Cambridge University Press.

28. Zaslavskaya, Tatyana. *The Second Socialist Revolution: An Alternative Soviet Strategy*. Trans. by Susan M. Davies with Jenny Warren. 1990. Indiana University Press.

C. Soviet System from Brezhnev to Gorbachev: Specialized Studies

1. Bialer, Seweryn, ed. *Politics, Society and Nationality Inside Gorbachev's Russia*. 1988. Westview.

2. Brown, Archie, and Michael Kaser, eds. *Soviet Policy for the 1980s*. 1982. Indiana University Press.

3. Brumberg, Abraham, ed. *Chronicle of a Revolution: A Western-Soviet Inquiry into Perestroika*. 1990. Pantheon.

4. Byrnes, Robert F., ed. *After Brezhnev: Sources of Soviet Conduct in the 1980s*. 1983. Indiana University Press.

5. Cocks, Paul, Robert V. Daniels, and Nancy Whittier Heer, eds. *The Dynamics of Soviet Politics*. 1977. Harvard University Press.

6. Cohen, Stephen F., Alexander Rabinowitch, and Robert Sharlet, eds. *The Soviet Union Since Stalin*. 1980. Indiana University Press.

7. Dallin, Alexander, and Gail W. Lapidus, eds., *The Soviet System in Crisis: A Reader of Western and Soviet Views*. 1991. Westview.

8. Gustafson, Thane. *Crisis Amid Plenty: The Politics of Soviet Energy Under Brezhnev to Gorbachev*. 1991. Princeton University Press.

9. Hewett, Ed A., and Victor H. Winston, eds. *Milestones in Glasnost and Perestroika: Politics and People*. 1991. Brookings.

10. Hoffmann, Erik P., and Robbin F. Laird, eds. *The Soviet Polity in the Modern Era*. 1984. Aldine.

11. Hoffmann, Erik P., ed. *The Soviet Union in the 1980s*. 1984. Academy of Political Science.

12. Juviler, Peter, and Hiroshi Kimura, eds. *Gorbachev's Reforms: Progress and Prospects*. 1988. Aldine.

13. Kelley, Donald R. ed., *Khrushchev and Gorbachev as Reformers*. 1992. Praeger.

14. Kelley, Donald R., ed. *Soviet Politics in the Brezhnev Era*. 1980. Praeger.

15. Lerner, Lawrence W., and Donald W. Treadgold, eds. *Gorbachev and the Soviet Future*. 1988. Westview.

16. Linden, Carl A. *Khrushchev and the Soviet Leadership: With an Epilogue on Gorbachev*. Updated ed. 1990. Johns Hopkins University Press.

17. McCauley, Martin, ed. *The Soviet Union Under Gorbachev*. 1990. St. Martin's.

18. Miller, R.F., J.H. Miller, and T.H. Rigby, eds. *Gorbachev at the Helm: A New Era in Soviet Politics?* 1987. Croom Helm UK/Routledge, Chapman and Hall.

19. Morrison, John. *Boris Yeltsin: From Bolshevik to Democrat*. 1991. Dutton.

20. Nogee, Joseph L., ed. *Soviet Politics: Russia after Brezhnev*. 1985. Praeger.

21. Nove, Alec. *Glasnost in Action: Cultural Renaissance in Russia*. 1989. Unwin Hyman.

22. Remington, Thomas F. *The Truth of Authority: Ideology and Communication in the Soviet Union*. 1988. University of Pittsburgh Press.

23. Rieber, Alfred J., and Alvin Z. Rubinstein, eds. *Perestroika at the Crossroads*. 1991. M. E. Sharpe.

24. Rigby, T.H. *The Changing Soviet System: Mono-Organizational Socialism from Its Origins to Gorbachev's Restructuring*. 1990. Gower Publishing Co.

25. Rigby, T.H., Archie Brown, and Peter Reddaway, eds. *Authority, Power and Policy in the USSR: Essays Dedicated to Leonard Schapiro*. 1985. St. Martin's.

26. Shlapentokh, Vladimir. *Soviet Intellectuals and Political Power*. 1990. Princeton University Press.

27. Shtromas, Alexander, and Morton A. Kaplan, eds. *The Soviet Union and the Challenge of the Future*. Vol. 1 (1988), Vol. 2 (1989). Paragon House.

28. Skilling, H. Gordon, and Franklyn Griffiths, eds. *Interest Groups in Soviet Politics*. 1971. Princeton University Press.

29. Solomon, Susan G., ed. *Pluralism in the Soviet Union: Essays in Honour of H. Gordon Skilling*. 1983. St. Martin's.

30. Tolz, Vera. *The USSR's Emerging Multiparty System*. 1990. Praeger.

31. Veen, Hans-Joachim, ed. *From Brezhnev to Gorbachev: Domestic Affairs and Soviet Foreign Policy*. 1987. St. Martin's.

32. White, Stephen. *Political Culture and Soviet Politics*. 1980. St. Martin's.

33. White, Stephen, and Alex Pravda, eds. *Ideology and Soviet Politics*. 1988. St. Martin's.

34. White, Stephen, Alex Pravda, and Zvi Gitelman, eds. *Developments in Soviet Politics*. 1990. Duke University Press.

35. Yeltsin, Boris. *Against the Grain*. Trans. by Michael Glenny. 1990. Summit Books.

III. The Economic System

1. Aganbegyan, Abel. *The Economic Challenge of Perestroika*. 1988. Indiana University Press.

2. Åslund, Anders. *Gorbachev's Struggle for Economic Reform*. Updated ed. 1991. Cornell University Press.

3. Bergson, Abram, and Herbert S. Levine, eds. *The Soviet Economy: Toward the Year 2000*. 1983. Allen and Unwin.

4. Bornstein, Morris, ed. *The Soviet Economy: Continuity and Change*. 1981. Westview.

5. Brezinski, Horst. *The Shadow Economy* [See Soviet case study]. 1989. Westview.

6. Desai, Padma. *The Soviet Economy: Problems and Prospects*. 1987. Blackwell.

7. Goldman, Marshall I. *USSR in Crisis: The Failure of an Economic System*. 1983. Norton.

8. Goldman, Marshall I. *Gorbachev's Challenge*. 1987 Norton.

9. Gregory, Paul R., and Robert C. Stuart. *Soviet Economic Structure and Performance*. 4th ed. 1990. Harper Collins.

10. Hewett, Ed A. *Reforming the Soviet Economy: Equality versus Efficiency*. 1988. Brookings.

11. Hewett, Ed A., and Victor H. Winston, eds. *Milestones in Glasnost and Perestroika: The Economy*. 1991. Brookings.

12. Hoffmann, Erik P., and Robbin F. Laird. *The Politics of Economic Modernization in the Soviet Union*. 1982. Cornell University Press.

13. Höhmann, Hans-Hermann, Alec Nove and Heinrich Vogel, eds. *Economics and Politics in the USSR: Problems of Interdependence*. 1986. Westview.

14. Hough, Jerry. *Opening Up the Soviet Economy*. 1988. Brookings.

15. Jones, Anthony, and William Moskoff, eds. *Perestroika and the Economy: New Thinking in Soviet Economics*. 1989. M.E. Sharpe.

16. Jones, Anthony, and William Moskoff, eds. *The Great Market Debate in Soviet Economics: An Anthology*. 1991. M.E. Sharpe.

17. Jones, Anthony, and William Moskoff. *Ko-ops: The Rebirth of Entrepreneurship in the Soviet Union*. 1991. Indiana University Press.

18. Lane, David. *Soviet Economy and Society*. 1985. New York University Press.

19. Nove, Alec. *Political Economy and Soviet Socialism*. 1979. Allen and Unwin.

20. Shmelev, Nikolai, and Vladimir Popov. *The Turning Point: Revitalizing the Soviet Economy*. 1989. Doubleday.

21. Simis, Konstantin M. *USSR: The Corrupt Society—The Secret World of Soviet Capitalism*. Trans. by Jacqueline Edwards and Mitchell Schneider. 1982. Simon and Schuster.

22. Spulber, Nicholas. *Restructuring the Soviet Economy: In Search of the Market*. 1991. University of Michigan Press.

A. Property and Planning

1. Berliner, Joseph S. *The Innovation Decision in Soviet Industry*. 1976. MIT Press.

2. Freris, Andrew. *The Soviet Industrial Enterprise: Theory and Practice*. 1984. Croom Helm.

3. Hedlund, Stefan. *Crisis in Soviet Agriculture*. 1984. St. Martin's.

4. Ioffe, Olimpiad S., and Peter B. Maggs. *The Soviet Economic System: A Legal Analysis*. 1987. Westview.

5. Johnson, D. Gale, and Karen M. Brooks. *Prospects for Soviet Agriculture in the 1980's*. 1983. Indiana University Press.

6. Kushnirsky, Fyodor I. *Soviet Economic Planning, 1965–1980*. 1982. Westview.

7. Maggs. Peter B., Gordon B. Smith, and George Ginsburgs, eds. *Law and Economic Development in the Soviet Union*. 1982. Westview.

8. Medvedev, Zhores. *Soviet Agriculture*. 1987. Norton.

9. William Moskoff, ed. *Perestroika in the Countryside*. 1990. M.E. Sharpe.

10. Smith, Gordon B., Peter B. Maggs and George Ginsburgs, eds. *Soviet and East European Law and the Scientific-Technical Revolution*. 1981. Pergamon.

B. Labor and the Environment

1. Kahan, Arcadius, and Blair Ruble, eds. *Industrial Labor in the USSR*. 1979. Pergamon.

2. Komarov, Boris. *The Destruction of Nature in the Soviet Union*. 1980. M. E. Sharpe.

3. Lampert, Nicholas. *Whistleblowing in the Soviet Union: A Study of Complaints and Abuses Under State Socialism*. 1985. Schoken Books.

4. Lane, David. *Soviet Labour and the Ethic of Communism*. 1987. Westview.

5. Lane, David and Felicity O'Dell. *The Soviet Industrial Worker*. 1978. Martin Robertson.

6. Lubin, Nancy. *Labour and Nationality in Soviet Central Asia: An Uneasy Compromise*. 1984. Princeton University Press.

7. McAuley, Alastair. *Women's Work and Wages in the Soviet Union*. 1981. Allen and Unwin.

8. Pryde, Philip R. *Conservation in the Soviet Union*. 1972. Cambridge University Press.

9. Ruble, Blair A. *Soviet Trade Unions*. 1981. Cambridge University Press.

10. Schapiro, Leonard, and Joseph Godson, eds. *The Soviet Worker from Lenin to Andropov*. 2nd ed. 1984. St. Martin's.

11. Singleton, Fred, ed. *Environmental Problems in the Soviet Union and Eastern Europe*. 1987. Lynne Rienner Publishers.

12. Stewart, John Massey, ed. *The Soviet Environment: Problems, Policies and Politics*. 1992. Cambridge University Press.

IV. Social and Cultural Development

1. Connor, Walter D. *The Accidental Proletariat: Workers, Politics, and Crisis in Gorbachev's Russia*. 1991. Princeton University Press.

2. George, Vic, and Nick Manning. *Socialism, Social Welfare and the Soviet Union*. 1980. Routledge and Kegan Paul.

3. Friedberg, Maurice, and Heyward Isham, eds. *Soviet Society Under Gorbachev*. 1987. M. E. Sharpe.

4. Jones, T. Anthony, ed. *Soviet Social Problems*. 1991. Westview.

5. Kagarlitsky, Boris. *The Thinking Reed: Intellectuals and the Soviet State from 1917 to the Present*. Trans. by Brian Pearce. 1988. Verso.

6. Kerblay, Basile. *Modern Soviet Society*. Trans. by Rupert Swyer. 1983. Pantheon.

7. Lane, David. *The End of Inequality: Stratification Under State Socialism*. 1971. Penguin.

8. Lane, David. *Soviet Society Under Perestroika*. 2nd ed. 1991. Unwin Hyman.

9. Madison, Bernice Q. *Social Welfare in the Soviet Union*. 1968. Stanford University Press.

10. Matthews, Mervyn. *Class and Society in Soviet Russia*. 1972. Walker.

11. Matthews, Mervyn. *Poverty in the Soviet Union: The Lifestyles of the Underprivileged in Recent Years*. 1986. Cambridge University Press.

12. Matthews, Mervyn. *Privilege in the Soviet Union: A Study of Elite Lifestyles Under Communism*. 1978. Allen and Unwin.

13. McAuley, Alastair. *Economic Welfare in the Soviet Union: Poverty, Living Standards, and Inequality*. 1979. University of Wisconsin Press.

14. Osborne, Robert J. *Soviet Social Policies*. 1970. Dorsey.

15. Pankhurst, Jerry G., and Michael Paul Sacks, eds. *Contemporary Soviet Society*. 1980. Praeger.

16. Rywkin, Michael. *Soviet Society Today*. 1989. M.E. Sharpe.

FOR FURTHER STUDY   159

17. Sacks, Michael Paul, and Jerry G. Pankhurst, eds. *Understanding the Soviet Union*. 1988. Allen and Unwin.
18. Willis, David K. *Klass: How Russians Really Live*. 1985. St. Martin's.
19. Yanowitch, Murray, ed. *New Directions in Soviet Social Thought: An Anthology*. 1989. M.E. Sharpe.
20. Yanowitch, Murray. *Controversies in Soviet Social Thought: Democratization, Social Justice, and the Erosion of Official Ideology*. 1991. M.E. Sharpe.

A. Daily Life in Soviet Society

1. Adelman, Deborah. *The "Children of Perestroika": Moscow Teenagers Talk About Their Lives and the Future*. 1991. M.E. Sharpe.
2. Binyon, Michael. *Life in Russia*. 1984. Pantheon.
3. Fisher, Wesley. *The Soviet Marriage Market*. 1980. Praeger.
4. Geiger, H. Kent. *The Family in Soviet Russia*. 1968. Harvard University Press.
5. Herlemann, Horst, ed. *Quality of Life in the Soviet Union*. 1987. Westview.
6. Kaiser, Robert G. *Russia: The People and the Power*. 1976. Atheneum.
7. Klose, Kevin. *Russia and the Russians: Inside the Closed Society*. 1984. Norton.
8. Kotkin, Stephen. *Steeltown, U.S.S.R.: Soviet Society in the Gorbachev Era*. 1991. University of California Press.
9. Lee, Andrea. *Russian Journal*. 1981. Random House.
10. Mace, David and Vera. *The Soviet Family*. 1964. Dolphin Books.
11. Millar, James R., ed. *Politics, Work, and Daily Life in the USSR: A Survey of Former Soviet Citizens*. 1987. Cambridge University Press.
12. Millar, James R., ed. *The Soviet Rural Community*. 1971. University of Illinois Press.
13. Pond, Elizabeth. *From the Yaroslavsky Station: Russia Perceived*. 3rd ed. 1988. Universe Books.
14. Shipler, David K. *Russia: Broken Idols, Solemn Dreams*. 1989. Times Books.
15. Shlapentokh, Vladimir. *Public and Private Life of the Soviet People: Changing Values in Post-Stalin Russia*. 1989. Oxford University Press.
16. Smith, Hedrick. *The New Russians*. Updated ed. 1991. Vintage.
17. Smith, Hedrick. *The Russians*. Rev. ed. 1984. Ballantine Books.
18. Taubman, William, and Jane Taubman. *Moscow Spring*. 1990. Simon and Schuster.
19. Treml, Vladimir. *Alcohol in the USSR*. 1982. Duke University Press.

B. Science and Education

1. Avis, George, ed. *The Making of the Soviet Citizen: Character Formation and Civic Training in Soviet Education*. 1987. Croom Helm.
2. Graham, Loren R. *Science, Philosophy and Human Behavior in the Soviet Union*. 1987, Columbia University Press.
3. Hutchings, Raymond. *Soviet Science, Technology, Design*. 1976. Oxford University Press.
4. Jacoby, Susan. *Inside Soviet Schools*. 1974. Hill and Wang.

5. Kneen, Peter. *Soviet Scientists and the State*. 1984. State University of New York Press.

6. Lubrano, Linda, and Susan Gross Solomon, eds. *The Social Context of Soviet Science*. 1980. Westview.

7. Medvedev, Zhores. *Soviet Science*. 1978. Norton.

8. Parrott, Bruce. *Politics and Technology in the Soviet Union*. 1983. MIT Press.

9. *Russian Education and Society: A Journal of Translations* (formerly *Soviet Education*). Edited by Anthony Jones. Published monthly by M.E. Sharpe since 1958.

10. Sorrentino, Frank M., and Frances R. Curcio. *Soviet Politics and Education*. 1986. University Press of America.

V. Foreign Policy and Defense

1. Laird, Robbin F., ed. *Soviet Foreign Policy*. 1987. Academy of Political Science.

2. Edmonds, Robin. *Soviet Foreign Policy: The Brezhnev Years*. 1983. Oxford University Press.

3. Grzybowski, Kazimierz. *Soviet International Law and the World Economic Order*. 1987. Duke University Press.

4. Kanet, Roger E. *Soviet Foreign Policy in the 1980's*. 1982. Praeger.

5. Laird, Robbin F., Fleron, Frederic J., Jr., and Erik P. Hoffmann, eds. *Soviet Foreign Policy*. 1991. Aldine.

6. Nogee, Joseph L., and Robert H. Donaldson. *Soviet Foreign Policy Since World War II*. 3rd ed. 1988. Pergamon.

7. Pravda, Alex. *Soviet Foreign Policy Priorities Under Gorbachev*. 1988. Routledge.

8. Ramundo, Bernard A. *Peaceful Coexistence: International Law in the Building of Communism*. 1967. Johns Hopkins Press.

9. Rubinstein, Alvin Z. *Soviet Foreign Policy Since World War II*. 4th ed. 1992. Harper Collins.

10. Shevardnadze, Eduard. *A New Vision for the World: Soviet Foreign Policy in the Age of Perestroika*. 1992. Pantheon.

11. Steele, Jonathan. *Soviet Power: The Kremlin's Foreign Policy—Brezhnev to Andropov*. Rev. ed. 1984. Simon and Schuster.

12. Ulam, Adam B. *Dangerous Relations: The Soviet Union in World Politics, 1970–1982*. 1983. Oxford University Press.

13. Von Beyme, Klaus. *The Soviet Union in World Politics*. 1987. St. Martin's.

A. Soviet–American Relations

1. Brzezinski, Zbigniew. *Game Plan: How to Conduct the U.S.-Soviet Contest*. 1988. Atlantic Monthly.

2. Garthoff, Raymond L. *Detente and Confrontation: American-Soviet Relations from Nixon to Reagan*. 1985. Brookings.

3. Horelick, Arnold, ed. *U.S.-Soviet Relations: The Next Phase*. 1986. Cornell University Press.

4. Jervis, Robert, ed. *Soviet-American Relations After the Cold War*. 1991. Duke University Press.

5. Legvold, Robert. *The Soviet Union and the Other Superpower: Soviet Policy Towards the United States, 1969 to the Present*. Forthcoming.

6. Leonhard, Wolfgang. *The Kremlin and the West: A Realistic View of Relations with the Soviet Union*. 1986. Norton.

7. Ryavec, Karl W. *United States–Soviet Relations* 1989. Longman.

8. Savigear, Peter. *Cold War or Detente in the 1980s: The International Politics of American-Soviet Relations*. 1987. St. Martin's.

B. Soviet–East European Relations

1. Braun, Aurel, ed. *The Soviet-East European Relationship in the Gorbachev Era*. 1990. Westview.

2. Brown, J.F. *Eastern Europe and Communist Rule*. 1988. Duke University Press.

3. Brown, J.F. *Surge to Freedom: The End of Communist Rule in Eastern Europe*. 1991. Duke University Press.

4. Dawisha, Karen. *Eastern Europe, Gorbachev and Reform: The Great Challenge*. 2nd ed. 1990. Cambridge University Press.

5. D'Encausse, Helene C. *Big Brother: The Soviet Union and Soviet Europe*. 1987. Holmes and Meier.

6. Gati, Charles. *The Bloc That Failed: Soviet-East European Relations in Transition*. 1990. Indiana University Press.

7. Gati, Charles. *Hungary and the Soviet Bloc*. 1986. Duke University Press.

8. Griffith, William E., ed. *Central and Eastern Europe and the West*. 1989. Westview.

9. Lovenduski, Joni, and Jean Woodall. *Politics and Society in Eastern Europe*. 1987. Indiana University Press.

10. Sodaro, Michael J. *Moscow, Germany and the West from Khrushchev to Gorbachev*. 1991. Cornell University Press.

11. Terry, Sarah Meiklejohn. *Soviet Policy in Eastern Europe*. 1984. Yale University Press.

12. Valenta, Jiri. *Soviet Intervention in Czechoslovakia, 1968*. 1979. Johns Hopkins University Press.

13. Volgyes, Ivan, ed. *The Uncertain Future: Gorbachev's Eastern Bloc*. 1988. Paragon House.

C. Military and National Security Policy

1. Colton, Timothy J. *Commissars, Commanders, and Civilian Authority: The Structure of Soviet Military Politics*. 1979. Harvard University Press.

2. Colton, Timothy J., and Thane Gustafson, eds. *Soldiers and the Soviet State: Civil-Military Relations from Brezhnev to Gorbachev*. 1990. Princeton University Press.

3. Erickson, John. *Commanders and Commissars: The Soviet Military System Under Challenge*. 1991. St. Martin's.

4. MccGwire, Michael. *Military Objectives in Soviet Foreign Policy*. 1987. Brookings.

5. MccGwire, Michael. *Perestroika and Soviet National Security*. 1988. Brookings.

6. Scott, Harriet Fast and William F. Scott. *The Armed Forces of the USSR*. 1984. Westview.

7. Sher, Alan B. *The Other Side of Arms Control: Soviet Objectives in the Gorbachev Era*. 1988. Allen and Unwin.

VI. Citizenship and Equality

1. Ginsburgs, George. *The Citizenship Law of the USSR*. 1984. Martinus Nijhoff.

A. Equality and Women

1. Atkinson, Dorothy, Alexander Dallin, and Gail W. Lapidus, eds. *Women in Russia*. 1977. Stanford University Press.

2. Browning, Genia K. *Women and Politics in the USSR: Consciousness Raising and Soviet Women's Groups*. 1987. St. Martin's.

3. Jancar, Barbara. *Women Under Communism*. 1978. Johns Hopkins. University Press.

4. Lapidus, Gail Warshofsky. *Women in Soviet Society*. 1978. University of California Press.

5. Mamonova, Tatyana, ed. *Women and Russia: Feminist Writings from the Soviet Union*. Trans. by Rebecca Park and Catherine Fitzpatrick. 1984. Beacon Press.

6. McAuley, Alastair. *Women's Work and Wages in the Soviet Union*. 1981. Allen and Unwin.

7. Sacks, Michael Paul. *Women's Work in Soviet Russia: Continuity in the Midst of Change*. 1976. Praeger.

B. Nationality Issues: General Perspectives

1. Allworth, Edward, ed. *Soviet Nationality Problems*. 1971. Columbia University Press.

2. Azrael, Jeremy. *Soviet Nationality Policies and Practices*. 1978. Praeger.

3. Conquest, Robert, ed. *The Last Empire: Nationality and the Soviet Future*. 1986. Hoover Institution Press.

4. Denber, Rachael, ed. *The Soviet Nationality Reader: The Crisis in Context*. 1992. Westview.

5. Dink, Nadia, and Adrian Karatnycky. *Hidden Nations: The People Challenge the Soviet Union*. 1990. Morrow.

6. Gleason, Gregory. *Federalism and Nationalism. The Struggle for Republican Rights in the USSR*. 1990. Westview.

7. Goldhagen, Erich, ed. *Ethnic Minorities in the Soviet Union*. 1968. Praeger.

8. Hajda, Lubomyr, and Mark Beissinger, eds. *The Nationalities Factor in Soviet Politics and Society*. 1990. Westview.

9. Karklins, Rasma. *Ethnic Relations in the USSR: The Perspective from Below*. 1986. Allen and Unwin.

10. Katz, Zev, Rosemarie Rodgers, and Frederick Harned, eds. *Handbook of Major Soviet Nationalities*. 1975. Free Press.

11. Mandelbaum, Michael. *The Rise of Nations in the Soviet Union*. 1991. Council on Foreign Relations.

12. Motyl, Alexander J. *Sovietology, Rationality, Nationality: Coming to Grips with Nationalism in the USSR*. 1990. Columbia University Press.

13. Motyl, Alexander J. *Will the Non-Russians Rebel?: State, Ethnicity, and Stability in the USSR*. 1987. Cornell University Press.

14. Nahaylo, Bohdan, and Victor Swoboda. *Soviet Disunion: A History of the Nationalities Problem in the USSR*. 1990. Free Press.

15. Olcott, Martha B., with Lubomyr Hajda and Anthony Olcott, eds. *The Soviet Multinational State: Readings and Documents*. 1990. M.E. Sharpe.

16. Ra'anan, Uri. *The Soviet Empire: The Challenge of National and Democratic Movements*. 1990. Lexington Books.

17. Simmonds, George W., ed. *Nationalism in the USSR and Eastern Europe*. 1977. University of Detroit Press.

18. Wimbush, S. Enders. *Soviet Nationalities in Strategic Perspective*. 1985. St. Martin's.

C. Nationality Issues: Case Studies

1. Akiner, Shirin. *Islamic Peoples of the Soviet Union*. 2nd ed. 1986. Metheun.

2. Allworth, Edward, ed. *Ethnic Russia in the USSR: The Dilemma of Dominance*. 1980. Pergamon.

3. Benningsen, Alexandre, and S. Enders Wimbush. *Muslim National Communism in the Soviet Union*. 1980. University of Chicago Press.

4. Benningsen, Alexandre, and S. Enders Wimbush. *Muslims of the Soviet Empire*. 1986. Indiana University Press.

5. Bilocerkowycz, Jaroslaw. *Soviet Ukrainian Dissent: A Study of Political Alienation*. 1988. Westview.

6. Carter, Stephen K., *Russian Nationalism*. 1990. St. Martin's.

7. Clemens, Walter, Jr., *Baltic Independence and Russian Empire*. 1991. St. Martin's.

8. Critchlow, James, *Nationalism in Uzbekistan*. 1991. Westview.

9. Dunlop, John B. *The New Russian Nationalism*. 1985. Praeger.

10. Fisher, Allan W. *The Crimean Tatars*. 1987. Hoover Institution Press.

11. Olcott, Martha B. *The Kazakhs*. 1987. Hoover Institution Press.

12. Raun, Toivo. *Estonia and the Estonians*. 1987. Hoover Institution Press.

13. Rywkin, Michael. *Moscow's Muslim Challenge: Soviet Central Asia*. 2nd ed. 1990. M. E. Sharpe.

14. Salitan, Laurie, P., *Politics and Nationality in Contemporary Soviet Jewish Emigration, 1968–89*. 1992. St. Martin's.

15. Senn, Alfred E. *Lithuania Awakening*. 1990. University of California Press.

16. Suny, Ronald Grigor. *The Making of the Georgian Nation*. 1988. Indiana University Press.

17. Walker, Christopher J., *Armenia: Survival of a Nation*. Rev. 2nd ed. 1990. St. Martin's.

18. Yanov, Alexander. *The Russian New Right: Right-Wing Ideologies in the*

Contemporary USSR. Trans. by Stephen P. Dunn. 1978. University of California, Institute of International Studies.

VII. Civil Rights and Duties

A. Social and Economic Rights

1. Andrusz, Gregory D. *Housing and Urban Development in the USSR.* 1984. Macmillan.
2. Brine, Jenny, Maureen Perrie, and Andrew Sutton. *Home, School and Leisure in the Soviet Union.* 1980. Allen and Unwin.
3. Dimaio, A.J. *Soviet Urban Housing.* 1974. Praeger.
4. Friedberg, Maurice. *Russian Culture in the 1980s.* 1985. Significant Issues Series, Vol. 7, No. 6. CSIS, Georgetown University.
5. Granick, David. *Job Rights in the Soviet Union: Their Consequences.* 1987. Cambridge University Press.
6. Grant, Nigel. *Soviet Education.* 4th ed. 1979. Penguin.
7. Hingley, Ronald. *Russian Writers and Soviet Society, 1917–1978.* 1979. Random House.
8. Matthews, Mervyn. *Education in the Soviet Union.* 1982. Allen and Unwin.
9. Moskoff, William. *Labor and Leisure in the Soviet Union.* 1984. Macmillan.
10. Tomiak, J.J., ed. *Soviet Education in the 1980's.* 1983. St. Martin's.
11. Zajda, J.I. *Education in the USSR.* 1980. Pergamon.

A-1. Studies on Health Care

1. Davis, Christopher, and Murray Feshbach. *Rising Infant Mortality in the USSR in the 1970's.* U.S. Department of Commerce, Bureau of the Census. 1980. U. S. Government Printing Office.
2. Field, Mark G. *Soviet Socialized Medicine.* 1967. Free Press.
3. Golyakhovsky, Vladimir. *Russian Doctor.* Trans. by Michael Sylvester and Eugene Ostrovsky. 1984. St. Martin's/Marek.
4. Hyde, G. *The Soviet Health Service.* 1974. Lawrence and Wishart.
5. Kaser, Michael. *Health Care in the Soviet Union and Eastern Europe.* 1976. Croom Helm.
6. Knaus, William A. *Inside Russian Medicine.* 1981. Everest.
7. Navarro, Vicente. *Social Security and Medicine in the USSR.* 1977. Lexington Books.
8. Ryan, Michael. *Doctors and the State in the Soviet Union.* 1990. St. Martin's.

B. Political and Civil Rights

1. Alexeyeva, Ludmilla. *Soviet Dissent: Contemporary Movements for National, Religious, and Human Rights.* Trans. by Carol Pearce and John Glad. 1985. Wesleyan University Press.
2. Bloch, Sidney, and Peter Reddaway. *Psychiatric Terror: How Soviet Psychiatry Is Used to Suppress Dissent.* 1977. Basic Books.
3. Chalidze, Valery. *To Defend These Rights: Human Rights and the Soviet*

Union. Trans. by Guy Daniels. 1974. Random House.

4. Cohen, Stephen F., ed. *An End to Silence: Uncensored Opinion in the Soviet Union.* Trans. by George Saunders. 1982. Norton.

5. Conquest, Robert. *Tyrants and Typewriters: Communiques from the Struggle for Truth.* 1989. Free Press.

6. Feldbrugge, F.J.M. *Samizdat and Political Dissent in the Soviet Union.* 1975. A. W. Sijthoff.

7. Fireside, Harvey. *Soviet Psychoprisons.* 1979. Norton.

8. Goldberg, Paul. *The Final Act: The Dramatic, Revealing Story of the Moscow Helsinki Watch Group.* 1988. Morrow.

9. Hopkins, Mark. *Russia's Underground Press: The Chronicle of Current Events.* 1983. Praeger.

10. Oleszczuk, Thomas A. *Political Justice in the USSR: Dissent and Repression in Lithuania, 1969–1987.* 1988. Columbia University Press.

11. Reddaway, Peter, ed. *Uncensored Russia: Protest and Dissent in the Soviet Union.* 1972. American Heritage Press.

12. *Reform and Human Rights: The Gorbachev Record.* Report Submitted to the Congress by the Commission on Security and Cooperation in Europe. 1988. U.S. Government Printing Office.

13. Rubenstein, Joshua. *Soviet Dissidents.* Rev. ed. 1985. Beacon Press.

14. Shanor, Donald R. *Behind the Lines: The Private War Against Soviet Censorship.* 1985. St. Martin's.

15. Solomon, Andrew. *The Irony Tower.* [On *glasnost* and Soviet art]. 1991. Knopf.

16. Tokes, Rudolf L., ed. *Dissent in the USSR.* 1975. Johns Hopkins University Press.

B-1. Memoirs and Studies of Dissidents

1. Amalrik, Andrei. *Notes of a Revolutionary.* 1982. Knopf.

2. Bukovsky, Vladimir. *To Build a Castle: My Life as a Dissenter.* Trans. by Michael Scammell. 1979. Viking.

3. De Boer, S.P., E.J. Driessen, and M. L. Verhaar, eds. *Biographical Dictionary of Soviet Dissidents.* 1982. Martinus Nijhoff.

4. Grigorenko, Peter. *Memoirs.* 1982. Norton.

5. Orlov, Yuri. *Dangerous Thoughts: Memoirs of A Russian Life.* Trans. by Thomas P. Whitney. 1991. William Morrow.

6. Ratushinskaya, Irina. *Grey Is the Color of Hope.* Trans. by Alyona Kojevnikov. 1989. Vintage.

7. Sakharov, Andrei. *Memoirs.* Trans. by Richard Lourie. 1990. Knopf.

8. Sakharov, Andrei. *Moscow and Beyond: 1986–1989.* Trans. by Antonina Bouis. 1991. Knopf.

9. Sharansky, Natan. *Fear No Evil.* Trans. by Stefani Hoffman. 1988. Random House.

10. Solzhenitsyn, Aleksandr I. *The Oak and the Calf: Sketches of Literary Life in the Soviet Union.* Trans. by Harry Willetts. 1980. Harper and Row.

11. Taagepera, Rein. *Softening Without Liberalization in the Soviet Union: The Case of Juri Kukk.* 1984. University Press of America.

B-2. Religion: General Studies

1. Boiter, Albert. *Religion in the Soviet Union*. 1980. Praeger.
2. Bourdeaux, Michael. *Gorbachev, Glasnost and the Gospel*. 1990. Hodder and Stoughton.
3. Bourdeaux, Michael, and Jane Ellis. *Religious Minorities in the Soviet Union*. Rev. 4th ed. 1984. Minority Rights Group.
4. Dunn, Dennis J., ed. *Religion and Modernization in the Soviet Union*. 1977. Westview.
5. Dunn, Dennis J., ed. *Religion and Nationalism in Eastern Europe and the Soviet Union*. 1987. Rienner, Lynne Publishers.
6. Fletcher, William C. *Soviet Believers: The Religious Sector of the Population*. 1981. The Regents Press of Kansas.
7. Hill, Kent. *The Soviet Union on the Brink: An Inside Look at Christianity and Glasnost*. 1991. Multnomah.
8. Lane, Christel. *Christian Religion in the Soviet Union*. 1978. Allen and Unwin.
9. Powell, David E. *Antireligious Propaganda in the Soviet Union*. 1975. MIT Press.
10. Ramet, Pedro. *Cross and Commissar: The Politics of Religion in Eastern Europe and the USSR*. 1987. Indiana University Press.
11. Ramet, Pedro, ed. *Religion and Nationalism in Soviet and East European Politics*. 2nd ed. 1989. Duke University Press.

B-3. Religion: Case Studies

1. Azbel, Mark. *Refusenik: Trapped in the Soviet Union*. 1981. Houghton Mifflin.
2. Bourdeaux, Michael. *Land of the Crosses: The Struggle for Religious Freedom in Lithuania, 1939–1978*. 1979. Keston College.
3. Ellis, Jane. *The Russian Orthodox Church: A Contemporary History*. 1986. Indiana University Press.
4. Freedman, Robert O., ed. *Soviet Jewry in the Decisive Decade, 1971–1980*. 1984. Duke University Press.
5. Freedman, Theodore, ed. *Anti-Semitism in the Soviet Union*. 1984. Freedom Library Press.
6. Gilbert, Martin. *The Jews of Hope: The Plight of Soviet Jewry Today*. 1985. Viking Penguin.
7. Grazulis, Nijole, ed. and trans. *The Chronicle of the Catholic Church in Lithuania: Underground Journal of Human Rights Violations, Nos. 1–9, 1972–74*. 1981. Loyola University Press.
8. Poliakov, Sergei. *Everyday Islam: Religion and Tradition in Rural Central Asia*. Edited by Martha B. Olcott. 1992. M.E. Sharpe.
9. Pospielovsky, Dimitry. *The Russian Church Under the Soviet Regime, 1917–1982*. Vol. 2. 1984. St. Vladimir's Seminary Press.
10. Vardys, V. Stanley. *The Catholic Church, Dissent and Nationality in Soviet Lithuania*. 1978. East European Quarterly.
11. Zaslavsky, Victor, and Robert J. Brym. *Soviet Jewish Emigration and Soviet Nationality Policy*. 1983. St. Martin's.

VIII. The Legislative and Administrative Systems

1. Adams, Jan S. *Citizen Inspectors in the Soviet Union: The People's Control Committee*. 1977. Holt, Rinehart and Winston.
2. Aspaturian, Vernon V. *The Union Republics in Soviet Diplomacy*. 1960. Institut Universitaire des Hautes Etudes Internationales.
3. Bahry, Donna. *Outside Moscow: Power, Politics and Budgetary Policy in the Soviet Republics*. 1987. Columbia University Press.
4. Cocks, Paul. *Controlling Communist Bureaucracy*. 1977. Harvard University Press.
5. Hopkins, Mark W. *Mass Media in the Soviet Union*. 1970. Pegasus.
6. Huber, Robert T., and Donald R. Kelley, eds. *Perestroika-era Politics: The New Soviet Legislature and Gorbachev's Political Reforms*. 1991. M.E. Sharpe.
7. Huskey, Eugene, ed. *Executive Power and Soviet Politics: The Rise and Decline of the Soviet State*. 1992. M.E. Sharpe.
8. Mickiewicz, Ellen P. *Split Signals: Television and Politics in the Soviet Union*. 1988. Oxford University Press.
9. Olcott, Martha B., with Lubomyr Hajda and Anthony Olcott, eds. *The Soviet Multinational State: Readings and Documents*. 1990. M.E. Sharpe.
10. Pipes, Richard. *The Formation of the Soviet Union*. Rev. ed., 1968. Atheneum.
11. Rosburgh, Angus. *Pravda: Inside the Soviet News Machine*. 1987. George Braziller.
12. Siegler, Robert W. *The Standing Commissions of the Supreme Soviet: Effective Co-Optation*. 1982. Praeger.
13. Smith, Gordon B., ed. *Public Policy and Administration in the Soviet Union*. 1980. Praeger.
14. Theen, Rolf H.W., ed. *The USSR First Congress of People's Deputies: Complete Documents and Records, May 25, 1989–June 10, 1989*. 4 vols. 1991. Paragon House.
15. Urban, Michael E. *More Power to the Soviets: The Democratic Revolution in the USSR*. 1990. Edward Elgar.
16. Vanneman, Peter. *The Supreme Soviet: Politics and the Legislative Process in the Soviet Political System*. 1977. Duke University Press.

A. Sources for Soviet Legislation in English Translation

1. Berman, Harold J. and John B. Quigley, Jr., eds. and trans. *Basic Laws on the Structure of the Soviet State*. 1969. Harvard University Press.
2. Butler, William E., ed., comp. and trans. *Basic Documents on the Soviet Legal System*. 2nd ed. 1991. Oceana.
3. Butler, William E., comp. and trans. *The Soviet Legal System: Legislation and Documentation*. 1978. Oceana.
4. *Collected Legislation of the USSR and Constituent Union Republics*. Ed. by William E. Butler. Published since 1979 by Oceana.
5. *Current Digest of the Post-Soviet Press* (weekly) (formerly *Current Digest of the Soviet Press*).
6. Foreign Broadcast Information Service. *Daily Report: Central Eurasia* (formerly *Daily Report: Soviet Union*).

7. Foreign Broadcast Information Service. *Joint Publication Research Service: Central Eurasia—Political Affairs* (bi-monthly) (formerly *Joint Publication Research Service: Soviet Union—Political Affairs*).

8. Foreign Broadcast Information Service. *Central Eurasia: Republic Affairs* (bi-weekly) (formerly *Soviet Union: Republic Affairs*).

9. Kavass, Igor I., comp. and ed. *Soviet Law in English: Research Guide and Bibliography, 1970–1987*. 1989. Williams S. Hein.

10. Kavass, Igor I., comp. and ed. *Gorbachev's Law: A Bibliographic Survey of English Writings on Soviet Legal Development, 1987–1990*. 1991. William S. Hein.

11. Matthews, Mervyn. *Party, State, and Citizen in the Soviet Union: A Collection of Documents*. 1989. M.E. Sharpe.

12. Simons, William B. ed. *The Soviet Codes of Law*. 1980. Sijthoff and Noordhoff.

13. Smirnov, L.N., ed. *Legislative Acts of the USSR, 1977–1979*. 1981. Progress Publishers.

14. Smirnov, L.N., ed. *Legislative Acts of the USSR*. Bk. 2. 1982. Progress Publishers.

15. Smirnov, L.N., ed. *Legislative Acts of the USSR*. Bk. 3. 1983. Progress Publishers.

16. Smirnov, L.N., ed. *Legislative Acts of the USSR*. Bk. 4. 1984. Progress Publishers.

17. Smirnov, L.N., ed. *Legislative Acts of the USSR*. Bk. 5. 1986. Progress Publishers.

18. *Statutes and Decisions: A Journal of Translations* (formerly *Soviet Statutes and Decisions*). Ed. Serge L. Levitsky. Published quarterly since 1964 by M.E. Sharpe.

19. Zile, Zigurds L., trans. and ed., *Ideas and Forces in Soviet Legal History*. 1992. Oxford University Press.

B. Local Government

1. Cattell, David T. *Leningrad: A Case History of Soviet Urban Government*. 1968. Praeger.

2. Friedgut, Theodore H. *Political Participation in the USSR*. 1979. Princeton University Press.

3. Hahn, Jeffrey W. *Soviet Grassroots: Citizen Participation in Local Soviet Government*. 1988. Princeton University Press.

4. Jacobs, Everett M., ed. *Soviet Local Politics and Government*. 1983. Allen and Unwin.

5. Lewis, Carol W., and Stephen Sternheimer. *Soviet Urban Management*. 1979. Praeger.

6. Morton, Henry W., and Robert C. Stuart, eds. *The Contemporary Soviet City*. 1984. M. E. Sharpe.

7. Savas, Emanuel S., and J. A. Kaiser. *Moscow's City Government*. 1985. Praeger.

8. Taubman, William. *Governing Soviet Cities: Bureaucratic Politics and Urban Development in the USSR*. 1973. Praeger.

IX. The Legal System

1. Alexeyev, Sergei. *Socialism and Law: Law in Society*. Trans. by Jane Sayer. 1990. Progress Publishers.

2. Barry, Donald D., ed., *Toward the "Rule of Law" in Russia?: Politics and Law in the Transition Period*. 1992. M.E. Sharpe.

3. Barry, Donald D., ed. *Law and the Gorbachev Era: Essays in Honor of Dietrich Andre Loeber*. 1988. Martinus Nijhoff.

4. Barry, Donald D., William E. Butler, and George Ginsburgs, eds. *Contemporary Soviet Law*. 1974. Martinus Nijhoff.

5. Barry, Donald D., George Ginsburgs, and Peter B. Maggs, eds. *Soviet Law After Stalin*. 3 vols. 1977–79. Sijthoff and Noordhoff.

6. Berman, Harold J., and John B. Quigley, Jr., eds. and trans. *Basic Laws on the Structure of the Soviet State*. 1969. Harvard University Press.

7. Berman, Harold J. *Justice in the USSR*. Rev. ed. 1963. Harvard University Press.

8. Butler, William E., ed., comp., and trans. *Basic Documents on the Soviet Legal System*. 2nd ed. 1991. Oceana.

9. Butler, William E., Peter B. Maggs, and John B. Quigley, Jr., eds. *Law After the Revolution*. 1988. Harvard University Press.

10. Butler, William E., ed. *Perestroika and the Rule of Law*. 1991. I.B. Tauris.

11. Butler, William E., ed. *Perestroika and International Law*. 1990. Kluwer Academic Publishers.

12. Butler, William E. *Soviet Law*. 2nd ed. 1988. Buttersworths.

13. Butler, William E., comp. and trans. *The Soviet Legal System: Legislation and Documentation*. 1978. Oceana.

14. Buxbaum, Richard M., and Kathryn Hendley, eds. *The Soviet Sobranie of Laws*. 1991. Institute of International and Area Studies of the University of California, Berkeley.

15. Chalidze, Valery. *The Dawn of Legal Reform: (April 1985 to June 1989)*. Ed. by Lisa Chalidze. 1990. Chalidze Publications.

16. Feldbrugge, F.J.M., ed. *The Distinctiveness of Soviet Law*. 1987. Martinus Nijhoff.

17. Feldbrugge, F.J.M., G. P. Van Den Berg, and William B. Simons, eds. *Encyclopedia of Soviet Law*. 2nd ed. 1985. Martinus Nijhoff.

18. Feldbrugge, F.J.M., and William B. Simons, eds. *Perspectives on Soviet Law for the 1980s*. 1981. Martinus Nijhoff.

19. Hazard, John N. *Managing Change in the USSR: The Politico-Legal Role of the Soviet Jurist*. 1983. Cambridge University Press.

20. Hazard, John N., William E. Butler, and Peter B. Maggs, eds. *The Soviet Legal System: The Law in the 1980's*. 1984. Oceana.

21. Holland, Mary, ed. "Legal Reform in the Soviet Union," special issue of *Columbia Journal of Transnational Law*. 1990, Vol. 28, No. 1.

22. Huskey, Eugene. *Russian Lawyers and the Soviet State*. 1986. Princeton University Press.

23. Ioffe, Olimpiad S. *Soviet Law and Soviet Reality*. 1985. Martinus Nijhoff.

24. Juviler, Peter H. *Revolutionary Law and Order: Politics and Social Change in the USSR.* 1976. Free Press.

25. Lipson, Leon, and Valery Chalidze, eds. *Papers on Soviet Law.* No. 3. 1981. Institute on Socialist Law.

26. Maggs, Peter B., and Olimpiad S. Ioffe. *Soviet Law in Theory and Practice.* 1983. Oceana.

27. "Perspectives on Legal *Perestroika*: Soviet Constitutional and Legislative Changes," special issue of *Cornell International Law Journal.* 1990, Vol. 23, No. 2.

28. Smith, Gordon B. *The Soviet Procuracy and the Supervision of Administration.* 1978. Sijthoff and Noordhoff.

29. Van den Berg, Ger P. *The Soviet System of Justice: Figures and Policy.* 1985. Martinus Nijhoff.

A. Criminal Law

1. Bassiouni, M. Cherif, and V. M. Savitskii. *The Criminal Justice System of the USSR.* 1979. Charles C. Thomas, Publisher.

2. Berman, Harold J., ed. *Soviet Criminal Law and Procedure: The RSFSR Codes.* Trans. by H. J. Berman and James W. Spindler. 2nd ed. 1972. Harvard University Press.

3. Chalidze, Valery. *Criminal Russia: A Study of Crime in the Soviet Union.* 1977. Random House.

4. Connor, Walter D. *Deviance in Soviet Society.* 1972. Columbia University Press.

5. Kaminskaya, Dina. *Final Judgment: My Live As a Soviet Defense Attorney.* 1982. Simon and Schuster.

6. Knight, Amy W. *The KGB: Police and Politics in the Soviet Union.* 1988. Unwin Hyman.

7. Neznansky, Fridrikh. *The Prosecution of Economic Crimes in the USSR, 1954–1984.* Ed. by Robert Sharlet. 1985. Delphic Associates.

8. Rand, Robert. *Comrade Lawyer: Inside Soviet Justice in an Era of Reform.* 1991. Westview.

9. Rubenstein, Joshua. *Soviet Dissidents.* Rev. ed. 1985. Beacon Press.

10. Solomon, Peter H., Jr. *Soviet Criminologists and Criminal Policy.* 1978. Columbia University Press.

11. Vaksberg, Arkady. *The Soviet Mafia: A Shocking Expose of Organized Crime in the USSR,* Trans. by John Roberts and Elizabeth Roberts. 1992. St. Martin's.

B. Civil and Other Branches of Law

1. Armstrong, George M., Jr. *The Soviet Law of Property.* 1983. Martinus Nijhoff.

2. Grzybowski, Kazimierz. *Soviet Private International Law.* 1964. A. W. Sijthoff.

3. Ioffe, Olimpiad S. *Soviet Civil Law.* 1988. Martinus Nijhoff.

4. Ioffe, Olimpiad S., and Mark A. Janis, eds. *Soviet Law and the Economy.* 1986. Martinus Nijhoff.

5. Levitsky, Serge L. *Copyright, Defamation and Privacy in Soviet Civil Law.* 1979. Sijthoff and Noordhoff.

6. Luryi, Yuri I. *Soviet Family Law.* 1980. William S. Hein.

7. Newcity, Michael A. *Copyright Law in the Soviet Union.* 1978. Praeger.

8. Shelley, Louise. *Lawyers in Soviet Work Life.* 1984. Rutgers University Press.

9. Simons, William B., ed. *The Soviet Codes of Law.* 1980. Sijthoff and Noordhoff.

10. Smirnov, L. N., ed. *Legislative Acts of the USSR.* Bks. 1–6. 1981–88. Progress Publishers.

Chronology of the Rise and Fall of the Soviet System, 1917–1991

1917

November
Bolshevik Revolution
Soviet Russian government formed; Lenin chairman
Decrees nationalizing landed estates, replacing tsarist judiciary with revolutionary tribunals, and outlawing opposition press

December
Formation of the *Cheka*, first Soviet secret police
Decree No. 1 on the Courts
Other decrees nationalizing banks, prohibiting stock trading, and secularizing marriage and divorce

1918

January
Constituent Assembly convened and dissolved by force
"Declaration of the Rights of the Toiling and Exploited Peoples" issued
Congress of Soviets appoints a constitutional drafting commission

February
Decree nationalizing land, water, forests, and natural resources

March
Seventh Congress of the Bolshevik Party

April
Decrees abolishing inheritance and nationalizing foreign trade

May
Civil War begins in Russia

June
Policy of War Communism begins
Decree nationalizing large-scale industry

July
Constitution of the RSFSR adopted, first Soviet constitution

August
Decree nationalizing apartment houses

September
Decree launching Bolshevik policy of terror

October
RSFSR Family Code, first Soviet law code

November
Decree on the strict observance of the law

December
RSFSR Labor Code

1919

8th Congress of Bolshevik Party (renamed Russian Communist Party)
New Program of Russian Communist Party
Decree creating forced labor camps
RSFSR Basic Principles for Criminal Law

1920

9th Party Congress
Bolsheviks victorious in the Civil War

1921

10 Party Congress: New Economic Policy adopted
Decree replacing economic requisitioning with a tax in kind
End of War Communism

1922

11th Party Congress
Soviet legal development underway: RSFSR Codes on Criminal, Criminal procedure, Civil and Land law; statutes on the Procuracy and judiciary
Special party commission headed by Stalin set up to draft a constitutional framework for a federal state
Treaty of Union adopted by RSFSR, the Ukraine, Byelorussia, and Transcaucasia, creating the USSR
Trial of the Socialist Revolutionaries, first political show trial

1923

12th Party Congress
Constitutional commission appointed to draft a constitution based on the Treaty of Union
RSFSR Civil Procedure Code
Statute on USSR Supreme Court

1924

Lenin dies
13th Party Congress
Constitution of the USSR ratified, first union constitution

1925

14th Party Congress: Industrialization policy adopted
New Constitution of the RSFSR ratified
Uzbek and Turkmen union republics created within the USSR

1926

New RSFSR Criminal Code (includes Art. 58 on political crimes)

1927

15th Party Congress: Collectivization policy adopted
Statute on the Collective Farm

1928

First Five-Year Plan for the economy launched
Shakhty trial, political show trial of foreign engineers
End of New Economic Policy

1929

Stalin ascendent in party leadership
Forced collectivization begins, industrialization accelerated

1930

16th Party Congress: Soviet state strengthened

1931

Trial of the Mensheviks, political show trial

1932

First Five-Year Plan completed early, Second Five-Year Plan begins
Statute on Protection of Socialist Property (includes the death penalty)

1933

RSFSR Corrective Labor Code (penitentiary law)

1934

17th Party Congress
Decrees on treason, the secret police, and the special boards (for administrative
    sentencing to forced labor)
Politburo member Kirov assassinated
Criminal procedure law amended to expedite political justice

1935

Massive purges under way
Series of show trials of major Bolshevik leaders begins
Constitutional commission appointed to draft a new constitution

1936

Draft constitution submitted for nationwide discussion
Stalin Constitution adopted
USSR now includes eleven union republics

1937

Third Five-Year Plan launched
New Constitution of the RSFSR
Procurator Vyshinsky presides over jurisprudence of terror

1938

Bukharin trial, last and greatest political show trial
Statute on Judiciary

1939

18th Party Congress

1940

Stalin, with Hitler's concurrence, forcibly annexes Lithuania, Latvia, and Estonia to
    the USSR

1941

Nazi armies invade the Soviet Union

1945

USSR and the allies victorious, ending World War II

1946

Stalin reimposes tight controls on Soviet society

1948

USSR completes domination of Eastern Europe; Stalinist model imposed, Cold
  War begins

1949

New purges begin in Leningrad
Soviet Union becomes an atomic power, tests first bomb

1952

19th Party Congress
Kremlin doctors arrested on political charges, Stalin plans new show trials

1953

Stalin dies, Khrushchev emerges as party leader
Secret police chief Beria tried and executed, terror abates
"Doctors' Plot" trial canceled, frameup revealed
Special boards for administrative purging abolished

1954

Secret police reduced in size and reorganized as KGB
Cultural thaw begins, limited *glasnost* (openness) permitted

1955

Khrushchev strengthens his leadership position
Legal de-Stalinization begins: new Statute on Procuracy
Large-scale political amnesties and rehabilitations begin

1956

20th Party Congress: Khrushchev criticizes Stalin in "secret speech"
Soviet forces suppress Hungarian Revolution

1957

Conservative leaders fail in coup attempt against Khrushchev
Khrushchev tries economic reform: industrial decentralization
Constitution amended, expanding union republics' authority to legislate on legal
  system
New Statute on USSR Supreme Court

1958

Party leader Khrushchev assumes chairmanship of government
Law reform accelerates: new USSR Fundamental Principles of Legislation on
  Criminal Law, Criminal Procedure, and on the Judiciary; new Statutes on
  Crimes against the State, and on Military Crimes

1959

21st Extraordinary Party Congress: de-Stalinization stepped up
Khrushchev signals need for constitutional reform
Syntax, one of the first underground journals appears

1960

New post-Stalin RSFSR codes of Criminal law and Criminal procedure enacted,
  models for other republics' codes

1961

22nd Party Congress: more criticism of Stalin

New Party Program and Party Rules approved

New legislation on populist forms of justice: comrades' courts and anti-parasite proceedings (against the willfully unemployed)

Criminal law amended, extending the death penalty to selected economic crimes

Political trial of ethnic nationalists in the Ukraine

1962

Constitutional commission chaired by Khrushchev, appointed to draft a new, post-Stalin constitution

Capital punishment added as a penalty for rape and for bribery

Troops fire on strikers in Novocherkassk

Cuban Missile Crisis, Khrushchev pulls back

1963

Conservatives restive, Khrushchev curbs *glasnost* in the arts

Kennedy and Khrushchev negotiate Nuclear Test Ban Treaty

Last meeting of Khrushchev's Constitutional Commission, work in progress on new charter

1964

Khrushchev ousted by a coup, Brezhnev new party leader

1965

Brezhnev attempts economic reform: enterprise reorganization

1966

23rd Party Congress: Party reforms rolled back

Brezhnev promises new constitution: 1962 Constitution Commission reactivated

Central planning system reaffirmed: price reforms

Siniavsky–Daniel trial, first post-Stalin show trial

Law on dissent and hooliganism strengthened

1967

50th anniversary of the Bolshevik Revolution

Emergence of unofficial human rights movement

Andropov becomes KGB chairman

Political trial of Bukovsky

Rehabilitation of Crimean Tatars and other minorities persecuted by Stalin

Solzhenitsyn criticizes censorship

1968

USSR and allies invade Czechoslovakia, overthrowing Communist reform movement

Dissidents demonstrate against invasion; put on trial

New legislation on family and land law

Main underground journal first appears

Sakharov joins dissident ranks

1969

New legislation on penitentiary, public health, and collective farm law

Formation of first unofficial human rights group

1970

New legislation on labor and natural resource law
Soviet Jewish emigration movement begins
Solzhenitsyn awarded Nobel Prize for Literature

1971

24th Party Congress

1972

50th anniversary of Treaty of Union forming USSR
Brezhnev signals need to complete work on new constitution
Nixon and Brezhnev sign SALT I accord on arms negotiations
Repression campaign against underground journals
Nationalist dissent erupts in Lithuania

1973

New legislation on production associations, on public education and invention law
Political trial of underground journal editors

1974

New law on internal passports, extending right to collective farmers for first time
Gulag Archipelago published in the West; Solzhenitsyn forcibly expatriated

1975

USSR signs Helsinki Final Act, including provisions on human rights
Political trial of Kovalev, human rights activist who worked with Sakharov
Sakharov awarded Nobel Peace Prize

1976

25th Party Congress: Brief progress report on drafting of new constitution
Dissidents form unofficial groups to monitor Soviet compliance with Helsinki Final
    Act
Political prisoner Bukovsky exchanged for imprisoned Chilean communist leader

1977

60th anniversary of the Bolshevik Revolution
New members added to Brezhnev's Constitutional Commission
New USSR constitution drafted, submitted for public discussion, modified, and
    adopted
Brezhnev adds title of chairman of Supreme Soviet Presidium
Crackdown on unofficial human rights monitoring groups

1978

New union republic constitutions adopted
Political trials of Helsinki "monitors," including Orlov, Shcharansky,   and
    Lukyanenko

1979

Brezhnev again attempts economic reforms: planning reforms
New legislation implementing USSR Constitution of 1977
USSR invades Afghanistan

1980

Constitutional implementation continues: several new laws
Sakharov protests Afghan invasion, exiled to Gorky
Labor unrest in Poland, rise of Solidarity trade union

1981

26th Party Congress
Martial law imposed in Poland

1982

Brezhnev dies, Andropov becomes party leader
Repression of dissidents intensifies

1983

Andropov launches major anti-corruption drive
Criminal law extensively amended, sanctions strengthened
Constitutional implementation: Statute on Labor Collective

1984

Andropov dies, Chernenko becomes party leader
Soviet Jewish, German, and Armenian emigration at low ebb

1985

Chernenko dies, Gorbachev becomes party leader
Party Central Committee adopts initial reforms
Gorbachev launches major anti-drinking campaign
Yeltsin appointed Central Committee Secretary
First Reagan–Gorbachev summit in Geneva
Jewish dissident Shcharansky prematurely released from prison, allowed
    to emigrate to Israel

1986

27th Party Congress: *perestroika* (restructuring) formally endorsed
Yeltsin elevated to Politburo
Chernobyl nuclear disaster in the Ukraine
Policy on *glasnost* (openness) advances in press and the arts
New legislation expanding private economic activity and cracking down on
    black market income
Second Reagan–Gorbachev summit in Iceland
Gorbachev releases Sakharov from internal exile
Political prisoner Orlov prematurely released
Ethnic demonstrations in Kazakhstan; police use force

1987

70th anniversary of Bolshevik Revolution: de-Stalinization resumes
Central Committee plenums on democratization, and radical economic reforms
Yeltsin expelled from leadership for criticizing slow pace of *perestroika*
Soviet-American nuclear disarmament treaty signed
Constitutional implementation: first law on judicial review of administrative
    decisions
New legislation on the state enterprise and public discussion of draft laws
Amnesty of political prisoners begins
Ethnic nationalists in Armenia and the Baltic republics demonstrate

1988

Gorbachev calls for a constitutional state
Special party conference accelerates constitutional reforms
Gorbachev becomes chairman of the Supreme Soviet Presidium
Constitution of 1977 extensively amended, creating a new legislative system
New legislation on cooperative businesses and regulation of public demonstrations

Constitution of 1977 extensively amended, creating a new legislative system
New legislation on cooperative businesses and regulation of public demonstrations
Soviet withdrawal from Afghanistan begins
Posthumous rehabilitation of Bukharin and other Old Bolsheviks purged
     by Stalin
Millennium of Christianity in Russia celebrated
Popular fronts organize in the Baltic republics
Armenian–Azerbaijani territorial dispute erupts in violence

1989

Semi-free elections to new Congress of People's Deputies;
Sakharov, Yeltsin and former prisoner Kovalev elected
First Congress of People's Deputies convenes, elects members of new
     Supreme Soviet; Gorbachev elected chairman of Supreme Soviet
Commission appointed to draft new constitution
Constitution of 1977 again extensively amended
Criminal law on political crime reformed
Soviet troops attack demonstrators in Tbilisi, Georgia; many deaths
Communal interethnic violence breaks out in Uzbekistan
Gulag Archipelago published for first time in USSR
Communism collapses in East Europe

1990

More constitutional revision, eliminating Party monopoly, and creating an execu-
     tive presidency
Gorbachev elected president of Supreme Soviet with additional powers
New legislation on freedom of the press and religion, and on constitutional over-
     sight and the emergency regime
RSFSR legislature elects Yeltsin its president
28th Party Congress; Yeltsin and other leading democrats resign   from the party
Soviet troops intervene in Baku, Azerbaijan; scores killed
Lithuania declares its independence, Gorbachev imposes economic embargo
Conservative reaction to decline of Soviet system grows
Gorbachev awarded Nobel Peace Prize
New Treaty of Union drafted to restructure federal relations
Foreign Minister Eduard Shevardnadze resigns, warns of dictatorship

1991

Winter: Gorbachev moves to the right

Security troops carry out assaults in Lithuania and Latvia to stem nationalism
Gorbachev calls out troops to block Yeltsin rally
Gorbachev proposes suspending new press law
First public referendum endorses concept of new union treaty

Spring: Gorbachev and Yeltsin join in reform alliance

Negotiations proceed on final version of new union treaty
Economy in steep decline
Yeltsin directly elected president of Russia
USSR Prime Minister Pavlov attempts to gain emergency powers

Summer: conservative backlash and defeat

Yeltsin and Gorbachev put pressure on party to reform
Last Bush–Gorbachev summit, strategic weapons treaty signed (START)
New union treaty ready to be signed; drafting of new constitution to follow
Conservatives attempt coup, offering constitutional justification
Yeltsin leads resistance, coup fails, Gorbachev freed, and conspirators arrested
Gorbachev resigns as party leader, party banned

Fall: Twilight of the USSR

Transitional government formed
Baltic states' independence recognized by USSR and other countries
Gorbachev attempts to hold union together, proposes new, looser version of union
    treaty
Most union republics declare independence
Disintegration of the USSR begins

The End: collapse of the Soviet system

Yeltsin and other new leaders form Commonwealth of Independent States,
    declare USSR dead
Gorbachev resigns union presidency, enters private life
Soviet Union ceases to exist, Russia reemerges.

Name Index

Subject Index

Absolutism
  Imperial Russian, 8
  communist, 9
Administrative-command system, 87
Administrative state, Russian, 114
Amalrik's paradox, 8, 112

Bolshevik Revolution, 9, 15, 46, 61,
  62, 120n

Campaigns
  anti-alcohol, 85
  anti-crime, 120n
  discipline, 55, 64, 65, 74, 77–81, 85,
    136n
  "Operation Trawl," 69, 70
  "upbringing," 74, 77–83, 139n
  vigilance, 76
Chile, 110
Civic culture, 7
Civil liberties, 6, 26, 36, 41, 42, 48,
  53, 58, 92, 95, 96, 142n
Civil-military relationship, 100
Civil society, 92, 149n
Closed society, ix
Collapse, decline, ix, x, 3, 101, 112,
  113, 118, 119n
Committee of Constitutional
  Supervision, 94, 143n, 146n
Committee of national salvation, 105,
  110, 146n
Commonwealth of Independent States,
  118
  constitutional continuity of, 149n
Communist Party of the Soviet Union,
  ix, 3, 4, 5, 8, 9, 20, 22, 28, 34, 42,
  43, 47, 53–55, 59, 65, 83, 85, 87,
  90, 93, 100, 105, 112, 141n

Communist Party of the Soviet Union
    (continued)
  as a metajuridical institution, 10
  as a social organization, 93
  Central Committee of, 15, 33, 58,
    62, 64, 65, 70, 74, 120n
  19th Conference of, 87, 106,
  Politburo of, 15, 56, 58, 65, 66, 72,
    80, 121n, 127n, 128n, 134n,
    147n
  Program (1961) of, 24
  20th Congress of, 19
  25th Congress of, 18
  26th Congress of, 62
  27th Congress of, 85
  28th Congress of, 147n
Congress of People's Deputies, USSR,
  93, 107, 114, 115, 148n
Constitution
  of 1809 (Speransky draft), 9
  of 1906 (first Imperial Russian), 9
  of 1918 (first Soviet, of RSFSR), 9,
    121n
  of 1924 (first union, of USSR), 10,
    90, 93, 121n
  of 1936 (Stalin Constitution), 10,
    15–18, 21–28, 33, 36, 44, 90,
    93, 95, 97, 120n, 121n, 124n,
    125n, 126n
  of 1977 (last Soviet), ix, x, xi, 10,
    13, 15, 18–24, 26, 29, 30, 34,
    49, 53, 54, 56, 60, 62, 64, 66,
    70, 71, 73, 78, 83, 86–88, 90,
    91, 93, 95, 99, 103, 105, 108,
    109, 111, 113, 114, 117, 120n,
    121n, 124n, 127n, 130n, 132n,
    140n, 142n, 144n, 146n, 148n

Robert Sharlet, professor of political science at Union College, Schenectady, N.Y., is a specialist on Soviet law and politics. He has published a number of books including *The New Soviet Constitution of 1977* and *The Soviet Union Since Stalin* (with Stephen F. Cohen and Alexander Rabinowitch) and volumes on the Soviet legal philosophers Pashukanis and Stuchka. Sharlet has held visiting appointments at Columbia, Yale, and the University of Wisconsin and was an exchange scholar at Moscow University Law School. He lectures frequently in Moscow.